Henry Brooke, Charles Kingsley

The Fool of Quality

The History of Henry, Earl of Moreland - Vol. II

Henry Brooke, Charles Kingsley

The Fool of Quality

The History of Henry, Earl of Moreland - Vol. II

ISBN/EAN: 9783743400764

Manufactured in Europe, USA, Canada, Australia, Japa

Cover: Foto ©ninafisch / pixelio.de

Manufactured and distributed by brebook publishing software (www.brebook.com)

Henry Brooke, Charles Kingsley

The Fool of Quality

THE

FOOL OF QUALITY:

OR,

THE HISTORY OF HENRY EARL OF MORELAND.

BY HENRY BROOKE, Esq.

A New and Revised Edition,

WITH AN INTRODUCTION

BY THE REV. W. P. STRICKLAND, D.D.,

AND

A BIOGRAPHICAL PREFACE

BY THE REV. CHARLES KINGSLEY, M.A.

COMPLETE IN TWO VOLUMES.

VOL. II.

NEW YORK:
DERBY & JACKSON, 119 NASSAU STREET.
1860.

ENTERED according to Act of Congress, in the year 1859, by

DERBY & JACKSON

In the Clerk's Office of the District Court of the United States for the Southern District of New York.

W. H. Tinson, Stereotyper.   Geo. Russell & Co., Printers.

THE FOOL OF QUALITY;

OR THE

HISTORY OF HENRY EARL OF MORELAND.

CHAPTER I.

WHEN I look back, my fair cousin, on the passages of my life, it is a matter of amazement to me, that a creature so frail, so feebly and so delicately constituted as man, with nerves so apt to be racked, and a heart to be wrung with anguish, can possibly endure under the weights of calamity that at times are laid upon him.

I had not yet dropped a tear. I was in a state of half stupid and half flighty insensibility; as one who, having lost every thing, had nothing further to look for, and therefore nothing to regard. But when I saw my dear old man, my best friend, my father, whelmed under such a depth of affliction, all the sluices of my soul and inmost affections were laid open, and I broke into an avowed passion of tears and exclamations, till, like David in his strife of love with Jonathan, I exceeded. I accused myself of all the evils that had happened to his house; and I devoted the day to darkness, and the night to desolation, wherein, by my presence and connections, I had brought those mischiefs upon him. The good man was greatly struck, and I think partly consoled, by the excess of my sorrows; and, all desolate as he was, he attempted to administer that comfort to me, which he himself wanted more than any who had life.

Break not your heart, my Harry—break not your heart, my child! he cried. Deprive me not of the only consolation that is left me; you are now my only trust, my only stay upon earth. A wretched merchant I am, whose whole wealth is cast away, save thee, thou precious casket, thou only remnant of all my possessions! My girl, indeed, was thy true lover, the tenderest of all mates; her love to thee, my son, was passing the love of woman; but we have lost her, we have lost her, and wailing is all the portion that is left us below.

As soon as the family heard the voice of our mourning, they too gave a loose to the impatience of their griefs, and all the house was filled with the sound of lamentation.

On the following day I summoned the chief medical artists, and got the precious remains of my angel embalmed. She was laid under a sumptuous canopy with a silver coffin at her bed's foot, and every night when the house was at rest I stole secretly from my bed and stretched myself beside her. I pressed her cold lips to mine; I clasped her corpse to my warm bosom, as though I expected to restore it to life by transfusing my soul into it. I spoke to her as when living; I reminded her of the several tender and endearing passages of our loves; and I reminded her also of the loss of our little ones, by whom we became essentially one, inseparably united in soul and body for ever.

There is surely, my cousin, a species of pleasure in grief, a kind of soothing and deep delight, that arises with the tears which are pushed from the fountain of God in the soul, from the charities and sensibilities of the human heart divine.

True, true, my precious cousin, replied the countess, giving a fresh loose to her tears. O Matilda! I would I were with thee!—True my cousin, I say; even now I sink under the weight of the sentiment of your story.

Upon the ninth night, continued Mr. Clinton, as I lay by the side of all that remained of my Matty, overtoiled and overwatched, I fell into a deep sleep. My mind notwithstanding, at the time, seemed more awake and more alive to objects than ever. In an instant she stood visible and confessed before me. I saw her clearer than at noonday, by the light which she cast with profusion abroad. Every feature and former trace seemed heightened into a lustre, without a loss of the least similitude. She smiled ineffable sweetness and blessedness upon me: and, stooping down, I felt her embrace about my heart and about my spirit; while, at the same time, I saw her bent in complacence before me. After a length of ecstatic pleasure, which I felt from her communion and infusion into my soul—My Harry, says she, grieve not for me! All the delights that your world could sum up in an age, would not amount to my bliss, no, not for an hour: it is a weight of enjoyment that, in an instant, would crush to nothing the whole frame of your mortality. Grieve not then for me, my Harry, but resign my beggarly spoils to their beggarly parent; ashes to ashes, and dust to dust! In my inordinate fondness for you, I have at length obtained a promise that my master and your master, my beloved and your lover, shall finally bear you triumphant through all the enemies that are set in fearful array against you. Having so said, I felt myself, as it were, compressed within an engine of love; and again, losing the remembrance of all that had passed, I sunk as into a state of oblivion. Towards the dawning, I was awakened by the clapping of hands and cries of lamentation. Starting up, I perceived Mr. Golding at the bedside, suspended over his Matty and me, and pouring forth his complaints.

There was a favoured domestic of his, a little old man, who had always kept a careful and inquisitive eye over every thing that was in or concerned our household. This Argus, it seems, at length suspected my nightly visits to the dead, and, lurking in a corner, saw me open and enter the chamber where the corpse was deposited. As he lay in his master's apartment, he took the first opportunity of his being awake to impart what he thought a matter of extraordinary intelligence to him.—Sir, says he, if I am not greatly deceived, my young master is this moment in bed with his dead lady.— What is this you tell me? cried Mr. Golding. No, John, no! what you say is impossible. All who live, love that which is living alone; whatever savours of death is detestable to all men.—As I am here, replied John, I am almost assured that what I tell you is fact.—Peace, peace, you old fool! said Mr. Golding; think you that our Harry is more loving than father Abraham, and yet Abraham desired to bury his dead out of his sight. I know not how that may be, said trusty John, but, if you are able to stir, I will help you to go and see. I am sure the thought of it melts the very heart within me.

Accordingly Mr. Golding, like old Jacob, strengthened himself, and arose, and, pained as he was, he came with the help of his John to the place where I lay.

Having for some time looked upon me, as I slept with his Matty fast folded in my arms, he could no longer contain his emotions, but he and John broke forth into tears and exclamations. O, my children, my children, my dearest children! he cried; why did ye exalt me to such a pitch of blessedness? Was it only to cast me down into the deeper gulf of misery—a gulf that has neither bank nor bottom?

As I arose, all ashamed to be detected in that manner, the good man caught me in his arms.—My Harry, my Harry, says he, what shall I pay you, my son, for your superabundant love to me and to mine? Could my wretchedness give you bliss, I should almost think myself blessed in being wretched, my Harry.

I now prepared to execute the late command of my angel, and to consign to earth the little that was earthly in her. But when our domestics understood that all that was left of their loved mistress was now going to be taken away from them for ever, they broke into tears anew, and set no bounds to their lamentations.

Her desolate father was desirous of attending the funeral, but on my knees I dissuaded him from it, as I was assured it would burst in twain the already overstretched thread of his age and infirmities. He then insisted on having the lid of the coffin removed, and, bending over, he cast his old body on the corpse; again he rose and gazed upon it, and clapping his hands, with a shout—Is this my world, he cried; the whole of my possessions? Are you the one that was once my little prattling Matty—the playfellow of my knees—the laugher away of care—who brought cheer to my heart and warmth to my bosom? Are you the one for whom alone I spent my nights in thought and my days in application? Is this all that is left, then, of my length of labours? O, my spark of life is quenched in thee, my Matty, my Matty! the flowing fountain of my existence is dried up for ever!

There is something exceedingly solemn and affecting, my cousin, in the circumstances and apparatus of our funerals; they are oppressive even to minds that are no way concerned or interested in the death of the party lamented. Though I grieved no more for my Matty—though I was as assured of her bliss as I was of my own being; yet, when the gloom of the procession was gathered around me—when I heard the wailing of the many families whom her charity had sustained—when I heard the bitter sobbings of the servants, whom her sweetness had so endearingly attached to her person—when all joined to bewail themselves as lost in her loss, my heart died, as it were, within me, and I should have been suffocated on the spot had I not given instant way to the swell of my sorrows.

The tempest of the soul, madam, like that of the elements, can endure but for a season. The passion of Mr. Golding, on the interment of every joy and of every hope that he could look for upon earth, within a few weeks subsided, or rather sunk into a solid but sullen peace; a kind of peace that seemed to say—There is nothing in this universe that can disturb me.

Harry, said he one evening, I have been thinking of the vision that I have had.—Vision, sir, said I; has my Matty then appeared to you?—Yes, he answered, she was the principal part of my vision for these twenty years past. The vision that I mean, my Harry, is the dream of a very long and laborious life. Here have I, by the toil of fifty years' application, scraped together and accumulated as much as in these times would set kings at contention, and be accounted a worthy cause for spilling the blood of thousands; and yet what are these things to me, or of what value in themselves, more than the stones and rubbish that make our pavement before the door? I have been hungering and thirsting after the goods of this world; I have acquired all that it could give me; and now my soul, like a sick stomach, disgorges the whole.—I then took one of his hands, and pressing it tenderly between mine—O, my father! I cried; my dear, dear father! O that I might be made sons and daughters, and every sort of kindred to you! All that I am and have should gladly be spent in bringing any kind of comfort to you, my father.

In about a fortnight after, as I entered his apartment to

bid him good-morrow, I observed that his countenance had much altered from what it was the evening before—that he looked deeply dejected and seemed to breathe with difficulty.

Are you not well, sir?—No, says he, my spirits are greatly oppressed. I find that I must leave you shortly; I believe that I must go suddenly; but where to? That is the question—the very terrible question—the only question of any importance in heaven or on earth.—Sure, sir, said I, that can be no question to you, whose whole life has been a continual course of righteousness, of daily worship to God, and goodwill to all men. If you have any sins to account for, they must be covered tenfold by the multitude of your charities.

Talk not, Harry, said he, of the filthy rags of my own righteousness. I am far from the confidence of the boastful Pharisee; alas! I have not even that of the poor and humble publican, for I dare not look up to say, "Lord, be merciful to me, a sinner!" wherefore, then, do you speak of having finished my course towards God and towards man? It is but lately, very lately, that I set out upon it, and I am cut short before I have got within sight of the goal. Yes, Harry, I fear, I know, I feel, that there is no salvation for me.

You amaze me, sir, said I; you terrify me to death! If there is not salvation for such as you, what a depth of perdition opens for the rest of mankind?

I would you could convince me, he cried. I want to be comforted; I desire comfort, any kind of consolation: but I feel my condemnation within myself. Moreover, I see every text of the gospel of the words of life terribly marshalled and set in broad array against me.—What text, sir? said I; I am sure I know of no texts that bring terror or condemnation to the just.—Ah Harry! he replied, justice is of the law and the circumcision, and has nothing to do with the new covenant or the new man. For, what says the great apostle?

1*

"Circumcision availeth nothing, neither uncircumcision, but a new creature." And Christ himself hath said, "Except a man be born again, he cannot see the kingdom of God." Again the same apostle saith, "I delight in the law of God after the inward man;" and again, "My little children, of whom I travail in birth, again until Christ be formed in you." Now if all these corresponding expressions of being "born again, a new creature, a new man, an inward man, Christ formed in us," etc., are to be glossed and explained away, as meaning little more than a state of moral sentiments and moral behaviour, there can be nothing of real import in the gospel of Christ.

Again, hear what the Redeemer saith, "Except ye be converted and become as little children, ye shall not enter into the kingdom of heaven." Again, "If any man will come after me, let him deny himself and take up his cross and follow me." Again, "Whosoever he be of you that forsaketh not all that he hath, he cannot be my disciple."

If these things, I cried, are to be taken according to the apparent sense and import of the letter, neither the teachers of the gospel, nor those who are taught, can be saved.

Therefore, replied he, it is said, that "Many be called, but few chosen." And again, "Enter ye in at the strait gate; for wide is the gate, and broad is the way that leadeth to destruction, and many there be which go in thereat; because strait is the gate, and narrow is the way which leadeth unto life, and few there be that find it." O my Harry, my Harry! our lives have been employed in seeking and "loving the world, and the things of the world," therefore "the love of the Father could not be in us." O that I had never been born! O thou God! whose tribunal at this hour is set up so tremendously against me, at length I feel the propriety of thy precepts, in rejecting the world and all that is therein; for what can they yield save a little food and raiment to bodily corruption, or incitements to that pride which cast

Lucifer into a gulf, that now opens before me without a bottom?

As I trembled and had nothing to answer, I proposed to bring some of our clergy to him. No, Harry! no, says he, I will have none of their worldly comforts; I will not cast my soul upon bladdered expectations. Can they persuade me that I am one of the few that are chosen? can they tell me wherein I have striven to enter at the strait gate, wherein many shall seek to enter, but shall not be able?

Here he sunk into a fit of agonizing desperation, so that a cold dew broke forth from all parts of his body, and fell, drop after drop, down his ghastly and fearful countenance. Never, madam, never did I feel such a kind of anguishing horror as I then felt; I was affrighted and all frozen to my inmost soul.—Haste, my dear sir, exclaimed Lady Maitland; make haste through this part of your narration, I beseech you! I also feel for myself; I am terrified to the last degree.

At length, continued Mr. Clinton, I recollect myself a little. My master, I cried; my father, my dearest father, since you will not take comfort in your own righteousness, take comfort in that of Him who was made righteousness for you. Do you not now reject the world? do you not now deny yourself?—I do, I do, he said; I detest the one and the other.—And do you not feel that you are wholly a compound of sin and death?—Ay, he cried; there is the weight, there is the mountain under which I sink for ever.—Come then to Christ, my father, heavy laden as you are, and he will questionless embrace you, and be rest to you, my father!—I would come, Harry, he cried; but I dare not, I am not able.—Strive, my father; do but turn to Him, and he will more than meet you. Cry out with sinking Peter, "Save, Lord, or I perish!" and he will catch you with the hand of his ever ready salvation.

Here his countenance began to settle into an earnest composure, and his eyes were turned and fixed upwards; while his old and enfeebled body continued to labour under the symptoms of near dissolution. At length he started, and seized my hand with a dying pressure—There is comfort, Harry; there is comfort! he cried, and expired.

I was now cast once more upon a strange and friendless world. All the interests of my heart were buried with this family; and I seemed to myself as without kindred or connections in the midst of mankind. Your dear mamma, indeed, sometimes called to condole with me, and water my losses with her tears; and in her, and you my cousin, young as you then were, was locked up and centred the whole stock that I had left of endearing sensations.

As the scenes of my former happiness served daily and nightly to render me more wretched by a sad recollection, I determined to quit my house, and to take private lodgings. For this purpose, I summoned Mr. Golding's domestics; and, as he had made no will, I first paid them their wages, and then gave them such pretended legacies as brought their tears and their blessings in a shower upon me.

As soon as I had discharged all except the two favourite servants of my master and my Matty, I desired that John, our little old man, should be sent to me.

John, said I, as he entered, here is a bill for five hundred pounds which our good old master has left you, in token of his acknowledgment of your true and loving services, and to help, with what you have saved, to soften and make easy the bed of death in your old age.—Do you mean to part with me, sir? said John, seemingly thankless and unconcerned about the gift which I had offered him.—Indeed, John, said I, in my present state of dejection, attendance of any kind would but be an encumbrance to me.—Then, sir, you may keep your bounty to yourself; for I shall break my heart before five-and-twenty hours are over.—Nay, John, said I, I

am far from turning you from me; stay with me as my friend
and welcome, but not as my servant; and I shall see the comfort of old times in always seeing you about me.—Thank you,
thank you, sir, he cried. I will not disturb you with my
tears; but I should die unblessed if I died out of your presence! So saying, he rushed from me in a fit of restrained
passion.

I then sent for my wife's maid, whom I formerly mentioned. She had just heard of my discharging the other
servants, and entered with a sad and alarmed countenance.—
Come near, Susan, I am going to part with you, said I; come
to me, and give me a farewell kiss. She approached with
downcast looks, when, taking her in my arms, I pressed and
kissed her repeatedly, and scarce withheld my tears.—Oh,
my girl, my Matty's precious girl! I cried, I am not forgetful of your love, your honour, and your disinterestedness
towards us. Here, my Susy, your darling mistress presents
you with this bill of a thousand pounds, and, if you choose,
I will give you cash for it within a quarter of an hour. This,
however, does not discharge me from my regard and attention to you. You are of a helpless sex, my Susy, that is subject to many impositions and calamities; wherefore, when
this sum shall fail you, come to me again—come to me as to
your friend, as to your debtor, Susy, and I will repeat my
remembrance, and repeat again, as you may happen to have
occasion; for while I have sixpence left, the favourite friend
of my Matty shall not want her proportion.

Here the grateful and amazed creature threw herself on
the floor. She cried aloud, while the family heard and
echoed to her lamentations. She clasped my knees, she
kissed my feet again and again. I could not disengage
myself, I could not force her from me.—Oh, my master! she
cried, my all that is left to me of my adored, my angel mistress! must I then be torn from you? must you live without

the service of the hands and heart of your Susy? But I understand your regard and care for me, my master. It is a cruel and naughty world, and must be complied with.

Here I compelled her to rise, and, kissing her again, I turned hastily to the chamber where my Matty's corpse had been laid; and bolting the door, and casting myself on the bed, I broke into tears, and at length wept myself to sleep.

While I was preparing to leave the once-loved mansion, I found in Mr. Golding's cabinet a parchment that much surprised me. On my marriage, he had proposed to make a settlement of his fortune upon me, which, however, I obstinately refused to accept; whereupon, without my privity, he got this deed perfected, which contained an absolute conveyance to me of all his worldly effects and possessions; and this again renewed in me the tender and endearing remembrance of each of those kindnesses and benefits which he had formerly conferred upon me.

I now found myself in possession of near a million of money, which, however, in my disposition of mind at the time, appeared no worthier than so much lumber in a waste room. And I know not how it was, that, through the subsequent course of my life, although I was by no means of an economical turn, though I never sued for a debt, nor gave a denial to the wants of those who asked, nor turned away from him that desired to borrow of me, yet uncoveted wealth came pouring in upon me.

It was not without some sighs and a plentiful shower, that I departed from the seat of all my past enjoyments. I took lodgings within a few doors of your father; and my little household consisted of my favourite Irishman, my little old man, two footmen, and an elderly woman who used daily to dress a plain dish of meat for us.

It was then, my fairest cousin, that your opening graces and early attractions drew me daily to your house; my heart was soothed and my griefs cheered by the sweetness of your prattle; and I was melted down and minted anew, as it were, by the unaffected warmth and innocence of your caresses.

As I had no faith in dreams, not even in that of my Matty, I thought it impossible that I should ever marry again. I therefore resolved, in my own mind, to make you my heir, and to endow you in marriage with the best part of my fortune. But you are a little pale, madam; you look dejected and fatigued. If you please, I will suspend my narration for the present, and in the morning, if you choose it, as early as you will, I shall renew and proceed in my insignificant history. Here, he pressed her hand to his lips. She withdrew with a tearful eye and a heaving heart; and the next day he resumed his narration, as followeth.

CHAPTER II.

Though you, my cousin, at that time, were a great consolation to me, and a sweet lightener of my afflictions, yet the griefs of heart which I had suffered were not without their effect. At length they fell on my constitution, and affected my nerves or spirits; I think our doctors pretty much confound the one with the other. Accordingly, I was advised to travel for change of air and exercise, and I was preparing for my journey, when there happened in my family the most extraordinary instance of an over-watchful providence that occurs to my memory.

My little old man John began to decline apace, and at length took to his bed, and, having a tender friendship for him, I went to sit beside him, and to comfort him the best I could. John, said I, are you afraid to die?—No, sir, not at all, not in the least; I long to be dissolved, and to be with our loving Lord.—Indeed, John, said I; I am inclined to think you have been a very good liver.—A dog, sir—a mere dog, desperately wicked, the vilest of sinners! I am a murderer too, my master; there's blood upon my head.— Blood! said I, and started.—Yes, sir, replied John; but then the blood that was shed for me, is stronger and more precious than the blood that was shed by me.—Blood, however, John, is a very terrible thing; are you not afraid to appear before the judgment-seat of Christ?—By no means, my dear master; I have long since laid the burden of my sins before him, for I had nothing else to bring to him, nothing else to offer him; and he has accepted them and me, and my conscience is at rest in him.—Then, John, there may yet be room for hope.—There is assurance, my master, for I have laid hold upon the rock, and cannot be shaken.

But how do you intend to dispose of your worldly substance?—All that I have, sir, I got with you and my old master; and where I found it, even there I resolve to leave it.—Indeed, John, I will not finger a penny of your money. How much may it amount to?—Eight hundred and thirty-seven pounds, sir, or thereabout.—And have you no relations of your own?—Not one living that I know of.—Then think of some one else, for no part of it shall lie on my conscience, I assure you.

I have read, somewhere or other, sir, of a great king who was advised of God, in a dream, to take the very first man whom he should meet the next morning, to be his partner in the government. Now, if it pleases you, my master, I will follow the like counsel; and, whosoever shall be the first found before our door, let that person be the owner and inheritor of my substance.—It shall be even as you say; I will go and see whom God shall be pleased to send to us.

Accordingly I went and opened our door, when a woman, who had nearly passed, turned about at the noise, and perceiving me, came up and said—A little charity, sir, for the sake of him who had not where to lay his head.

I was strongly affected by the manner in which she addressed me, and, eyeing her attentively, I observed that she was clean though meanly apparelled; wherefore, to make a further trial whether our adventure was likely to prove prosperous or not, I slipped a guinea into her hand, and desired her to go about her business. Accordingly, she curtsied and went from me a few steps, when, looking into her hand, she turned suddenly back—Sir, sir, says she; here had like to have been a sad mistake; you meant to give me a shilling, and you have given me a whole guinea.—It was, says I, a very great mistake, indeed; but be pleased to come in, and we will try to rectify our errors.

Here I took her into the chamber where John lay, and, having constrained her to sit down, I put my hand in my pocket. Here, good woman, said I; here are ten guineas for you, to make you some amends for the mistake I was guilty of in giving you but one. The poor creature could scarcely credit her senses, but raising her eyes in ecstasy, and dropping from the chair upon her knees, she was proceeding to bless me; but I peremptorily insisted on her retaking her seat. Mistress, said I, be pleased to stay your prayers for the present; what I want from you is the story of your life; tell me who and what you are, without suppressing any circumstance, or concealing the faults of which you have been guilty, and I will make you the mistress of twenty guineas, that shall be added to what you have already received.

Sir, said she, you frighten me; my story is a very unhappy and a very foolish story, and cannot be of the smallest consequence to you. Sure, you are too much of the gentleman to desire to ensnare me; and, indeed, I know not of any thing whereby I may be ensnared. Wherefore, bountiful sir, unto you as unto heaven I will open my whole soul, without seeking to know why you look into the concerns of such a worm as I am.

I am the daughter of a farmer in Essex; my maiden name was Eleanor Damer. I was married, early in life, to a man who kept a chandler's shop, in a little lane that led to Tower Hill, his name was Barnaby Tirrel.—Barnaby Tirrel! exclaimed John; are you very sure that his name was Barnaby Tirrel?—Peace, John I cried; whatever you may know of this man, or of any other matter, I command you not to interrupt the woman till she has finished her story. She then continued.

I had neither brother nor sister, sir, except one brother—a twin-brother, and we loved one another as though there was nobody else in the world to be loved.

About three years before my marriage, my brother Tommy, then a sweet pretty lad, took to a seafaring life, and went from me, I know not where, upon a voyage that I was told was a very great way off; and so I cried, day and night, as many tears after him as would have served me to swim in.

My husband was very fond of me, and when he used to see me cry while he spoke of my Tommy, he would kiss me and try to comfort me, and say, that he wished for nothing more than his return to old England, that he might welcome him and love him as much as I did.

One night, on the ninth month of my marriage, as I sat moping and alone, my husband being abroad upon some business, I heard a knocking at the door, which was opened by our little servant-girl. And then, before you could say this, in leaped my brother, and catched me fast in his dear arms.

I gave a great shout for joy, you may be sure; and pushing my Tommy from me, and pulling him to me again and again, we embraced, and cried, and kissed, and embraced and kissed again, as though we never could be tired.

In the meanwhile, the door being open, my cruel Barnaby entered, unperceived by either of us; and seeing a strange man so fond and familiar with me, he opened a long clasped knife which he had in his pocket, and rushing up, he gave my darling brother three stabs in the body before he could speak a word or turn about to defend himself. Then, casting down the knife, in a minute he was out of the house, and I never saw him more.

For a time I stood like a stone, and then, giving a great shriek, I fainted and fell on my brother as he lay weltering in his blood.

Our little Mary, in the while, being frightened almost to death, ran about like a wild thing, and alarmed the street. Our neighbours crowded in, and sent for the next surgeon. My brother's wounds were probed and dressed, and he was laid in our spare bed.

Meantime, being forward with child, I fell into strong and untimely labour, and after very grievous travail was delivered of a boy, who was christened and called James, after my dear and lately deceased father.

No pains of my own, however, kept me from inquiring after that dear and lamented brother who had been killed as I supposed, for his love to me. But his youth and natural strength carried him through all dangers. In three months he was up and about, as well as ever; and in less than three more he set out on another voyage, from whence he never, never, O never returned!

Before he went abroad, my dear and sweet fellow had left me a note of hand for the receipt of his wages. But in five years after I heard that he was cast away, or killed by the Barbary people: and though I went and went again in the middle of my wants, and in the middle of my sorrows, to ask and to petition for his pay from the Admiralty, I never could get an answer of any profit or any comfort.

My little Jemmy, however, grew, and throve, and prated apace, and was my only prop under all my afflictions. My husband, indeed, had left me in pretty circumstances; and, had he but stayed with me, we should have prospered above our fellows. But what can a woman do, single, weak, and unprotected? I was imposed upon by some; by others I was refused payment for the goods that I had given; and at length I was reduced to poverty, and obliged to shut up shop.

Meantime I had spared no cost on the bringing up of my Jemmy. I had given him school learning, and he now was grown a very towardly and clever boy; and having taken to messages, my sweet fellow every night used to bring to me whatever he had earned in the daytime.

In the loss of my husband and brother, in the loss of my Barnaby, and in the loss of my Tommy, to be sure I had grief upon grief; so that my health went from me, and next my strength went from me, and I was not able to work at the washing business as before. But this didn't signify much while my child had his health; for he had now got a porter's place in the custom-house, and, young as he was, he willingly carried heavy burdens to have the pleasure of bringing home his hard earnings to his mammy. But about six weeks ago, may it please your honour, my dear boy fell ill of a quartan ague, as they call it, under which he and his mother's heart still continue to labour.

As soon as she had ended her short narrative—Well, John, said I, methinks this business will do; in my opinion you have got a very worthy inheritor of your fortune; what say you to it, John?—First, sir, let me ask her a question or two, if you please. Honest woman, draw your chair a little nearer to me, I pray you. And now, tell me the truth. Did you ever love your husband?—Yes, dearly, indeed very dearly did I love him; for he had loved me very dearly till that miserable night. But when, as I thought, he had killed my brother, I hated him as much as I had ever loved him before. But then again, when my Tommy had recovered of his wounds, I sent far and near to inquire after him and find him out; and when I could learn no tidings of him, I put it into all the printed papers that Thomas Damer was well recovered, and that Barnabas Tirrel, who had wounded him, might return without danger, to his wife and infant.

And he is returned! shouted John—he is returned, my Nelly! Your barbarous and bloody husband, who stabbed your brother, and left you and your infant to famish, he is returned to you, my Nelly; and, in his death, he shall make you amends for all the sufferings which he brought upon you during his lifetime! But, my master, my dearest master, send immediately for my child, my Jemmy, I beseech you, that, bad as I am myself, I may give him a father's blessing before I die.

I was surprised and affected, madam, beyond expression, by incidents that were at once so wonderful and so tender; and I directly sent servants and a sedan chair for James, with orders to have him carefully and warmly wrapped up; for what his mother told me of him had already given me a very strong prejudice in his favour.

Meanwhile, Mrs. Tirrel had sunk on her knees by her husband's bedside, and was plentifully pouring forth her tears upon him; partly for joy of having found him, and partly for grief of having found him in that condition.

O, my Nelly, my Nelly! cried Barnabas; had I known who the person was whose blood I drew that terrible night, I would sooner have thrust my knife into my own heart than into any part of the body of that dear brother of yours. But I was old and ugly, you know; and you were young and handsome; and jealousy is a mad devil that rages in the breast like hell-fire; it never knew how to spare, but tears and consumes every thing that comes within its reach.

At length James was brought to us; and as we were in his father's apartments, a chamber in no way adorned, James entered without any respect to persons. He was a tall and comely youth, but very pale and lean; and as it was one of his well days, he walked in without help. He had barely been told that his mother sent for him in a hurry; so that he entered with a visible alarm in his countenance.

What is the matter, my dear mother? says he. Alas! I am little able to help you at present. I hope nothing has happened that is suddenly distressful. Nothing amiss, my child, more than that your dear father, for whom I have sought and been sighing this many a year—your father lies dangerously ill in this very bed, my Jemmy.—Am I then so blessed, cried the boy, as to see and embrace a father?—O my child! exclaimed the old man, and eagerly stretched his arms towards him, come to my bosom, thou only offspring of my bowels! I may now say, with blessed Jacob, Let me die, let me die, since I have seen thy face, and thou art alive, my son!

I would at any time give a thousand pounds, my cousin, for a tenth of the enjoyment that I then had, in the feelings which God poured into the hearts of this little family, on their so very unexpected and marvellous meeting. It appeared to me, however, that young James even exceeded his parents in love; and this gave me such a cordial attachment to him, that from that hour to this we have never been sundered. He never failed nor forsook me; and at this very day he is my respected friend, and the superintendent of my family.

John, otherwise Barnabas, continued to linger for about a fortnight longer, and then departed quite happy, and without a groan. During the same space, also, James was daily attended by my own physician, and was nearly re-established in his health.

Being then intent on my departure, I sent for Mrs. Tirrel. Mrs. Tirrel, says I, I should be much inclined to take your James along with me, if I did not think you would grieve overmuch in his absence.—No, no, sir! said she; I would to heaven I were myself a young man for your sake. I desire no better either of him or for him, than that he should live and die faithfully and lovingly in your service.

When Mr. Clinton came to this part of his story, a messenger entered in fearful haste, and delivered a letter to Lady Maitland. As soon as she had run it over—My dearest sir, she cried, I must leave you this instant. I lately made you an offer of a hundred thousand pounds; and now I know not that I have so many shillings upon earth. I am here informed that the trustee of all my affairs has absconded, and made his escape to France; but I must hurry to town, and inquire after this business. So saying, she curtsied and suddenly withdrew, without giving her cousin time to make a tender of his services.

The next morning Mr. Clinton ordered his chariot to the door, and hastened to attend her ladyship at her house in London, but there he was told that she had set out for Dover about an hour before; and he returned much dejected and grieved on her account.

In about three weeks after, Mr. Clement with his young pupil came home, quite lightened of the money they had taken abroad. Mr. Fenton, for so we shall call him again, gave Clement a friendly embrace, and took Harry to his caresses, as though he had returned from a long and dangerous voyage.

Well, Clement, said Mr. Fenton, what account have you to give us of your expedition?—An account, sir, that would be extremely displeasing to any man living except yourself: in short, our young gentleman here, has plunged you above a thousand pounds in debt, over the large sums that we carried with us.—I hope the objects were worthy, said Mr. Fenton.—Wonderfully worthy, indeed, sir; I never saw such tender and affecting scenes.—Then I shall be overpaid and enriched by the narration.

Here, Harry inquired impatiently for Mrs. Clement and his friend Ned; and being told that they were on a visit to the Widow Neighbourly, he took a hasty leave for the present, and away he flew to embrace them.

As soon as he was gone—Sir, said Mr. Clement, I cannot think that there is in the world such another boy as yours. I will leave to himself the detail of our adventures in the several prisons; they had such an effect on his heart, that they cannot but have made a deep impression on his memory; so I shall only tell you of what happened in our way to London.

As we were chatting and walking leisurely along the road, a poor man before us happened to drop in a fit of the falling-sickness. When Harry saw the writhings and convulsions in which he lay, he turned pale, and looked vastly frightened, and seizing me under the arm, he cried—Come —come away! and hurried me off as fast as he could. But we had not gone far till his pace began to abate, and stopping, and hesitating—Let us turn, let us turn, Mr. Clement, he cried; let us go back again and help the poor man! We then returned hastily, and, raising his head, we kept him from bruising it against the ground. I then forced open his clenched hands, and having chafed the palms awhile, he began to recover, and soon came to himself. Meanwhile Harry's fright was not yet quite over. He seemed willing to get away from the object of his terror, and putting his hand in his pocket, and giving him all the silver he had, he wished him better health, and away he went.

We had not gone above half a mile further, when I saw a little girl, in a field on the right hand, endeavouring to drive a cow through a small gate into the road, in order to be milked, as I suppose, by her mother; but the cow kicked up her heels, and proved wanton and refractory, and ran hither and thither and would not be guided. The poor child then set up a cry of as bitter distress as if all that was valuable in the world was going to ruin. Harry gave a ready ear to the sound of lamentation, and, seeing the plight that the poor thing was in, he suddenly crossed the road, above ankle deep in dirt, and leaping the ditch, he proved nimbler than the cow, and driving her through the pass, he turned her into the way that the child would have her go.

That morning, indeed, was to Harry a morning of petty adventures. By the time that we approached the suburbs, we had nearly overtaken a grown girl who carried a basket of eggs on her head. A great lubberly boy just then passed us by at a smart pace, and tripping up the girl, gave the basket a tip with his hand, and dashed all the eggs into mash against a stony part of the road, and, again taking to his heels, run on as before. Immediately Harry's indignation was kindled, and setting out at top speed, he soon overtook him, and gave him several smart strokes with his little cane across the shoulders. The fellow then turned upon Harry, and gave him a furious blow with his fist over the head, while I hastened to his relief, as I perceived that the other was quite an overmatch for him. But before I arrived, our hero had put a quick end to the combat; for, springing from the ground, he darted his head full into the nose and mouth of his adversary, who instantly roared out, and, seeing his own blood come pouring down, he once more took to flight, while Harry continued to press upon him, and belaboured him at pleasure, till he judged that he had beaten him to the full value of the eggs.

Meanwhile the poor girl, wholly unmindful of what passed, remained wailing and wringing her hands over the wreck of her merchandise. The voice of a siren could not so powerfully have attracted and recalled Harry from the length he had gone; he returned with speed to her, and I followed.— My poor girl, says he, where were you going with those eggs?—To market, master, says she.—And what did you expect to get for them?—About five shillings, sir; and I had promised my daddy and mammy to lay it out in shoes and stockings for my little brothers and sisters; and so I must now bear all the blame of the poor things going barefoot. Here she again set up her wailings, and her tears poured down afresh.

Harry then desired me to lend him ten shillings, and turning to the mourner—Hold out your two hands, my poor girl, he cried; then putting five shillings into each hand, Here is the payment for your eggs, said he; and here are five shillings more, though I fear it is too little to pay you for all the tears they cost you.

Never did I see so sudden, so great a change in any countenance. Surprise, gratitude, ecstasy flashed from her eyes, and gave a joyous flush to the muscling of her aspect. She hurried her money into her bosom, and dropping on her knees in the dirt, and seizing hold of Harry's hand, she squeezed and kissed it repeatedly, without being able to utter a word; while Harry's eyes began to fill, and, endeavouring to disengage himself, he made off as fast as he could from such thanks as he thought he had no way deserved.

This, sir, was the last of our adventures going to London. But had you seen us, on our return, about two hours ago, you would have wondered at the miry plight into which we were put, by helping passengers up with their bundles that had tumbled into the dirt, or by assisting to raise cattle that had fallen under their carriages; for Master Harry would compel me to be as busy and active in matters of charity as himself.

However, sir, I am to tell you that Harry, with all his excellences of person, heart, and understanding, will be accounted a mere idiot among people of distinction, if he is not permitted to enter into some of the fashionable foibles and fashionable vices of the age.

We were taking a walk in the Mall, when we were met by the Earl of Mansfield, who expressed great joy at seeing his old acquaintance, as he called him; and he pressed us so earnestly to dinner, that we could not, in manners, refuse him.

There was a vast concourse of company, especially of the little quality of both sexes, who came to pay their respects to young Lord Bottom and his sister the Lady Louisa.

Harry was received and saluted by Lady Mansfield and the young lord, without any appearance of the old animosity. Some time after dinner a large packet of letters was brought in to the earl, and, making his excuse to Harry alone, he rose from the table and retired to his closet.

Lord Bottom and his sister then led the young males and females to an adjoining apartment, where several card-tables were laid; and I began to tremble for the credit of my pupil on the occasion, as I knew him to be a novice in such matters.

In the mean time, the remaining ladies and gentlemen divided into two or three parties at ombre; and I sauntered about the room, admiring the prints of the Ariadne and the Aurora, that were taken from Guido, as also some capital paintings that the earl had brought from Italy.

I had spent above an hour in this pleasing amusement, and had nearly made the tour of the whole dining-room, when, as I stood at a little distance behind my lady's chair, seeming inattentive to any thing that passed, Lord Bottom entered on tiptoe, and tripping up to his mother, and tittering and whispering in her ear—What do you think, mamma? said he; sure Master Fenton is a fool, a downright fool, upon my honour! He does not know a single card in the whole pack: he does not know the difference between the ace of hearts and the nine of clubs. I do not think either that he knows any thing of the difference or value of coin; for, as we passed through the hall to-day, a beggar asked for a halfpenny, and I saw him slip a shilling into his hand. Indeed, mamma, he is the greatest fool that ever I knew; and yet, poor fellow, he does not seem to know any thing of the matter himself.

During this oration of Lord Bottom on the virtues of his new friend, I felt my whole body glow and tingle with concern; and soon after Harry entered with the rest of the small quality.—Master Fenton, cries my lady, I beg to speak with you.—Don't you know the cards, my dear?—No, indeed, madam.—Can't you play at dice?—No, madam.—Can you play at draughts, polish, or chess?—Not at all, madam.—Why then, my dear, I must tell you that all your father's fortune will never introduce you among people of any breeding or of any fashion. Can you play at no kind of game, Master Harry?—A little at fox and geese, madam.—And pray, my dear, said my lady smiling, which of the parties do you espouse?—The part of the geese, madam.—I thought as much, pertly cried out my Lord Bottom; whereupon a loud laugh was echoed through the room.

Here my lady chid the company, and calling Harry to her again, for he had gone something aloof—Tell me, I pray you, said she, why you espouse the part of the geese.—Because, madam, I always wish that simplicity should get the better of fraud and cunning.

The countess here looked astonished; and having gazed a while at him, and caught and kissed him eagerly—You are a noble fellow, she cried, and all must be fools or mad that ever shall take you for the one or the other.

The elder gentry here laid their cards aside, and desired the young ones to set about some play. Lady Louisa proposed draw-gloves, or questions and commands, and to it they went.

Among the females was one Miss Uppish, sole heiress to a vast fortune. Though her person was deformed, her face was the picture of confident disdain; and scarce any one could speak to her, or look at her, without being told of the contempt she had for them, by the side glance of her eye, the writhing of her neck, and tossing up of her head.

In the course of the play, our Harry was commanded to put the candle into the hand of Miss Uppish, and then to kiss the candlestick; which command he obeyed literally, by giving her the candle, and kissing the candlestick which he held in his own hand.

Hereupon, a great shout was set up in the young assembly, and—O the fool, the senseless creature; the fool, the fool, the fool! was repeated throughout; while Lord Bottom laughed, and danced about in the impatience of his joy.

I was amazed that Harry's countenance seemed no way disconcerted by all this ridicule. At length Lady Mansfield called him to her. How, my dear, could you be guilty of such an error? she said; did not you know that, when you gave the candle into the hand of the young lady, she became the candlestick, and it was her you should have kissed? Harry then approached to her ladyship's ear, and in a pretty loud whisper, said—I did not like the metal, madam, that the candlestick was made of. Again Lady Mansfield looked surprised, and said—You are a sly rogue, a very sly rogue, upon my honour; and have sense enough to dupe the wisest of us all.

Jemmy Bottom, cried my lady aloud, come here! I can't but tell you, Jemmy, that you have behaved yourself extremely ill to your young friend here, who might have improved you by his example, as much as he has honoured you by his visit. I must further tell you, Jemmy Bottom, that, whenever you pique yourself on degrading Mr. Fenton, you only pride in your own abasement, and glory in your shame. Hereupon I got up, and, leaving our compliments for the earl, I carried off my young charge, for fear of our falling into any further disgrace.

While Harry is abroad, said Mr. Fenton, be pleased to

give me a general sketch of the manner in which you disposed of your money.—In the first place, sir, answered Clement, you will find by this list, that, for little more than the five hundred pounds alotted, we released ninety-five prisoners, whose debts amounted from forty shillings to about twelve pounds per man. These, in the general, had been journeymen tailors or weavers, or professors of other inferior crafts; and, as they wanted means of encouragement for exercising their respective occupations in jail, they subsisted on the pence which they got by begging at the grates, or on their dividends of occasional sums which were sent for their relief by charitable individuals. Nearly all of them were thin in flesh, and extremely shabby in clothing; and yet they could hardly be said to excite compassion, as they appeared so cheerful and unfeeling of their own wretchedness. Neither was there one of them, that I could learn a single circumstance of, whose story was worth reciting.

Some, however, were of a quality much superior to this class. Among others, there was a French marquis and a German prince; the prince had been put under arrest by his caterer, and the marquis by his tailor; so that something less than fifty pounds set them both at liberty.

While the keeper of the Fleet Prison was making out a list for us of the principal debtors, Harry and I took a turn about the court, and observed two fellows in liveries bearing several smoking covers up the stone stairs to a front dining-room. This surprised me, and gave me the curiosity to inquire what prisoners it could be who lived in so expensive and superb a manner.—Sir, said the under-keeper, there are few men now at liberty near so wealthy as this gentleman, who has done us the honour to set up his staff of rest in our house. His name is Sink. He is an attorney and an old bachelor, turned of sixty years of age. He is in for several sums, amounting to upwards of nine thousand pounds, and he is reputed to be worth above double that money.

During the last twenty years, he behaved himself with the strictest probity towards all men, and with the strictest appearance of piety towards God. In the dark, in frost and snow, and all inclemencies of weather, he never missed attending morning service at church. He was equally solicitous to be at evening prayer; and, whatever company he chanced to have with him, or how important soever the business in which he was engaged, the moment he heard the bell ring he would huddle up his papers and break away without ceremony. He was eager in his inquiries to know where the sacrament was soonest to be administered, and he never missed receiving it at least once in a week. Whenever he heard any profaneness or obscenity in the streets, he would stop to reprove and expostulate with the offender. In short, he so perfectly counterfeited or took off, as they call it, the real Christian, that many looked to see him, like Enoch or Elijah, taken alive into heaven.

This perpetual parade of sanctity gave him such an eclat and unmeasurable credit, that he was left trustee and executor in a multitude of wills; and numbers also deposited their substance in his hands, in order to be laid out at interest on securities, and so forth.

Three months since, about the dawning, as his butcher happened to pass by his door, he heard it open, and turning, saw a number of porters come out heavy laden. This gave him a kind of suspicion. He let them all pass, and, walking softly after, he stepped up to the hindmost, and offered him half-a-crown on condition of his telling him where they were carrying those parcels. That I will, said the porter; for the secret, if such it is, is nothing to me, you know. In short, we are carrying them to the wharf, to be put on board a boat that waits to take them in.

The butcher said no more, but hurried away to the baker, and, as they both run to the office, they met the brewer by the way. They took out their respective actions, and, taking a constable with them, they seized on good Mr. Sink, as he was stepping into a coach and six to make the best of his way to Dover. He would have paid them their money and discharged their actions on the spot; but here the master, in whom he trusted, happened to leave him in the lurch. As he had turned all his effects into money, and his money into paper, he had not at hand wherewith to pay his instant creditors. So they hurried him to jail, and before the banks were open the matter was blown, and action after action came pouring fast upon him.

When he found himself thus at bay, he cast aside his disguise, and set them all at defiance. His creditors have since offered to accept ten shillings, and some of them to accept five shillings, in the pound; but he swears that he will never pay them a groat; for he is now as liberal of his oaths and impious execrations, as he was lately of his more impious profanation of gospel phrases. And thus he daily revels in the sensual consumption of those wretches whom he hath so inhumanely defrauded; while hundreds of orphans and widows, and other miserables, perish for want of the sustenance which one infernal appetite devours without remorse. Nay, several of his creditors are, at this very time, famishing in this prison, while they see him feasting so lavishly upon their spoils.

The gorge of my soul, cried Mr. Fenton, the very gorge of my soul rises against this demon! Can nothing be done to bring him to punishment? Our parliament will surely interfere in such a calling exigence; they will send to the several banks and take up all the deposits that have been made in his name.—Alas, sir! said Clement, he was already

2*

aware of such possibilities, and has entered all his lodgments in feigned names, and to bearer upon demand.

Indeed, continued Clement, I heartily wished at the time that the laws of the Grecians and Romans had been in force among us, by which the debtor was given up to be set to labour, whipped, or tortured, at the pleasure of the creditor.

God forbid! God forbid! exclaimed Mr. Fenton.

When we see mankind divided into the rich and the poor, the strong and the weak, the sound and the sickly, we are apt to imagine that health, strength, or opulence was given to those, and infirmity, want, and weakness appointed to these, as marks of the peculiar favour or disfavour of Providence.

God, however, knows that there is nothing permanently good or evil in any of these things. He sees that nothing is a good but virtue, and that nothing is a virtue save some quality of benevolence. On benevolence, therefore, he builds the happiness of all his intelligent creatures; and in this our mortal state (our short apparatus for a long futurity), he has ordained the relative differences of rich and poor, strong and weak, sound and sickly, etc., to exercise us in the offices of that charity and those affections, which, reflecting and reflected, like mutual light and warmth, can alone make our good to all eternity.

Benevolence produces and constitutes the heaven or beatitude of God himself. He is no other than an infinite and eternal Good Will. Benevolence must, therefore, constitute the beatitude or heaven of all dependent beings, however infinitely diversified through several departments and subordinations, agreeable to the several natures and capacities of creatures.

God has appointed human power and human wealth, as

a ready and sufficient fund for human want and weakness; to which fund, therefore, they have as good a right to resort as any other creditors have to respective trusts or deposits; for though poverty and weakness are not creditors by the laws of man, they are creditors by the eternal laws of nature and equity, and must here, or hereafter, bring their debtors to account.

Every man when he becomes a member of this or that society, makes a deposit of three several sorts of trusts, that of his LIFE, that of his LIBERTY, and that of his PROPERTY.

Now as every man, in his separate or independent state, has by nature the absolute disposal of his property, he can convey the disposal thereof to society, as amply and absolutely as he was, in his separate right, entitled thereto.

This, however, cannot be said of his life, or of his liberty. He has no manner of right to take away his own life, neither to depart from his own liberty; he cannot therefore convey to others a right and authority which he hath not in himself.

The question then occurs, by what right it is that the legislative and executive powers of community appoint some persons to death, and others to imprisonment? My answer is short, and follows:—

It is the right, perhaps the duty, of every man, to defend his life, liberty, and property, and to kill or bind the attempters. This right he can, therefore, convey; and on such conveyance it becomes the right and duty of the trustees of society to put to death or imprison all who take away, or attempt the life, liberty, or property of any of its members.

This right, however, extends to criminal matters only; and it does not yet appear to me upon what reason, or right rule, founded in nature or policy, the several societies of mankind have agreed to deliver up their members to slavery, to stripes, tortures, or imprisonment, for matters merely civil, such as debts.

Several of the states of Greece, though accounting the rest of the world as barbarians, and even the Roman republic, during the times of its most boasted policy and freedom, gave up insolvent debtors (without inquiring into the causes or occasions of such insolvency) as slaves, or absolute property, into the hands of their creditors, to be sold at will, or put to labour, or starved, macerated, or tortured, in order to give value in vengeance, which they could not give in coin or other equivalent commodities.

The Jewish or Mosaic law, though allowing sufficiently, as Christ says, for "the hardness of that people's hearts," yet gave perfect enlargement to all Jews who were bondmen, and perfect remission to all Jews who were personal debtors, on every seventh or sabbatical year, and on every seventh or sabbatical year, or jubilee, all prisons were thrown open; all slaves, though foreigners or aliens, set at liberty, and even the lands were enfranchised, however mortgaged, or labouring under debt and execution; that all things, animate or inanimate, might have an earnest of that immunity and perfect freedom which God originally intended, and keeps in store for all his creatures.

The laws of Egypt permitted no member to deprive the public of the life, liberty, or labour of any other member, except he were a criminal not fitting to live, or to be suffered to walk at large. In all cases of debtor and creditor, they equitably appointed value for value, as far as the substance of the debtor could reach; and, in case of insufficiency, the insolvent party was obliged to leave in pledge the mummies, or preserved bodies, of his deceased ancestors, till, by industry or good fortune, either he or his posterity should be enabled to redeem them—a matter of refined as well as charitable policy; as nothing was held more infamous among the Egyptians than their inability to produce the mummies of their forefathers.

The laws of Holland, by their late qualifications, seem to acknowledge the iniquity, or inadequateness, of depriving a man of the possibility of earning, merely because he has not an immediate ability to pay. Sensible, therefore, that all men are debtors to God, and reciprocally debtors and creditors to each other, they have ordained that he who imprisons an insolvent debtor shall pay the proper penalty of his malevolence or indiscretion, by maintaining the party from whom he takes the ability of maintaining himself.

It must be admitted that, were our laws less severe with respect to debtors, were people less afraid of the jail on failure of payment, there would be less credit, and consequently less dealing in this so wondrously wealthy and trading a nation. But if our credit were less, would not our extravagance lessen also? Should we see such princely tables among people of the lower class? would so much claret, spirits, and ale, intoxicate a kingdom? should we see the value of a German prince's ransom gorgeously attiring each of our belle-dames, if neither merchant, butcher, brewer, laceman, mercer, milliner, nor tailor, would trust?

Many of our poor city dealers are yearly undone, with their families, by crediting persons who are privileged not to pay, or whose remoteness or power places them beyond the reach of the law. For by the return of *non-invent.* generally made upon writs, one would be apt to imagine that no single sub-sheriff knew of any such thing as a man of fortune, within his respective county, throughout the kingdom of Great Britain.

Before money became the medium of commerce, the simple business of the world was carried on by truck, or the commutation of one commodity for another. But when men consented to fix certain rateable values upon money, as a ready and portable equivalent for all sorts of effects, credit was consequently introduced, by the engagements of some to pay so much money in lieu of such commodities, or to deliver such or such commodities on the advance of so much money; and states found it their interest to support such public credit by enforcing the performance of such engagements.

By the common law of England, no person except the king could take the body of another in execution for debt; neither was this prerogative of the crown extended to the subject till the statute of Marlbridge, chap. 23, in the reign of Henry III.

Many contract debts through vanity or intemperance; or borrow money, or take up goods, with the intention of thieves and robbers, never to make return. When such suffer, they suffer deservedly in expiation of their guilt. But there are unavoidable damages by water, by fire, the crush of power, oppressive landlords, and more oppressive lawsuits, death of cattle, failure of crop, failure of payment in others; with thousands of suchlike casualities, whereby men may become bankrupt, and yet continue blameless. And in all such cases one would think that the present ruin was sufficient calamity, without the exertion of law to make that ruin irreparable.

As all the members of a community are interested in the life, liberty, and labours of each other, he who puts the rigour of our laws in execution, by detaining an insolvent brother in jail, is guilty of a fourfold injury; first, he robs the community of the labours of their brother; secondly, he robs his brother of all means of retrieving his shattered fortune; thirdly, he deprives himself of the possibility of payment; and lastly, he lays an unnecessary burden on the public, who, in charity, must maintain the member whom he in his cruelty confines.

However, since the severity of law is such, that he whose misfortunes have rendered him insolvent must "make satisfaction," (for so the savages esteem it,) by surrendering his body to durance for life, it is surely incumbent on our legislators and governors to make the condition of the unhappy sufferers as little grievous as may be.

But this most Christian duty, this most humane of all cares, is yet to come. When a debtor is delivered up into the fangs of his jailer, he is consigned to absolute and arbitrary slavery; and woe be to the wretch whose poverty may not have left him a sop for Cerberus. How more than miserable must be the state of those unhappy men, who are shut in from all possible redress or appeal against the despotic treatment of their savage keepers, whose hearts are habitually hardened to all sense of remorse, and whose ears are rendered callous by incessant groans!

We are credibly informed that it is usual with such keepers to amass considerable fortunes from the wrecks of the wretched: to squeeze them by exorbitant charges and illicit demands, as grapes are squeezed in a vine-press while one drop remains; and then to huddle them together into naked walls and windowless rooms; having got all they can, and nothing further to regard, save the return of their lifeless bodies to their creditors.

How many of these keepers exact from their distressed prisoners seven and eight shillings per week, for rooms that would not rent at a third of that sum in any other part of this city! At times, nine of those wretched prisoners are driven to kennel together in a hovel, fit only to stable a pair of horses, while many unoccupied apartments are locked up from use. Even a sufficiency of the common element of water is refused to their necessities, an advantage which the felons in Newgate enjoy. Public or private benefactions are dissipated or disposed of at the pleasure of the keepers, regardless of the intention or order of the donors. And the apartments appointed to these miserable men are generally damp or shattered in the flooring, and exposed, by breach or want of windows, to the inclemency of night-air, and all the rigour of the season.

But what avail their complaints if the legislature have not authorized, or made it the duty, of some especial magistrates to examine into and redress these crying abuses?

But tell me, continued Mr. Fenton, were there any prisoners of consideration among the confined debtors?—A few, sir, of note, and many who had been well to pass in the world. Among these, indeed, it was that every scene and species of misery was displayed. There you might see, as you have said, numerous families of wretches, whose thin and tattered garments but ill defended their shivering bodies from the inclemency of the elements, that blew through shattered windows or came pouring from unstanched roofs.

These people fared incomparably worse than those of the vulgar herd; for, being ashamed to beg at the grates, they had nothing to subsist on save their scanty portions of such charities as happened to be sent in from time to time, and this scarcely supplied them with a sufficiency of water, black bread and offal; while the recollections of their former affluence added sharp and bitter poignancy to the sense of their present wants. But here comes my pupil; he will be more particular on scenes with which his heart was so meltingly affected.

Harry then entered, with Mrs. Clement caressing him on the one side, and his old dependent Ned hanging about him on the other.

As soon as Clement and his Arabella had embraced, and all were settled and seated—Well, Harry, said Mr. Fenton, will you favour us with some account of your expedition? Have you ever a pretty story for me, my Harry?—Several stories, sir, said Harry, that were sweet pretty stories when

I heard them; but Mr. Clement had better tell them, they would be sadly bungled if they came through my hands, sir. —The company will make allowances, replied Mr. Fenton; let us have these stories in your own way, Harry, just as your memory may happen to serve you.

On the second day, sir, as my tutor and I were walking in the court-yard of the Fleet Prison, whom should I spy but my old master, Mr. Vindex, walking very sad to and again by the wall. He was so pale and shabby, and so fallen away, that I did not rightly know him till I looked at him very earnestly. My heart then began to soften and warm towards the poor man; for it told me that something very sorrowful must have happened, before he could have been brought to that condition. So I went up to him, with a face, I believe, as melancholy as his own.

How do you do, good Mr. Vindex? said I. I should be glad to see you, if I did not see you look so sad. He then stared at me for some time, and at length remembering me, he looked concerned, and turned away to shun me; but I took him lovingly by the hand, and said—You must not leave me, Mr. Vindex; won't you know your old scholar, Harry Fenton?—Yes, says he, casting down his mournful eyes, I know you now, master; I know I used you basely, and I know why you are come; but reproach me and insult me as much as you please, all is welcome now, since I cannot lie lower till I am laid in the earth.

I do not mean to insult you; this tear will witness for me that I do not mean to insult you, my dear Mr. Vindex; and so I wiped my eye. Here are twenty guineas to put warm clothes upon you in this cold weather. Little and low as I am myself, I will try to do something better for you; and so give me one kiss in token that we are friends.

The poor dear man then opened his broad eyes in a wild stare upon me, with a look that was made up half of joy and half of shame. He then kneeled down, as I supposed, that I might reach to kiss him, and taking me into his arms—You are not born of woman; you are an angel, an angel! he cried; and so he fell a-crying, and cried so sadly, that I could not for my heart but keep him company.

I did all I could to pacify and make him cheerful, and getting him up at last—You must not part with me, Mr. Vindex, said I; we must dine and spend the day together. Here is Mr. Clement, my tutor; you and he too must be friends.

I then led him by the hand into a large ground room that Mr. Close, the chief keeper, had appointed for us; and I ordered dinner to be hastened and brought up. As soon as we were all seated, I began to laugh and joke, after my foolish way, in order to make poor Mr. Vindex merry. When I found that it would not do—Mr. Vindex, said I, be so kind to let me know what the money may come to for which you are confined?—A terrible sum, indeed, my darling, said he; no less than a hundred and fifty-two pounds. I then put my hand in my pocket, and taking out two bills and a little matter of money that made up the sum, I put it into his hand, saying, My friend shall never lie in jail for such a trifle as this.

Having looked for some time at the bills with amazement, he turned to my tutor with a doubtful and shamed face—Is this young gentleman, sir, said he, duly authorized to dispose of such vast matters as these?—He is, says Mr. Clement; he is the carver and disposer of his father's fortune at pleasure; and I am confident that his father will think himself doubly paid, in the use that his noble son has made of his privilege this day.

A gleam then, like that of sunshine, broke through his sad countenance, as through the clouds of a dark day. And are you the one, he cried—Are you the one, Master Harry, whom I treated so barbarously? You may forgive me, my little cherubim ; you indeed may forgive me ; but I never—I never shall forgive myself!—O Mr. Vindex ! said I, I would very nearly undergo the same whipping again to do you twice the kindness, and make you love me twice as much as you now love me.

Dinner was now served, and, calling for wine, I filled him a bumper in a large glass, which he drank to the health of my glorious dada, as he called you, sir. Upon this we grew very merry and friendly among one another ; and when dinner was over, I begged him to tell me how he came to be put into confinement.

O, Master Harry ! he cried, I have suffered all that I have suffered very justly—very justly, for my harsh and cruel usage of you, Master Harry.

After the affair of the hobgoblins, as you know, the shame to which I was put by my fright and by my scourging began to be whispered, and then to be noised about the town. The boys at length catched the rumour, and began to hoot at me; and the more I chastised them the more they gathered about me, and shouted after me—A rod for the flogger ; a rod for the flogger!

No disease is so deadly, no blasting so baneful, as contempt to a man in the way of his profession. My boys grew disorderly, and behaved themselves in school without respect to my person, or regard to my government. Even my intimates shunned me, and would cast at me a side glance of smiling scorn as they passed. My school then melted from me like snow in a fog. Even my boarders forsook me. I stood at a high rent; my effects were seized by the landlord. It was in vain that I solicited payment from the parents of my scholars. No one who was indebted to me would give me a penny; while all that I owed came like a tumbling house upon me, and so I was cast into this prison, from whence your bounty has set me free.

My poor broken-hearted wife would have accompanied me to jail; but, as I had not wherewithal to give her a morsel of bread, I sent her to an old aunt, who had the humanity to take her in.

Alas, alas! poor Mr. Vindex, said I; had I guessed any part of the mischiefs that our unlucky pranks have brought upon you, I would have put both my hands into the furnace of Nebuchadnezzar rather than have had art or part in such a wickedness; for herein we acted the fable of the frogs and the boys—that which was play to us was death to you, Mr. Vindex.

In conscience, now we are indebted to you for every misfortune we caused you; and, as you are not yet paid for the half of your sufferings, I here give you my hand and word to make up a hundred and fifty pounds more for you; and for this I will not accept the smallest thanks, as I think it is no more than an act of common honesty.—And I, cried Mr. Fenton, I hold myself indebted to you a thousand pounds, my noble Harry, for that single sentiment.—That's well—that's well, sir! cried Harry, leaping up and clapping his hands; I shall now be clear in the world with all my poor creditors!

Thus, sir, continued he, it rejoiced my heart greatly to send poor Mr. Vindex away in such triumph; while my tutor and I went two or three doors off to see a mighty pretty young creature, who was said to be confined with her ancient father. And I will tell you their story, with two or three other stories, more on account of the incidents that happened while we were there, than of any thing else that was wonderful or uncommon in them.

On tapping at the door, we were desired to walk in, and saw a female with her back to us, weaving bone lace on a cushion, while an elderly man, with spectacles on, read to her in Thomas à Kempis. They both rose to salute us. Mr.

Clement then stepped up, and seeing what they were about, cried—God cannot but prosper your work, good people, since you employ your time to his purposes, both on earth and in heaven. As an earnest of his kindness to you, he sends you by us a considerable charity, which you shall receive as soon as you inform us who and what you are, and how you came here.—Blessed be the messengers of my God! cried out the father, whether they come with happy or with heavy tidings! I say, with old Eli—"It is the Lord, let him do what seemeth him good."

O father! I was quite charmed when the daughter turned to me; there was such a sweetness, such a heavenly harmlessness, in her face, that I could have kissed her, and kissed her, again and again.

As I had brought a glass and the remainder of our bottle with me, we all got about a board that was half stool and half table, and, after a round or two, the good man began his story.

My father's name was Samuel Stern. He had a clear estate of nine hundred and fifty pounds a year in Sussex; and had by my mother three daughters and four sons, of whom I was the second.

My father, unhappily, was a loyalist; and when the troubles broke out between King Charles and the parliament, he took up all the money he could at any interest, and raised a company at his own cost, which he headed on the part of his royal master.

After some successful skirmishes, his head was split in two by the broadsword of a trooper at the battle of Naseby. Immediately all our servants forsook us, each carrying away with him whatever came to hand; and quickly after, the soldiers of the Commonwealth came, carried off all the cattle, and left nothing of our house except the bare walls.

In the mean time, we poor children huddled together into

the garden, and there separating, ran and crept under bushes and hedges, as so many chickens endeavouring to gain shelter from the kite.

As soon as the noise of the tumult was over, we rose and looked about fearfully; and, getting together again, we helped one another through the garden hedge, and made as fast as we could to the cottage of a neighbouring farmer, who had been our father's tenant. Here we were received coldly, and fared but very hardly for that night. On the next day, however, in order to get quit of us, as I suppose, the man went among our relations, and prevailed on one to take a son, and another to take a daughter, till we were all divided among them; and so we entered on a kind of service to our kindred—a service, as I believe, that is found on experience to be much harder and more insulting than any service to a stranger.

I forgot to tell you, gentlemen, that our mother deceased before our father engaged in arms, insomuch that we became orphans in all respects. I fell to the share of an uncle by my mother's side. He had a small estate of about a hundred and twenty pounds yearly income, with one son, and a daughter whom I thought very lovely.

My uncle appointed me overseer of his labourers, as also his occasional clerk, for casting accounts and inditing his letters, etc.; but when it was intimated to him that there was a secret liking between his daughter and me, he called me aside, and, taking up a book of profane poems, he kissed it, and swore by the contents thereof, that if ever I married his daughter he would not give us a groat.

If you ever knew what love was, said he to Mr. Clement, you must know that it breaks over stronger fences than these. In short, we were wedded, and turned out of the house without any thing to live upon except about the value of twenty pounds in small matters, which had been given to my wife from time to time, by Lady Goodly, her godmother.

We made the best of our way to London. My wife understood needlework, and as I knew that my father-in-law was quite irreconcilable, I joined myself to a house-painter, to whom I gave my time for nothing, on condition of his giving me a sight into his business.

In the third year my dear wife brought this poor creature into the world; but happily, she did not encumber mankind with any more of our wretched and depending progeny.

All our care and delight was fixed on this our little daughter, and we thought nothing of any pains or labour that might serve to introduce her, like herself, into the world.

As soon as Charles II. had ascended the throne, our relations were fully assured that we should be restored to our ancient rights and possessions; and they contributed, as it were, for their own credit, to set us forth in a suitable manner for appearing at court. There, accordingly, we attended, from time to time, for the space of twelve months, and got a number of woeful memorials presented to his majesty; but his majesty was so deeply engaged in his pleasures, or so fearful of offending the enemies of his house, that he gave no attention to our wrongs. There may be also something in the breasts of the great that excites them to acts of bounty rather than acts of justice; for these, as they apprehend, might be accepted as matter of debt and not as matter of favour.

Being tired of a fruitless suit, I returned to my former employment, and, by industry and frugality, I lived with my little family quite happy and contented.

About ten months ago, two men came to our lodgings. The one was in a rich livery, and, having inquired for my daughter, presented her with a note to this effect:—"Lady

Diana Templar sends Diana Stern the enclosed bill of twenty-five pounds, in order to put her into some little way of livelihood." As my poor dear child had no cause to suspect any fraud or evil intention in the case, she desired the men to return her most humble thanks and duty to her ladyship, and away they went.

As this lady was a distant relation of my wife's father, my daughter in a few days dressed herself in her best, and went to return thanks to her ladyship in person, but was told that she was gone to her seat in the country.

In the mean time she laid out her supposed bounty in furnishing a little front shop with some millinery wares, and was already beginning to get some custom, when one evening two bailiffs entered, laid an action upon her, and, taking her up in their arms, hurried her into a coach that drove up to the door.

My wife and I had rushed out on hearing our child shriek; and, seeing a coach set off with her at a great rate, we ran after as fast as we could, shouting, and screaming, and crying—Stop the coach—stop the coach! At length a bold fellow who was passing caught one of the horses by the bridle, and, while the coachman lashed at him, he took out his knife and cut the reins in two. A mob then began to gather; whereupon a well-dressed man, who was in the coach, leaped out and made his escape, but the coachman was not so lucky; the people pulled him from the box, and having beaten and kicked him, they dragged him through the kennel.

Meanwhile we got our child out, and then the mob overturned the coach, and, jumping upon it, broke and dashed it all to pieces. We then thought that we had nothing further to apprehend, and, taking our child between us, we turned back and walked homeward; but, alas! we were not permitted to enter. The two bailiffs met us, and, producing their writ, again arrested our daughter at the suit, as they said, of Jonathan Delvil, Esq., for the sum of twenty-five pounds, which he had lent her on such a day. So they conducted her here, while my wife and I accompanied her, weeping and sobbing all the way.

I then took these poor apartments to cover us from the weather, and, as my wife grew suddenly sick and faint, I hastened back to our lodgings and had our bedding brought hither.

It was now evident that the pretended gift of Lady Templar was no other than a diabolical scheme of the villain Delvil to get my darling within his fangs; and I cursed my own stupidity for not perceiving it at first; but blessed be God, however, in all events, that my lamb was still innocent —was still unsullied.

What with grief and with fright together, my dear wife took to her bed, from whence she never rose, but expired on the fifth day, blessing and pressing her daughter to her bosom. My poor infant then fell as dead beside her mother, and could not be recovered from her fit in many hours; and indeed it was then the wish and the prayer of my soul, that we might all be laid and forgotten in one grave together.

As soon as my darling was recovered, however, I again wished to live for her sake, that I might not leave her without a comforter or protector in the midst of a merciless and wicked world.

In order to pay the nurse-keeper, the doctor, and apothecary, as also to defray the funeral expenses, I left my child with the nurse-keeper, and, going to our former lodgings, I sold all her millinery matters at something under a third of prime cost; and having discharged the lodgings, and paid my jail debts, I prepared to lay my precious deposit in the womb of that earth which is one day to render her back incorruptible to eternity.

When the corpse was carrying out at the door, my child

fell once more into fits, and I was divided and quite distracted about what I should do, whether to stay with the living, or pay my duty to the dead. But I will no longer detain you with melancholy matters, since all worldly griefs, with all worldly joys also, must shortly be done away.

As soon as I understood that Lady Templar was returned to town, I waited upon her, and giving her an abridgment of our manifold misfortunes, I produced the note that had been written in her name; but she coldly replied that it was not her hand, and that she was not answerable for the frauds or villanies of others.

Meanwhile, my dear girl accused herself as the cause of all our calamities, and pined away on that account as pale as the sheet she lay in. She was also so enfeebled by her faintish and sick fits, that she was not able to make a third of her usual earnings; and as I, on my part, was also disqualified from labouring in my profession, since I did not dare to leave my child alone and unsheltered, we were reduced to a state of the greatest extremity.

One day word was brought me that a gentleman, a few doors off, desired to speak with me; and as they who are sinking catch at any thing for their support, my heart fluttered in the hope of some happy reverse. Accordingly I followed the messenger. His appearance in dress and person was altogether that of the gentleman.

He ordered all others out of the room, and requesting me to sit beside him, in a half whispering voice he began:—I am come, Mr. Stern, from one whom you have great reason to account your greatest enemy: I come from Mr. Delvil, at whose suit your daughter now lies in prison. I started.—Be patient, sir, he said. He knows your distresses—he knows all your wants—he knows also that he is the author of them; yet I tell you that he feels them as if they were his own, and that it was not his enmity, but his love, that occasioned them.

He depends on his old uncle Dimmock for a vast fortune in expectation. He saw your daughter, and loved her; he saw her again, and loved her to madness. He inquired her family, her character, and found that he had nothing to expect from any licentious proposal. He feared, however, that all must love her as he did, and, to prevent other pirates, he made use of the stratagem which, contrary to his intentions, has brought you here. He never meant any thing dishonourable by your daughter. Had he carried her clear off, you might all have been happy together at· this day; and, if you consent, he will marry her here in the presence of a few witnesses, who shall be sworn to secrecy till his uncle's death; and he will instantly pay you down three hundred pounds in recompense for your sufferings, and will settle one hundred pounds annuity on your child for life.

I must own that, to one in my circumstances, this proposal had something very tempting in it. But who is this Mr. Delvil? said I. I know him not; I never saw him.—I am the man, sir, said he. I would have discharged my action as I came to this place; but I dare not permit your daughter to get out of my custody; for, at the loss of my fortune— at the loss of my life—I am determined that no other man living shall possess her.—I then promised him that I would make a faithful narration to my child of all that had passed, but told him, at the same time, that I would wholly subscribe to her pleasure; and so we parted.

As soon as I represented this matter to my Diana—O no! my papa, she cried; it is impossible—it never can be; I would do any thing—suffer any thing—but this, for your relief. Would you act the marriage of the lamb and the wolf in the fable? If such have been the consequences of this gentleman's affection for us, what have we not to expect from the effects of his aversion? I would prefer any kind of death to a life with such a man. And then, my mother, she cried, and burst into tears—my dear mother whom he has murdered! Though he were worth half the world, and would marry me publicly in the face of the other half, it will not be—it cannot be, indeed, my papa!

Hereupon I writ Mr. Delvil almost a literal account of my daughter's answer. It is nearly five weeks since this happened, and we have not heard any thing further of him. In this time, however, we got acquainted with a family at the next door, whose converse has been a great consolation to us. There is a father and mother, and seven small children—boys and girls; they are very worthy people, and of noble descent; but how they contrive to live at all I cannot conceive, for they have no visible means of making a penny. Had we not known them, we should have thought ourselves the poorest of all creatures. We must own them more deserving of your charity than we are.

Here poor Mr. Stern ended; and you cannot think, dada, how my heart leapt with love towards him, on his recommending others as more deserving than himself. So I resolved at once what to do, and taking two fifty pound notes from my pocket-book—You shall not be under the necessity, Mr. Stern, says I, of marrying your pretty lamb here to the ugly wolf; so here is fifty pounds to pay your action and fees, and other small debts.

On taking the note he looked at it very earnestly; and when he saw it was a true note, he opened his eyes and his mouth so wide, and stood so stiff, without stirring hand or foot, that he put me in mind of Lot's wife who was turned into a pillar of salt. However, I did not seem to mind him, but turning to his daughter, and shewing her the other note, Miss Diana, says I, here is fifty pounds for you also, in order to set you up in your little shop again; but you shall not have it without a certain condition.—What condition, master? she said, smiling.—The condition, says I, of putting your arms about my neck, and giving me one or two sweet kisses. She then looked earnestly at me with eyes swimming with pleasure; and starting suddenly to me, and catching me to her bosom, she kissed my lips and my forehead, and my head, again and again; and then set up as lamentable and loud a cry as if her father had lain a corpse before her.

Mr. Stern then lifted up his eyes, and dropping on his knees—O my God! he cried, how bountiful art thou to a wretch who is not worthy the least of all thy mercies! Hereupon the daughter turned, and seeing the posture of her father, she fell on her knees before him, and throwing her arms about him, he folded her in his also, and they wept plentifully upon each other.

How comes it that crying should be so catching? However it be, Mr. Clement and I could not contain; and I shall love him better during life for the tears that he shed on that occasion.

On hearing a smart rapping, Mr. Stern rose and opened the door, where a footman, almost breathless, delivered him a letter. The letter was to the purpose that Mr. Delvil was ill of a quinsy, that he had but a few hours to live, and requested Mr. Stern to bring his daughter to him, that, by marriage, he might give her a lawful title to his fortune. No, papa! cried Diana; living or dead, nothing shall ever bribe me to give my hand to a man who has had a hand in the death of my dearest mother.

Mr. Clement, however, thought it advisable that Mr. Stern should attend the messenger, to see if Mr. Delvil was really ill, or whether this might not be some new-contrived treachery.

This was a day of successes to poor Mr. Stern. We had promised to stay with his Diana until his return; and he had not been long gone till some one tapped at the door.

I opened it, and saw an exceeding old and reverend man; he was dressed all in black, and his white head looked like snow on the feathers of a raven. Is Tom Stern here? said he.—No, sir, said I, he is gone into town.—I thought he was a prisoner. No, sir, it is not he, but his daughter who is under confinement.—Will you give a feeble old man leave to sit with you, gentlemen? and so down he sat. Come here to me, child, says he to Diana; are you a daughter of Tom Stern?—I am, sir, so please you.—And what was your mother's name?—Ann Roche, sir; but, alas! she is not living,—I was the cause of her death; she broke her heart, good sir, on my being put to jail.—I hope, child, said the old gentleman, that you were not imprisoned for any thing that was naughty.—No, sir, no! cried Mr. Clement, it was her honesty alone that brought and kept her here; had she been less virtuous she might have been at liberty, and flaunting about in her coach.

The old man then put on his spectacles, and ordering her to draw nearer; he took a hand in each of his, and, looking intently in her face—What is your name, my dear? said he; Diana, honoured sir.—That is a pretty and chaste name, for an unchristian name. Indeed, Diana, you are a sweet babe, and the prettiest little prisoner that ever I saw. I will pay all your debts, and give you a thousand pounds, over, if you will come along with me, and be my prisoner, Diana.—Ah, sir! cried the girl, it is too much to have broken the heart of one parent already; I would not leave my dear father for any man with all the money in all the world.—You do not leave your father, he cried, by going with me, Diana. I am your true father, the father of Nanny Roche, the father of her who bore you—your own grandfather, my Diana.

Here she sunk on her knees, between his knees, begging and beseeching his blessing; while his hands and eyes were lifted in prayer over her. He then raised her, and placing her gently on his knee, clasped her in his aged arms; while she threw hers about his neck, and joining her cheek to his, sobbed aloud, and poured her tears into his bosom. The old gentleman, however, did not express his concern by word or sob, or even any change of his countenance; and yet his tears fell fast down his reverend and delightful features, upon his grandchild.

This was a very pleasing, though a very affecting sight. As soon as the height of their passion was something abated, Miss Diana turned her eye towards me, and said—You were pleased, my grandpapa, to promise that you would pay my debts, but that is done already. This angel here was sent to prevent all others; and he further presented me with this bill for £50, to set me up in a better shop than I kept before.

I rejoice, cried the old man, I rejoice to find that so much of heaven is still left upon earth. But you, my Diana, are now in a condition rather to give charity than receive it from any. Your dear uncle Jeremy, who traded to the West Indies, lately died of the smallpox on his passage homeward. You are the heir of his fortunes, and the heir of my fortune; you are the whole and sole lady of all our possessions. But, tell me, how much did this young gentleman advance in your favour?—A hundred pounds, sir.

He then took out a banker's note of a hundred pounds, and, having offered it to me, I did not dare to refuse it, for fear of offending the honour of the respectable old gentleman; so I held it in my hand after a doubting manner.—My dear Miss Diana, says I, I will not be put to the pain of taking this back again, but on the condition of your telling me to whom I shall give it?—O, she cried out instantly, to the babies, to the sweet babies at the next door! I wish to heaven I had as much more to add to it for their sakes.

I then inquired the name of her favourite family at the next door, and being told that it was Ruth, I looked over my list, and found that Mr. Ruth was in for above seven hundred pounds. This grieved me very much, as such a sum nearly amounted to the half of our whole stock. However, I comforted myself with the hope that God would send some one else to make up to this poor family what should be wanting on my part.

Mr. Stern just then returned. I beg pardon, said he, gentlemen, for detaining you so long, but I could not avoid it. The unhappy man is actually dying a very terrible death, indeed, in his full strength, and almost in his full health, stifling and gasping for air, which the swelling of his glands will not suffer to pass.

As soon as I entered, he beckoned to me, and put this paper sealed into my hand. And again, observing that I was agitated and deeply concerned for the state in which he laboured, he reached out his hand to me, and grasping my right hand, put this ring upon my finger. This paper contains, under his hand and seal, a discharge of the action which he laid upon my daughter, as also a conveyance to us of the cash notes enclosed, amounting to three hundred pounds, in consideration, as he recites, of our losses and unjust sufferings. And so, my dear Mr. Fenton, I here return you your £100 with all possible acknowledgments, and a sense of the obligation that will never leave me during life.

Sir, said I, you must excuse me; I am already paid. That gentleman yonder compelled me to accept of the very sum you offer.

Mr. Stern then started, and turning, he saw his uncle; and, eyeing him inquisitively, at length recollected who he was. He then stepped up, and falling on his knees before him—O, sir! he cried, your pardon, your pardon! 'Tis all I presume to ask; I dare not hope for your blessing.

Tom, said the old gentleman, I wanted to be even with you; I wanted to seduce your daughter, as you seduced mine. But your daughter, Tom, though come of very rebellious parents, would not be seduced. However, as I have taken a liking to her, she must come along with me, whether she will or no. And as Jacob said to Joseph concerning Ephraim and Manasseh, she shall be mine and not thine, Tom; and my name and the name of my fathers shall be named upon her, according to her inheritance. But if you have any affection for this, my child, Tom, and are unwilling to part with her, you may follow her, and welcome.

Soon after we got up, and, having congratulated this happy family on the blessing of their meeting and reconciliation, I stepped to the old gentleman, and catching him about the neck, tenderly took my leave of him, as I did also of Mr. Stern. But when I went to take leave of the fair Diana, she drew some steps backward, and her eyes and sweet features beginning to swell, she again run forward, and catching me in her dear arms—O, my darling, my darling, my darling! she cried; am I then going to lose you, it may be never to see you more! were it but once in a week, in a month, in a year, to behold you, even that would keep me alive for all the remainder. O my best, my most generous, my first preserver! it is you who might be the seducer—who might make me and others run after you barefoot. But if we must part, my little angel, do but promise to know me in heaven, and there your poor Diana will meet you, never to part any more.

What could I say or do, sir, in answer to the dear girl? My heart swelled almost to bursting while she caressed and wept over me. At length, with words as well as my tears would give me leave to pronounce them, I demanded the name of the place to which she was going, and promised to pay her a visit as soon as possibly I could. We then parted very melancholy, notwithstanding all our success; and, going out, I wiped my eyes, and begged Mr. Clement to order tea and coffee, with a comfortable entertainment, for the family at the next door, while I should go in and introduce myself as well as I could.

Having tapped gently at the door, it was opened by a little ragged boy of about five years old. Mrs. Ruth sat full in my view, and her three little daughters stood before her, while she examined them in the Old Testament questions of who was the first man, and the wisest man, and the strongest man, and the oldest man, and, above all, the man after God's own heart?

Mrs. Ruth was a fine woman, and had a great deal of humble dignity about her. I bowed to her as I entered, and, going familiarly up, I took her by the hand and kissed it.—Allow me, madam, said I, to introduce a little neighbour to you. I lodge within a few doors, and shall think myself happy in being acquainted in your family.—Alas! my dear, says she, there are very few who seek acquaintance with calamity.—They who wish to relieve it seek acquaintance with it, madam.

Having eyed me all over with an earnest kind of surprise —You look, my love, said she, to be very good-natured, and, I daresay, will be very charitable when you come to have the ability.—The little ability I have, madam, shall be strained for your service. In the mean time, pray pardon the freedom I have taken in ordering tea and coffee into your room, with some cakes and sweetmeats for these pretty misses. I will only trouble you, madam, with one guest more; it is Mr. Clement, my tutor, who, good man, has been no stranger to poverty or distress.

Here she called Mr. Ruth from an inner room.—Give me leave, my dear, says she, to introduce a young stranger to you; from what world he comes I know not, but I am sure that he is not wholly of the world that we have lived in.

Mr. Ruth's countenance spoke at once the meekness of Moses and the patience of Job. Having saluted, we both sat down.—Mr. Ruth, said I, I have a message to you and your lady from your sweet, pretty neighbour, Mr. Diana Stern. In token of her respect and affection for you, she presents you with this cash-note of a hundred pounds.— Diana Stern! cried out Mr. Ruth; why, master, she is nearly as poor as ourselves.—By no means, sir, I assure you; her grandfather has come to town; she is worth several thousands, besides a considerable estate to which she is heiress.—O the dear creature! the dear angel! cried Mrs. Ruth; I will instantly go and pay her my acknowledgments. So up she got, and out she run, before I could prevent her.

As soon as she was gone—Mr. Ruth, says I, my father is much fonder of me than I deserve. He has given me a little money to dispose of at pleasure among the confined debtors; and, though I may not have enough to answer your occasions, yet my father is so very good and so very generous, that if you give me the sum of your debts, with the story of your distresses, his heart, I am sure, will melt, and he will set you clear in the world.

He made no answer, however, to this my offer, but, lifting up his eyes, he cried—Well mightest thou say, great Saviour of the simple, "Suffer little children to come unto me, for of such is the kingdom of heaven." O thou babe of the manger! "thou first-born of many brethren;" here, indeed, is a dear and true little brother of thine; but he speaks in his simplicity, and not according to knowledge! Then, turning towards me—Can you guess, my darling, said he, what you undertake to do for me? I question if the charities of all this nation would be sufficient, when united, to effect my deliverance. Nothing—nothing, but the arm of the Almighty can do it. He will do it, indeed, in death; but what then shall become of my wife and seven infants? that truly is terrible—is worse than death to think of!

While we were speaking, two sweet little fellows came in, the eldest very nearly of my size, but both clad in very thin and poor-looking apparel. Having kneeled for their father's blessing, they slipped behind us; and, turning my head to observe them, I was quite ashamed, and drew it back again on perceiving that the poor things were unlading their pockets of old crusts and broken meats, which I supposed they had begged for the family.

Mrs. Ruth just then returned, and her countenance looked something dejected. She took her seat by her husband, and, continuing a while silent, she put her handkerchief before her eyes, and began in broken words—Can you guess, my dear, said she, what sort of a creature this is whom we have got among us? This little heavenly impostor, to lighten our obligation, would have persuaded us that the hundred pounds was the gift of another; but it is all his own bounty—it is all his own graciousness. Come, my daughters—come, my children, kneel down and return your thanks to this your patron, your benefactor, your little father here!

O, sir, you would have pitied me sadly had you seen me at this time! The poor dear things came, all in a cluster, pressing, and catching, and clasping, and clinging about me, while my love and my very heart was torn, as it were, to fritters among them. So I took them one by one in my arms, and kissed and embraced them very cordially, calling them my brothers and sisters. I then took out another hundred-pound note, and giving it to the eldest of the daughters—Here, my dear, said I, I always loved the little misses better than the little masters; here is for yourself and your sisters, to clothe you in a way more becoming your family. And then, taking a note of equal value, I gave it to the eldest son, for himself and his brothers, as I said, to help to educate them in a manner more agreeable to the house from whence they came.

Mr. and Mrs. Ruth looked so astonished at me, and at each other, that for a while they were not able to utter a syllable; and, just as they began to make their acknowledgments, I cried—Hush, hush! here comes my tutor.

Mr. Clement just then entered, followed by several servants, who carried a tea equipage, cold fowl, baked meats, with pastries and some wine.

Having introduced Mr. Clement, we all got round the table, and after a tea and a further regale, I besought Mr. Ruth to give us the story of his misfortunes.

My father, said he, was baron of Frankford. He left my brother with the title, four thousand five hundred pounds a-year entailed, however, upon me, in case of his dying without male issue; and he left me a small inheritance of four hundred pounds yearly, to support in some measure the appearance of a gentleman.

As my concern bordered on my brother's estate, we saw one another every day, and continued for several years in straight and tender amity.

Being both invited one day to dine with other company, at the house of a neighbour called Mr. Heartless, a question happened to be started over the bottle, whether the method of setting an egg on end was originally the invention of Columbus. or whether it was communicated to him by some other, and I unhappily espoused the opinion that was opposite to that of my brother.

Now, though the question was not worth the very shell of the egg about which we debated, yet we entered as warmly into it as though a province had lain at stake; for it is not truth or instruction that disputants seek after—it is victory alone that is the object of their contention.

After some warm words and personal retorts had passed between my brother and me, he started into sudden passion, and gave me the lie; whereupon, reaching across the table, I gave him a tap on the cheek with the flat of my fingers, then rising furiously from his seat, he swore a fearful oath, and cried—I will ruin you, Harry, though it cost me my estate; I will ruin you, Harry Ruth, with all who are yours.

The very next day he mustered his tenants and labourers, and, coming upon me with a little army, he laid most of my fences level with the earth.

When I complained of this violence to my next neighbours, Mr. Heartless and Mr. Hollow, they protested they would stand by me against such outrageous proceedings to the last of their fortunes. They then advanced me, between them, five hundred pounds for the purpose. I immediately commenced suit against my lord's tenants. But, though I cast them all with costs, I unhappily found that nearly all my money was sunk in the contest.

Meantime, scarce a day passed wherein I was not served with a subpœna from chancery, to answer such or such a bill, to which my brother had procured me to be made a party. And he also entered a suit against me himself, in order to invalidate my father's will, whereby I claimed my little patrimony.

When I told this to my friend Mr. Hollow, he broke into a loud laugh. Your title! cried he; the world cannot invalidate your title, Mr. Ruth; I will let you have a thousand pounds upon it to-morrow; and this I was under the necessity of accepting soon after.

Contention serves, with mutual hands, to shut every door against reconciliation. The more I had loved my brother, the more I now detested him. Instead of any submission or overture to appease him, my lips uttered, in daily invectives, the overflowings of my heart; as I also was assured that, on his part, he wished me nothing less than eternal perdition. Thus we burned, on both sides, with unquenchable fire, and the kingdom of Satan was fully opened within us.

At length my body was imprisoned, at the suit of my neighbour Heartless, for £750, and my lands were taken under execution, at the suit of my neighbour Hollow, for the sum of £2000. But I soon was informed that all this money was my brother's, who had advanced it from time to time, to those his clandestine correspondents, in order to hasten and deepen my destruction. When I understood this I raged—I was all on fire; and I took a horrid pleasure in the notion of having the fangs of a tiger, that I might tear my brother piecemeal, and my false friends limb from limb, and feast my spirit on their pangs, and mine eyes on their carnage.

But when I turned a look on my wife and seven infants, grief joined with rage to rend me by a double distraction. I cursed the lot to which I was appointed upon earth, and I should have sought some desperate means of putting an end to my torments and existence together, but that I dreaded, by my death, to give pleasure to my brother, ten times more than I dreaded the pain of death itself.

O my friends! had all that ever were sainted come and preached to me the peace of our Lord Christ at that season, it would have been no more than beating the air, or striving with so many sponges to make an impression on a block of marble. It is distress alone that, by oppression, makes impression—that preaches the internal doctrine of sensible mortification, and humbles a proud spirit by plucking away all its props.

At first, I was a worm under the foot of my God. I

turned and struggled, and writhed, and fought with all my force against the crusher. But, alas! all was in vain; he was too mighty for me, and opposition served only to add to my anguish.

At length I was compelled to acquiesce, rather through the want of power than the want of will to resist. And I lay, as it were, without motion under his dispensations; at the same time that my heart reproached him in secret.

Having sold all our moveables, and even our wearing apparel, for sustenance, we were reduced to the necessity of sending our eldest boys to beg fragments of victuals at kitchen-windows, to keep us from utterly famishing. This I held to be such a further shame and disgrace as stung my soul to the quick; I therefore began to kick against these pricks also; but finding that the more I spurned, the stronger I was held and pressed into the dust, I gave up all resistance, and contented myself with grieving and weeping under the hand of the Almighty.

From hence I gradually sunk into a state of resigned serenity, which, although without sunshine, was yet without disturbance. My fury smoothed its crest, my passions subsided, and I felt nothing more of rancour against my brother, or resistance against my God.

The activity of the soul will find itself employment. As I had now no further prospect or concern upon earth, I began to turn my thoughts and attention towards heaven. I locked myself into yonder closet. I threw myself into the dust. I have sinned, I cried—I have greatly sinned, O God! I am nothing—I am crushed even lower than the nothing that I am; spare, spare me from a deeper perdition, I beseech thee!

I felt that my prayer was heard; peace descended upon me like dew upon the night; the day-star began gradually to dawn to my soul; the dark kingdom of Satan gave way before the kingdom of the Son of light and love; and I would no more have entertained any one of my former passions than I would have taken burning coals and have buttoned them up in my bosom.

I was greatly delighted, father, with this part, and some more of Mr. Ruth's story: and I got him to repeat it over and over, that I might remember it the better.

I now, continued he—I now pitied my brother as much as ever I had hated him. I grieved for having caused the loss of his peace. I wished to restore it to him. I wrote a penitential acknowledgment of my faults. I besought his pardon, in the humblest manner, for the unfortunate blow. I subscribed to the justice of my subsequent sufferings; and I sent my son here, to attend his lordship with my lowly address.

The triumph which this humiliation gave to my brother, supplied him with patience to go through my memorial. But then conceiving, as I suppose, that it was dictated by mercenary meanness and hypocrisy, he tore it to pieces and dashed it into the fire. Then returning to my child the box which had so inflamed the soul of his lordship, he kicked my poor little fellow out of his house.

My child came home to me weeping sadly; but I consoled him the best I could, and mingled my tears with his; not in any resentment for the treatment received, but through grief for the inveteracy of my unhappy brother. O my God! I cried, I no longer repine at my abasement, at the weight of my sufferings and mortifications! I bless thee for them, O God! they have proved my best friends, my most salutary physicians. Cruel and stern, indeed, is the porter who stands at the iron gate of pain; but O, it opens upon regions of inward delight; for He who clothed himself with the cross is all glorious within.

My happy experience of this truth opened for me a new

prospect in the mystery of God's dispensation to mortals, and threw a number of shining lights on those very articles of gospel-redemption which had formerly appeared to me so exceptionable and gloomy. If God, said I to myself, hath suffered man to fall, he hath also provided for him every possible means of recovery and restoration.

Wherefore, when sin came into the world, God also sent suffering, its inseparable attendant, to be a cure and an antidote to the poison thereof. If sin, therefore, hath thrust the kingdom of heaven from within us, suffering comes as God's forerunner; it relaxes and unfolds the brazen gates of our polluted temple, that Christ, our righteousness, may enter, the very hem of whose garment is salvation to every soul that lays hold upon it.

Here I took Mr. Ruth about the neck, and kissing him, said, that I was sure my father would be willing to pay his whole debt, in return for the sweet instructions which he had given to his Harry.—You speak of your father, my dear, said he, as though he were the representative of God in the Gospel, who forgave to his servant ten thousand talents. What you have given me already, master, is beyond any human bounty that I ever heard of. I shall, therefore, lay by two of these notes, till I am better informed how far your good father may be satisfied with the donation.

Soon after we took leave, for the present, of this honourable family. We then went among the other principal debtors, whose distresses indeed were great, though their stories, except one, had little singular in them. In order to make our money go as far as we could, we hurried here and there through the town, compounding with the several creditors, from eight to ten and twelve and fifteen shillings in the pound; so that, for about six hundred pounds, we discharged a number who were indebted to the amount of a thousand.

On Tuesday about noon, in the last week, I stepped to Mr. Ruth's, to see if the family had been decently clad, agreeable to my request. There I found him and his four sons clothed in warm and clean, though very coarse, apparel; and he told me that his wife had gone abroad with her three daughters, in order to put them also into a suitable condition.

While I sat with him, a young woman came in, of a very genteel appearance, though in a plain dress. Don't you remember the girl, sir, said she, to Mr. Ruth, who used to come to you over night, in a green kerchief and a little red mantle?—I should be very ungrateful, indeed, said he, if any change of dress could conceal from my remembrance that sweet and charitable countenance.—O sir! she cried, the few shillings that I have brought you, from time to time, came from a very affectionate hand, though from a hand you would little suspect of any affection towards you; they came from your loving niece, Belinda Ruth, who has shed many a shower of tears on your misfortunes.—May heaven be her portion, cried out the good man, since earth has nothing equal to so much goodness!—Indeed, sir, continued the girl, the little that your niece sent you was procured with much difficulty and danger to herself; for from the time that, on her knees and with a deluge of tears, she petitioned her father in your behalf, he kept a watchful eye over her, and took from her all family trusts, so that she had nothing wherewith to supply you except the price of some cast gowns, and of other little matters that she feigned to have lost. Moreover, my lord swore vehemently, that if ever she furnished you with the value of a farthing, or kept any kind of correspondence with you or with yours, he would disown and turn her into the public streets.

You alarm me greatly, cried out Mr. Ruth. Is any thing amiss—has any thing happened to my dear child? She was a lovely little lamb—a little angel from her cradle, though I should not know her now if she stood erect before me. I hope, I say—tell me——proceed, I beseech you!

There was a servant, sir, a man whom your niece thought very faithful, and therefore intrusted with the secret of my coming to you, that he might attend and see me safe back again. This fellow, presuming on the confidence that was placed in him, would this morning have taken liberties with his young mistress. This she resented in a becoming manner, and threatened to complain of his insolence to her father. The revengeful villain instantly ran and told the affair to his lord, with many aggravations, as though his daughter was robbing him of all his substance. Thereupon she was hastily called, and having in part confessed the charge, my lord drew his sword in his fury, whereupon, giving a shriek and a sudden spring, she got out of his presence, and has sent me to know, sir, if you will be pleased to receive her?

Yes, cried Mr. Ruth, to my bosom, to my heart! with the same pleasure and welcome that a convict receives pardon on the hour of execution.

Just then Mrs. Ruth entered, with her three daughters, who, running up to their father, dropped together on their knees before him for a blessing.

While his hands and eyes were raised in prayer over them, the young stranger stepped earnestly up, and falling on her knees beside the daughters, she broke into tears, and cried aloud—Bless me, bless me also, O my father! I am your niece, your Belinda. My father is no more! Yours, my lord, is the title, yours all the possession! I now, in my turn, depend on your bounty for a morsel of bread.—My brother, my brother dead! exclaimed Mr. Ruth.—He is, my lord, she replied; he was suffocated by his rising choler, and expired on the spot.

While the young lady spoke, Mrs. Ruth looked as quite

terrified by the tidings of such a sudden elevation; and clapping her hands together, and lifting her eyes, she cried—It cannot be, it is impossible! Ours the title, ours the fortune! —O my God!—O my husband!—O my children!—and down she dropped.

CHAPTER III.

WHILE Harry was speaking, Ned saw a woman standing before one of the windows; and looking earnestly at her, he gave a sudden jump, and dancing about, cried—O, sir, sir! my mammy, my mammy! there's my mammy, as sure as day!

Run, Ned, instantly, cried Mr. Fenton, and call James to me. James, yonder's the woman who stole Ned from his parents; have an eye to her, do not let her escape! Order Frank to take a horse and go with all speed to Mr. and Mrs. Fielding, that they may come and know, of a surety, whether Ned is their child or not—Stay a moment; as soon as you have given Frank his orders, take the rest of the servants and lay hold on this bad woman; bring her into the house by force, and confine her in one of the back rooms till Mr. Fielding arrives. By all Ned's account, she must be a very sad creature, and deserves no favour.

James went out with alacrity upon his commission; and having executed matters with his accustomed punctuality, he returned to the company.

O, sir! cried James, it is impossible that this woman should be Ned's mammy, as he called her. This is some unhappy decayed gentlewoman, as innocent of the fact, I dare answer, as the child unborn. I am sorry, with all my heart, that I had her used so roughly. Besides, sir, she is so deaf that she can't answer to anything of which she may be accused.

When we took her in hand she was terribly frighted. Come, says I, 'mistress, you must now give an account of all your wickedness.—Ennis, says she, Ennis? No, but Enfield; five miles beyond Enfield, with the Rev. Mr. Catharines.—I know nothing, said I aloud, of your Enfields or your Catharines; but I tell you that you must now answer for the life that you have led.—Dead, dead! says she, God forbid! A dear and good master he was to me, I am sure. I have lived with him these five years, and he gave me money enough to bear my charges; but I fell sick at St. Alban's and spent all, and I have been these three days creeping along, and begging wherewithal to keep life in me on the way.

As you say, James, cried Mr. Fenton, this account seems pretty feasible; a deaf servant, however, is something uncommon. Go to her yourself, Ned, and observe her more exactly; for if what she says has any truth in it, it is impossible she should be your mammy.

Ned accordingly went, but returned under evident confusion and difficulty.—I don't know what to think, sir, of this matter, cries Ned. When I look at the gentlewoman's face, I could swear, twenty times over, to every feature; but, when I look at her dress and manners, I could again almost swear against her face.

Ned's perplexity added greatly to Mr. Fenton's curiosity. He got up in haste and went in person to inspect the party. When he entered, he saw a young woman who looked very pale and sickly, but of a genteel appearance, and neatly though plainly dressed. She cast upon him a sensible and penetrating look, and curtsying to him, with downcast eyes—Sir, said she, your presence tells me that you are master here. I know not for what offence your people have confined me; but if it is on any suspicion of misbehaviour, I have here the certificate of a worthy man and a great saint, who vouches at least for the innocence of my conduct.—

Here she presented him with a paper that contained the following words:

"I certify that the bearer hath served me upwards of five years, in quality of housekeeper and intendant of my family; and that she is a young woman of distinguished piety and merit, and departs, at her own desire, on some business to London. Given under my hand, etc.
"MARMADUKE CATHARINES, Cl."

On reading this, Mr. Fenton bowed, and made a motion with his hand for her to sit down. He then took a pen and paper that lay beside him, and wrote to the purpose, that he requested her to allow him to detain her certificate for about an hour; after which he would return it, and endeavour to make her amends for the unbecoming treatment which his people had given her.

On casting her eye over the paper, she made a low curtsy, and said—I shall willingly attend, sir, during your pleasure; but hope, in the mean time, that your charity will afford me a morsel or two of the fragments of your last meal.

Mr. Fenton then pulled a bell, and having ordered some cold meats and wine to be served, he bowed, and withdrew to his company.

Ned, said he, as he entered, this woman is just as much the empress of Russia as she is your mammy. Here, Mr. Clement, look at this certificate; I have no reason to doubt the truth of the character given in it, for her person and manners are every way conformable. I am sorry at heart that I sent in such a hurry for Mr. and Mrs. Fielding; I have thereby raised a sort of expectation in them, and it may be very mortifying to have that expectation so suddenly and so wholly defeated.

Some time after, a coach and six frothing horses drove up to the door, and Mr. and Mrs. Fielding alighted, with a kind of impatience and trepidation apparent in their countenance. As soon as Mr. Fenton had duly received and seated them— My dear madam, says he to Mrs. Fielding, I think myself very unhappy in having given you a deal of unnecessary trouble. My poor Ned here, has been utterly mistaken in the person of the woman whom he took to be his mammy. The certificate of her certain residence bears a date even previous to that in which we found him; and her deportment is more than a thousand testimonies against her being of the wandering or dissolute class of people. Be pleased, Mr. Fielding, to look over this certificate; I think it has all the marks of its being genuine.

The moment that Mr. Fielding cast his eyes on the paper, A well-known character, indeed! he exclaimed. It is the hand of Mr. Catharines, my tutor, my friend; the man of the world, excepting yourself, Mr. Fenton, for whom I have the dearest respect and affection. No question can be made of any thing to which he sets his affirmative.

Alas! cried Mrs. Fielding, then all the hopes we had conceived must again be cast aside. Here comes our nurse, too, poor woman, in great haste; I sent her word that we had found the person whom we suspected to have stolen our child, and desired that she would meet me here directly.

While Mrs. Fielding spoke, nurse entered panting, and almost breathless; and, without saluting or taking any notice of the company—Where, she hastily cried, where is the boy, madam, whom you suppose to be your child?

Ah, nurse! said Mrs. Fielding, we were quite mistaken in the woman whom we suspected to be the kidnapper, and so that affair is all over again.

I have nothing to say, cried nurse, to this woman or

t'other woman; but you must not have another body's child put upon you. If he is indeed your son, I shall know him in an instant; I should know him from all the children that ever were born.—Why, nurse, cried Mrs. Fielding eagerly, do you know of any natural mark or mole, or spot, by which you could guess at him?—He had no such spot upon him, madam; but, if he be a living boy, he has a mark of my own making that never will out, and that's the reason that I never dared to tell you of it.—What mark, nurse, what mark? tell me instantly, I beg you.

Why, madam, you must know as how the weather was very cold, it being twelfth day in Christmas holidays. So you and my master were from home on visiting, and I had a rousing fire down, and my child stood by my knee, being just then twelve months nineteen days old, and as sturdy a fellow of his age and inches as any could desire to see. So the cat, all at once, threw down some crockery ware behind me. Up I started, to be sure, and run to save the vessels; but, hearing my child scream, I turned much nimbler back again, and found him fallen with his little neck against the upper bar of the grate. It was well that I didn't die on the spot, for then he must have died, too. So I whipped him up in my arms, but he shrieked and roared terribly. So I got some softening cream and spread it over the burn, and I put a plaster upon that again; and I covered the place from day to day so well with his cap, that neither you nor my master knew any thing of the matter. But the shape of his hurt went so deep into my heart and into my memory, that, as I was saying, and still say, I should know him by it again among all the children in all the world.

Go then, my dear nurse, cried Mrs. Fielding; go immediately, and examine if this boy has your mark upon him.—Is this the master, madam, whom you suspect to be your son?—It is, nurse, it is; my heart took a liking to him the first moment I saw him; he, too, was stolen from his parents, and may as well be my son as the son of another.

Here nurse made a hasty step or two toward Ned, but suddenly stopping and turning pale—Ah, madam! she cried, I wish you would go and try yourself; the wound, if he has it, is just under his right ear; for if I should find, indeed, that he is my very child, I shall certainly run mad on the very spot for joy.—I dare not try, nurse, I dare not try for the world, said Mrs. Fielding; I am already all of a tremble, I know not how.

Nurse, then plucking up a little resolution, stepped suddenly to Ned, and turned up his hair; when, giving a loud scream, she had just the power to cry out—My child, my child, my child! and dropped down in an anguishing fit of hysterics.

Mrs. Fielding, on hearing her nurse cry out, rose hastily from her chair, and would have gone to embrace her son, but falling instantly back, she fainted away. The poor nurse, however, was not so happy. She broke forth at times into convulsive peals of laughter, that made the house ring; and again she fell into fits of weeping, so outrageous and bitterly desolate, as no heart under the temper of adamant could support.

While the family were all in bustle, applying remedies to their patients, Mrs. Fielding recovered, and hearing the cries of her nurse, she went and kneeled down by her, and wept with her and over her, while her tears proved a seasonable restorative to herself.

As soon as Mr. Fielding found that his lady was well recovered, he turned to Ned, and lifting his hair, observed the remarkable seam that the burn had made. It is, it is my child! he tenderly cried. O my God! how is this? wherein have I deserved thy smallest notice or regard, that thou shouldest thus visit me with thy wonders, and by thy mercies put me to confusion of face?

Here Ned kneeled respectfully down for a blessing, which his father silently called upon him with lifted hands and eyes. He then raised him, and sitting down took him fondly to his bosom. Thou art, thou art my son, my beloved son, he cried; my first and my last, the only offspring of my bowels! Thou shalt no more be a wanderer, no more be a beggar, my babe! Thrice blessed be our meeting, and tenfold blessed thy future fortune! O that our lives, my child, might be made one whole oblation to him from whom this amazing salvation hath come!

By this time the nurse's distemper was greatly abated, though she still continued extremely low and feeble, and did not seem to recollect, except by faint glimmerings, any matter that had passed. Mr. Fielding then proposed to take her to town to the physicians, observing that there was room enough for her and Ned, in their carriage; and, as Mrs. Fielding made no exception, the coach was ordered to turn directly to the door.

Poor Ned, during this time, was as a person who fluctuated between the dread of leaving known and certain enjoyments, and the hopes of possessing somewhat that he had not yet tasted.

Mr. Fielding then stepped up, in a kind of quick rapture, to Mr. Fenton. He caught him in his arms—My dearest sir, he cried, I love, I respect, I revere you, even next to my God! What can I return you? what shall I say to you? All that I am or have, sinks out of sight from your benefits.—I am blessed, my dear sir, I am blessed beyond expression, replied Mr. Fenton, in being made an humble instrument of happiness to a worthy man.—O sir! cried Mr. Fielding, what events next to miraculous! We came to your door, but we were not permitted to pass; our carriage broke for the purpose; you then told us of this foundling; but what likelihood that among millions he should happen to be ours? You then proposed an expedient for ascertaining the persons from whom he was kidnapped. This expedient failed. God, however, would discover him, and had foreordained the means. He set upon him an indubitable mark for the purpose; none knew of this but his nurse, and she has revealed it. Had any one of these many circumstances been wanting, our child must have continued a stranger to us for ever.—Indeed, sir, said Mr. Fenton, they are all concurring proofs that you are under the especial eye of Providence. But, sir, I fear we shall have a heavy loss of our friend, Ned; for, though he does not want his small faults, he is a worthy-hearted child, and a very pleasant companion.—O sir! cried Mr. Fielding, you and Master Fenton have a right to command both him and us at all times. But come, Ned, take leave for the present of your best friends.

Here Ned, with filling eyes, stepped respectfully to Mr. Fenton, and, kneeling before him, took each of his hands and kissed them, crying—My father! my father! whereupon Mr. Fenton tenderly raised him, and, pressing him affectionately to his bosom, cried—God be good to you, my son, and make you a blessing to your true parents, and to all your kin!

Ned then turnèd to Harry, and taking him by both hands, and looking him fondly in the face—O Master Harry, Master Harry! he cried; I never shall be able to say the word farewell to you, my Master Harry! I was hungry and you fed me, I was naked and you clothed me, I was a stranger and you took me in; the whole world to me was fatherless and friendless, when you were father and mother, and a whole world of friends to me, my true lord and master, Harry! Are you not my owner? am I not your property, your own hard bought bargain? Did you not purchase me with your stripes, and with your precious blood, and will you suffer me to be taken away from you, my heart's master?

Here Harry, swallowing his passion as well as he was able, clasped Ned in his arms and cried—My brother, my brother, my friend and brother for ever! Then turning to Mr. and Mrs. Fielding, and wiping his eyes—I hope, madam, I hope, sir, says he, that you will excuse my young friend here, for his partiality to a family who have loved him long and very dearly; in a little time, to be sure, he will love and respect you both, above all the world, though put altogether. Though I grieve to part with him, I heartily rejoice at his being found, and acknowledged to be the child of such worthy parents; and I hope, I say, that you will not be offended at his concern for parting with his old friends.

No, my noble creature, cried Mr. Fielding, we are delighted at the proof that he gives of his gratitude, and at the strength of his attachment, where he has been so highly obliged.

Oh, sir! Oh, madam! says Ned (kissing the hands of his parents), did you but know the value of what I lose, when I leave, when I leave—and here he burst afresh into tears.

Mrs. Fielding then took Ned in her arms, and tenderly embracing him, cried—We do, my love, we do know the value of the family that you leave; and it is the first and the dearest wish of my heart, that we should all become as one family and as one household. This angel here, as you say, is your rightful owner; and we owe him more on that account than our whole fortune can pay, and he shall have you as long and as often as ever he pleases; but for this night, my darling, it would be very unkind not to go with your good nurse, your true and loving mammy, who has suffered so much for your sake; and her case requires that we should take her immediately to the doctor's.

Here Ned acquiesced; and having taken a weeping leave of all the family, not forgetting the meanest servant in the house, he stepped slowly into the coach, sat down by his nurse, and away they drove.

As soon as the family of the Fieldings were gone, Harry withdrew to his chamber and locked himself in, while Mr. Fenton went to enfranchise his late prisoner.

He first returned the certificate to her, and then presenting her with twenty guineas, he bowed and made a motion with his hand to the door, intimating that she was at liberty to depart when she thought proper.

Having looked several times, with silence and surprise, now at Mr. Fenton, and again at the money—I should be very ill deserving of your bounty, sir, she said, should I attempt any longer to impose upon you. I am not deaf, as you supposed; it was only an artifice which I made use of, when taken into custody, to avoid answering questions. But you look so altogether the gentleman, and the kind-hearted Christian, that I think I ought to have no reserve of any kind towards you.

Be pleased then, said Mr. Fenton, as far as prudence will allow, to let me know who and what you are

I hope, sir, she replied, that I am very far from being what I was, otherwise I should be the very vilest of the vile. Wherefore, if you will allow a weakly woman to sit, I will tell you the whole of my short story, with the same openness that I made confession of my sins to Him from whom alone I can look for remission.

She then narrated to Mr. Fenton the substance of her history—it was a tale of sorrow, of passion, and of sin. She had been under housekeeper in the Fielding family, where she had formed an attachment to a worthless and profligate young man in the neighbourhood, who had asked her in marriage; but this union Mr. Fielding had strenuously opposed on account of the man's character being so very bad; and her lover soon married another. On this she left her service full of ire and bent on vengeance; she had fallen into poverty through unhappiness and neglect of herself; and, hovering round the house whose master she conceived had so injured her, she kidnapped his child in the absence of the nurse, who had left him on the lawn for a moment. For two years she had subsisted by soliciting alms, and had taught little Ned to assist in her evil trade of mendicancy: till one day, the parish officers coming on her track, she deserted the child near Mr. Fenton's gate, and escaped. Shortly after, being taken ill near Enfield, she was carried into the workhouse, where, during a long sickness, she had been attended by the Rev. Mr. Catharines, an old and pious clergyman, who first taught her to see the errors of her life, and into whose service she passed on the recovery of her health, an altered and a happier character in every respect. To his house she had been now returning after a visit to a friend near London, when she had suddenly fallen sick on the way, and spent all her money, and in that condition she had been seen and recognised by Ned, and brought into Mr. Fenton's house.

Her story was an ample confirmation of the discovery made by nurse; and Mr. Fenton, having taken it all down in a certified form, dismissed her, in a day or two after she was rested and refreshed, in one of his own carriages, back to her master, Mr. Catharines, to whom, as well as to the Fieldings, he wrote an account of the whole matter.

When he had folded and sealed his letters, he took bills from his pocket to the amount of thirteen hundred pounds, and on Harry's return from London presented them to him

Here, my dear, said he, here is what will enable you to be more than just to your engagements—it will enable you to be generous also. And I desire, my Harry, in matters of charity, that you may never stint the sweet emotions of your heart, for we have enough, my child, and we are but the stewards of the bounty of our God.

Here Harry's speech was stopped, but his silence was more eloquent than a thousand harangues. He suddenly threw his arms about his dear father, and, hiding his face in his bosom, he there vented the tears of that pleasure, love, and gratitude, with which he found himself affected.

On the afternoon of the following day, Harry and Arabella went to drink tea with the Widow Neighbourly, who received them with a countenance that spoke an uncommon welcome. Some other company had arrived before them, and rose on their entrance. When all were again seated, Mrs. Neighbourly very affectionately questioned Harry concerning his father.

On hearing the name of Master Fenton, an elderly gentlewoman started. Pray, madam, said she eagerly, is this Master Fenton, the son of that noble gentleman who lives on the hill?—He is, madam, said Mrs. Neighbourly.—My God! exclaimed the stranger, can this suckling be the father of the orphan and the widow? Is this he who goes about turning sorrow into joy? who wipes the tears from the afflicted, and heals the broken of heart? Permit me then, thou beloved child of the Father which is in heaven, permit me to approach and throw myself at the feet of my preserver!

So saying, she rose with a rapturous motion, and dropping at Harry's knees, she clasped his legs and kissed his feet, before he could prevent her.

Poor Harry, much to be pitied, sat astonished, abashed, and distressed to the last degree. At length, recollecting, and disengaging himself with difficulty—My dear madam, he cried, you hurt me greatly; what have I done that you should put me to so much pain?

Babe of my heart, she cried, I am the wife of your Vindex—your own Vindex—whom you redeemed from beggary and slavery—whom you restored to his wretched partner—whom you restored to his infant daughter—all pining and perishing apart from each other, but now united by you, my angel in joy and thanksgiving!

Here her words were suffocated, and, throwing herself back in the chair, she was not ashamed to give way to her tears, and, putting her handkerchief to her face, she vented her passion aloud.

Harry then rising, and going tenderly to her, put his arms about her, and kissed her forehead, and then her lips.—You owe me nothing, my dear Mrs. Vindex, said he, I am still greatly in your debt. I was the very naughty boy who brought your misfortunes upon you. But I am willing to make you amends, and that will do me a great pleasure, instead of the punishment which I deserve.

The tea-table was now laid, and Mrs. Vindex grew more composed when her husband entered, leading his daughter by the hand, a very pretty little girl of about six years old. Harry instantly sprung up, and running, and throwing himself with a great leap upon him, he hung about his neck, crying—How glad I am to see you, my dear Mr. Vindex!—Boy of boys, cried Vindex, am I so blessed as to have you once more in my arms!

The company then rose and saluted Mr. Vindex, and congratulated him on his return to his ancient habitation. But Harry took him aside, and having cautioned him in a whisper not to take any notice of what should pass, he stole a bill for one hundred and sixty pounds into his hand, saying softly—It is good first to be honest, so there is what I owe you. And here also is a small matter for your daughter; I did not know till now that we had such a sweet little charge in our family. So saying, he slipped to him another bill of fifty pounds, and then, turning from him, stepped carelessly to his seat, as though nothing had happened.

Meantime the astonished Vindex was greatly oppressed. He did not dare to offend Harry by any open intimation of his recent bounty, and yet he could feel no ease till the secret should be disclosed. He therefore stole softly to the back of our hero's chair, where, unperceived of Harry, he displayed the bills to the company, beckoning at the same time in a way that forbade them to take any notice; then raising his hand over his head, and lifting his eyes towards heaven, he blessed his benefactor in a silent, ardent ejaculation, and, taking an empty seat, joined in with the company.

While they were in chat, the little Susanna slipped unnoticed from beside her mamma, and veering over towards Harry, she went on one side, and then on the other, and surveyed him all about; then, coming closer, she felt his clothes, and next his hands, in the way, as it were, of claiming acquaintance with him. At length, looking fondly up to his face, she lisped and said—Me voud kiss oo, if oo voud ask me.— indeed then, said Harry, me vill kiss oo, fedder oo vill or no. And so, catching her upon his knee, he pressed her to his bosom, and kissed her over and over again.

You all see, cried Mr. Vindex, it is not one of the elders with whom our Susanna has fallen in love.—My sweet babe! cried Mrs. Vindex, her little heart instinctively led her to her best friend, to the one of all living who best deserved her love.—Miss Susanna, said Mrs. Clements, puts me in mind of some very delicate lines in Milton, respecting our Virgin Mother; for she also refused to kiss the loveliest man that ever was created, at least till she was asked.

———"And though divinely brought,
Yet innocence and virgin-modesty,

> Her virtue and the conscience of her worth,
> That would be woo'd, and not unsought be won;
> Not obvious, nor obtrusive, but retired,
> The more desirable."

It is happy, said Mrs. Neighbourly, for our weakly and over affectionate sex, that God has been pleased to fix a monitor within us, who struggles against our inclinations, who fights against our affections, and is, with difficulty, won over to acquiesce in our desires. I know not else what might become of the most of womankind.

But then, said Mrs. Vindex, are we not rather to be pitied, that, even when our propensities are warrantable, we are prohibited by custom from giving any intimation thereof to the object; while the licentious reprobate, man, roves and riots at large, and unreproved, beyond the pale over which it is treason for us to look?

I do not pity you, ladies, said Mr. Vindex—I do not at all pity you on account of any restraints that custom has laid you under, respecting chastity, or its environs called decorum. The chastity of woman is the only basis upon which the order, honour, and peace of the world can be built; it twists the sacred and endearing cord of society; without it there could be no amity, no brotherhood upon earth. But then, surely, there is much respect and tenderness due to those from whom such advantages are derived. Whereas I have observed, on the contrary, that the most amiable of your sex are generally mated to tyrants; to men who, being born and appointed their protectors, pervert every end of nature and duty, and treat with injury, contempt, and insult, the gentle saints whom they should have cherished with their most respectful endearments.

The question yet occurs, said Arabella, whether your devils of husbands find us angels, or make us such. Tyrants are like files, they serve to smooth and polish whatever they are applied to. I was once in company with a man who was called the saint-maker; he had married five shrews in succession, and made grizels of every one of them before they died.

But pray, ladies, said Harry, are there no tyrants among the wives? I lately took a walk to Tower-hill, and growing hungry, I turned in to a little shop of groceries, where a slender, skinny woman, of about four feet high, stood behind the counter. Taking out a sixpence, I threw it on the board, and desired her to give me the value in almonds and raisons. She had scarce weighed my merchandise when a huge, jolly-looking Quaker came up to the hatch-door, but seemed fearful of opening it. The moment the little woman had cast her eye towards him, she exclaimed, in a shrill and exasperated accent—Art thee there, thou rogue, thou hangdog, thou gallows-faced vagabond? when, gathering up the whole dignity and importance of his person, and clapping a hand on each side, he cried with an undaunted air, "I tell thee, Mary, I fear thee not!" Ah, thou villain! she vociferated, dares thee then appear in my presence? Get thee back to thy fellows and husseys on whom thee spendest my substance! Still, however, he kept his ground, and courageously repeated, " I tell thee, Mary, I fear thee not!"

Not fear me, sirrah! sirrah, not fear me! says she; we shall see that in a twinkling. So saying, she whipped up the measuring-yard, and, scudding round the counter, she flew to the door. But he was already vanished as fast as his fat sides would let him. And, to tell you the truth, ladies, there was something so authoritative and tremendous in the little body's voice and manner, that I was glad to get out and to scamper after him.

The company laughed heartily, and Mr. Vindex added—I forget the hero's name—a great general he was, and I think a Frenchman. He won every battle abroad, but was sure to be beaten in his turn also, as often as he returned home to his wife.

Well said Hercules and the distaff, cries Harry! But to the point; the bravest man I know is one Peter Patience, a currier, who lives in the suburbs. My tutor and I were walking one day through Islington, when we perceived the likelihood of a scuffle at a distance.

As we approached, we saw one man making up with great fury to another, who would have avoided him; and who, retiring backward across the street, parried his blows, and kept him off as well as he could. His enraged adversary would then have closed in upon him; but, grasping his shoulder with a long and very strong arm, he still held his enemy aloof, who nearly spent all his efforts and blows in the air.

Never did I see so living a representation of heaven and hell, as was visible in the faces of those two men. The muscles of the one were frightfully distorted, his eyes shot fire, and his mouth frothed with madness; while the countenance of the other was as a lake in a summer's evening, that shews heaven in its bosom, and reflects all the beauties of nature around it.

Be quiet, Ben! he said; you know that I would not hurt you! you know that I love you. What a fool the man makes of himself. Are you not sensible that I could demolish you with a single blow? but I cannot find in my heart to do it. Be quiet, Ben! I say; I see you want to vex me; but I won't be vexed by you, my dear Ben.

While the gentle Peter was thus expostulating with his exasperated friend, Mrs. Patience, as it should seem, had seen all that passed from an upper casement; and flying down-stairs, and rushing out at the door, she seized her husband behind by the hair of his head, and tore and cuffed away at a terrible rate.

Poor Peter, finding himself thus between two fires, gave a slight trip to his male assailant; who instantly fell with his shoulder against the pavement, and, rising with difficulty, limped homeward, muttering curses all the way.

Then Peter, turning meekly to the lady mistress of his house—Gatty, my love, says he, what have I done to provoke you?—Oh! she cried, you mean-spirited, hare-hearted, milk-livered poltroon! I'll teach you what it is to suffer every fellow to pommel you!—Sirrah, sirrah (and still she cuffed), I'll have you tied down at the foot of the market cross, with notice on your breast, for all who pass to spit on you!

Then, quite angry to see the man so abused, to whom I had taken such a fancy, I rushed in between man and wife, and seized Mrs. Patience by both her hands; but, wrenching one of them from me, she gave me a round cuff on the side of my head. I was, however, too well used to cuffs to matter that much; and so, catching one of her hands on both of mine, I gave her a pluck to me, and a foot at the same time, and laid her on the broad of her back in the kennel.

My friend Peter looked quite astonished at this, and fearing what might happen to me on the rising up of his wife, he tucked me like a gizzard under the wing of a turkey, and off he scoured with me down the street; while Mr. Clement also made pretty nimbly after us, for fear, as I suppose, that Mrs. Patience, when on her legs, might take him for one of our company.

As soon as we had turned a corner, and were out of harm's way, honest Peter set me down.—My friend, says I, if you would be advised by me, you will not be in a mighty hurry to get back to your wife. I see a house of entertainment yonder, and I wish to be further acquainted with you. —Adad, said he, you are the boldest little body that ever I knew; you performed a feat to-day that made me tremble

for you. Had any other man, though, used my wife so——
but I pass that matter over ; I see you are too great a hero
to be threatened by any one, and I should consider that you
did what you did for my sake.

So saying, we all went into a sort of a tavern, and, being
shewn to a little parlour, I called for a pint of white wine.

As soon as we were seated, I took my new acquaintance
very lovingly by the hand. My dear friend, said I, I have
conceived a great respect and fondness for you, and should
be glad to know who and what you are.—I am a currier by
trade, sir, and my name is Peter Patience.—You are patience
itself, indeed, said Mr. Clement; but your wife, as I think,
has taken the whole trade of the currier into her own hands.

Peter laughed, and replied—She is a dear and a sweet girl
as ever lay by the side of a man, and she loves me as she loves
her own soul. Her blows were sweet blows to me ; they
were the blows of her affection. For, though I did not matter the strokes of my friend Benjamin a single fillip, yet
every one of them went to her heart, and she wanted to
frighten me from ever taking the like again.

But pray, says I, how happened the quarrel between you
and your friend Benjamin, as you call him ?—Why, there it
is, too, said Peter ; he also beat me, out of his downright
and true-hearted kindness to me.

As this is holiday in the afternoon among us trades-folk,
Ben Testy invited me to a share in a can of flip, at the Cat
and Bagpipes over the way. Just as we sat down—Peter,
says he, I am told that your Gatty is with child.—I believe
it may be so, says I.—I am glad of it, Peter, with all my
heart ; and so now remember that I bespeak myself gossip.
—Why, that may happen, says I, just as matters shall turn
out. If the child is a boy, you shall be one of the god-
fathers, and welcome ; but if it is a girl, this cannot be, for
my uncle Geoffry has already engaged himself, and I have

some expectations from him.—And so, says he, you refuse to admit me for your gossip.—If it is a girl, says I, you see that I cannot.—Oh! he cried, I had forgot, I was a rascal for proposing it; you are of high blood, have high relations, and so scorn to have connections with a poor tradesman like me.—That is not the case, indeed, my dear Ben, but——Confound your dears! says he, I will have no more of them. You are a covetous scoundrel, and value money more than love!—Well, says I, but will you be patient, will you hear reason, my friend?—Friend, friend, says he, my curse upon all such friendships! I see into you now. You're an ungrateful, unloving, cold-hearted villain, and I would sooner be godfather to a child of the Turk. So saying, he struck at me, and repeated his blows across the table. But, as I saw that his choler was inflaming more and more, I got up and retreated, merely intending to defend myself till his passion should be spent upon me. But you saw what happened, gentlemen, which I am heartily sorry for, as I fear that my poor dear fellow is much hurt.

Well, said my tutor, I have heard many definitions and many disputes concerning the word courage, but I never saw the thing itself till this day. Pray, Mr. Peter, were you never angry?—Scarce ever, sir, that I remember, at least on my own account; for I do not fear any man that steps upon the earth, and what is it then that should make me angry?—A man may be angry, said Mr. Clement, from other motives sure besides that of fear. God himself can be angry, and yet he cannot possibly fear.

I am feelingly assured, sir, replied the valiant Peter, that God was never angry in his whole life; and that is a long time that has neither beginning nor ending.—Don't you believe the Gospel? says Mr. Clement; the Scripture assures us, in a hundred places of the anger of God against impenitent sinners.—I am the son of a clergyman, sir, said Peter and mayhap could quote Scripture as well as another. The Scriptures were written for man; but how should man understand them, if they were not written according to his own language and to his own passions? I will ask you a question, sir, Can you be angry at a mite or a worm, which you can crush into nothing at pleasure?—I think not, said my tutor.—No, certainly, said Peter, because you cannot fear a thing that has not power to offend you. Now, all the world is but as a worm or a mite to God, and neither man nor angels can disturb or affect him with any thing, except delight, on their acceptance of that happiness which he desires to give to all his creatures.

Ay, but, says Mr. Clement, you see that God's anger and indignation was so great against sin, that nothing could satisfy for it save the death of his beloved Son.—Ay, but, says Peter, the Scripture which you quote tells you, that it was not his anger but his love that sent him to us. "For God so loved the world," a very sinful world, indeed! "that he gave his only begotten Son to take his death upon the cross." And I am as fully assured as I am of my own being, that the same gracious God who has already redeemed poor sinners, would willingly redeem the poor devils also if they could but find in their hearts to desire his salvation.

Here, catching and clasping his hand—My dear Peter, said I, I embrace and wish from my heart that your doctrine may be true. I have many tutors, Mr. Peter, and my father pays them all, with pleasure for the instructions that they give me. Tell me then, Mr. Peter, what must he give you for the lesson which you have taught me?—What lesson, my hero?—A very precious lesson, says I; a lesson that will always teach me " to despise myself for a coward whenever I shall be angry."

Peter then sprung up without speaking a word, and hugged, and clasped, and kissed me with all his affections.

Then, plucking a button from the upper part of my coat—I will accept of this token, my darling, says he; and will look at it many a time in the day for your sake.

But, Mr. Peter, said I, I think it would be my advantage to keep up an acquaintance with you, and this cannot be so well done while your dear Gatty is angry with me. You must therefore promise me to carry a token to her also, as an olive-branch of that peace which I want to be made between us.—I will, my love, says he; I never refuse to give or accept the favours of a friend.—You must be upon honour, then, not to reject what I offer you.—I am upon honour, he said.

I then slipped something into his hand, at which he looked and looked again; and then cried out from the overflowings of a good and grateful heart—You are either of the blood-royal, or ought to be so! For the man was very poor, though so very sensible and well descended, and so he looked upon a little as a great matter.

Here Harry closed his narration, and all the company gathered about him, and nearly smothered him with their caresses, in which little Susanna came in for her full share.

On the following day, Harry introduced his friend Vindex and family to his dear father, who received them with a graciousness that soon dispelled that awkward diffidence, and humbling sense of obligations, under which the late unhappy preceptor apparently sunk.

As soon as it was known abroad that Mr. Vindex enjoyed the patronage and good countenance of Mr. Fenton and his family, his former friends resorted to him, his acquaintance was sought by all the neighbourhood, his credit was restored, his school daily increased, and, like Job, his latter end was far more blessed than his beginning.

Within a few weeks Mr. and Mrs. Fielding, with their sister Phœbe, our friend Ned, and a splendid equipage, called and breakfasted at Mr. Fenton's; and, soon after, Mr. Fenton and his Harry, with Mr. and Mrs. Clement, attended their visitants to St. Alban's, where, all together, they spent the happiest night; only that this happiness was blended at times with the affecting consideration of parting in the morning.

For two succeeding years and upwards little interesting happened, save that our hero increased in stature and all personal accomplishments, and had happily got over the measles and smallpox. He was now nearly master of the Latin and Greek languages. He could outrun the reindeer, and outbound the antelope. He was held in veneration by all masters of the noble science of defence. His action was vigour, his countenance was loveliness, and his movement was grace.

Harry by this time was also versed in most of the select and interesting portions of history. Mr. Clement had instructed him in the use of the globes and maps; and, as he there led him from clime to clime, and country to country, he brought him acquainted with the different manners, customs, laws, politics, governments, rise, progress, and revolutions of the several nations through which they passed. Finally, said Clement, you see Master Fenton, that the mightiest states, like men, have the principles of growth, as likewise of dissolution, within their own frame. Like men, they are born and die—have their commencement and their period. They arise, like the sun, from the darkness of poverty to temperance, industry, liberty, valour, power, conquest, glory, OPULENCE, and there is their zenith. From whence they decline to ease, sensuality, venality, vice, corruption, cowardice, imbecility, infamy, SLAVERY. And so, good-night!

Mr. Fenton now judged it full time to give our hero an insight into the nature of the constitution of his own country; a constitution of whose construction, poise, action, and counteraction, the lettered Mr. Clement had scarcely any notion, and even the learned in our laws and the leaders in our senate but a very confused idea.

For this especial purpose he called Harry to his closet. —You are already, my love, said he, a member of the British state, and, on that account, have many privileges to claim, and many duties to perform towards your country in particular, independent of your general duties to mankind.

Should it please God to bless your friends with the continuance of your life for eight or ten years longer, you will then be a member of the legislature of Great Britain, one of the highest and most important trusts that can be confided by mankind.

Here, my Harry, I have penned, or rather pencilled, for your use, an abstract in miniature of this wonderful constitution. But, before I give it for your study and frequent perusal, I would give you some knowledge of the claims whereon it is founded; as also of the nature of man in his present depraved state, and of his several relations as a subject and as a sovereign.

Man comes into this world the weakest of all creatures, and while he continues in it is the most dependent. Nature neither clothes him with the warm fleece of the sheep nor the gay plumage of the bird; neither does he come forth in the vigour of the foal or the fawn, who, on the hour of their birth, frisk about and exult in the blessing of new existence.

Sacred history seems to intimate that man was originally created invulnerable and immortal; that the fire could not burn him, stones wound, air blast, nor water drown him. That he was the angelic lord and controller of this earth, and these heavens that roll around us; with powers to see at once into the essences, natures, properties, and distinctions of things; to unfold all their virtues, to call forth all their beauties, and to rule, subdue, and moderate these elements at pleasure.

These, truly, were godlike gifts, illustrious powers and prerogatives, and well becoming an offspring produced in the express image of an all-potent, all-wise, and all-beneficent Creator.

True, sir, said Harry; but then we see nothing now of all this greatness and glory. Man, on the contrary, is himself subjected to all the elements over which, you say, he was appointed the ruler. He has every thing to fear from every thing about him; even the insects and little midges fearlessly attack and sting this boasted lord of the creation; and history shows, from the beginning of the world, that the greatest of all enemies to man is man.

This, replied Mr. Fenton, is continually to remind him of the depraved and guilty state into which he has fallen. Man, indeed, is now no better than the remains of man; but then these remains are sufficient to prove the lustre and dignity of his original state. When you behold the ruins of some lofty and spacious palace, you immediately form an idea of the original beauty and stateliness of the structure. Even so, in our present feeble and fractured state, a discerning eye may discover many traces and fragments of man's magnificent ruin; thoughts that wing infinity, apprehensions that reach through eternity, a fancy that creates, an imagination that contains an universe, wishes that a world hath not wherewithal to gratify, and desires that know neither ending nor bound.

These, however, are but the faint glimmerings of his once glorious illumination. All his primitive faculties are now lapsed and darkened; he is become enslaved to his natural subjects; the world is wrested out of his hands; he comes as an alien into it, and may literally be called "a stranger and pilgrim upon earth."

All other animals are gifted with a clear knowledge and instant discernment of whatever concerns them; man's utmost wisdom, on the contrary, is the bare result of comparing and inferring; a mere inquirer called reason, a substitute in the want of knowledge, a groper in the want of light; he must doubt before he reasons, and examine before he decides.

Thus ignorant, feeble, deeply depraved, and the least sufficient of all creatures in a state of independence, man is impelled to derive succour, strength, and even wisdom, from society. When he turns a pitying ear and helping hand to the distressed, he is entitled, in his turn, to be heard and assisted. He is interested in others, others are interested in him. His affections grow more diffused, his powers more complicated; and in any society or system of such mutual benevolence, each would enjoy the strength, virtue, and efficacy of the whole.

You have, sir, said Harry, here drawn an exceeding sweet picture of society, and you know I am but a fool and a novice in such matters; but if any other man breathing had given me such a description, I should, from all my little reading, have withstood him to the face. Look through all the states and associations that were ever upon earth; throughout the republics of Greece, Italy, Asia Minor, and others, the most renowned for urbanity and virtue; and yet what do you find them, save so many bands of public robbers and murderers, confederated for the destruction of the rest of mankind? What desolation, what bloodshed, what carnage from the beginning! what a delight in horrors! what a propensity in all to inflict misery upon others! The malignity of the fiends can, I think, pierce no deeper!

Neither is this, sir, as I take it, the extent of their malevolence. For when any of these bands, or states, as you call them, have conquered or slaughtered all around them, they never fail, for want of employment, to fall out among themselves, and cut the throats of their very confederates; and this puts me in mind of what is said by the Prince of Peace, "The prince of this world cometh, and has no part in me." And again he says to the purpose, that fathers and sons, and mothers and daughters, shall be divided against each other; and that "a man's enemies shall be those of his own household."

I lately met with a fragment of an epic poem that struck me wonderfully at the time; and I recollect some of the lines that contain, in my opinion, the most genuine, the truest picture that ever was drawn of the state of mankind.

> "Man comes into this passing world in weakness,
> And cries for help to man—for feeble is he,
> And many are his foes. Thirst, hunger, nakedness;
> Diseases infinite within his frame;
> Without, inclemency, the wrath of seasons,
> Famines, pests, plagues, devouring elements,
> Earthquakes beneath, the thunders rolling o'er him;
> Age and infirmity on either hand;
> And death, who shakes the certain dart behind him!
> These, surely, one might deem, were ills sufficient.
> Man thinks not so; on his own race he turns
> The force of all his talents, exquisite
> To shorten the short interval, by art,
> Which nature left us—Fire and sword are in
> His hand, and in his heart are machinations,
> For speeding of perdition. Half the world,
> Down the steep gulf of dark futurity,
> Push off their fellows, pause upon the brink,
> And then drop after."

Say then, my dearest father, tell me whence comes this

worse than flinty, this cruel-heartedness in man? Why are not all like you? Why are they not happy in communicating happiness? If my eyes did not daily see it in fact, as well as in history, I should think it impossible that any one should derive pleasure from giving pain to another. Can it be more blessed to destroy than to preserve, to afflict than to gladden, to wound than to heal? My heart wrings with regret for being cast into a world where nation against nation, family against family, and man against man, are perpetually embattled, grudging, coveting, grasping, tearing every enjoyment, every property, and life itself, from each other.

Here Harry for a while held his handkerchief to his eyes, while his fond uncle dropped a silent tear of delight at beholding the amiable emotion of his beloved.

Take care, my Harry, rejoined Mr. Fenton; beware of the smallest tincture of uncharitableness! You see only the worse part, the outward shell of this world; while the kernel, the better part, is concealed from your eyes. There are millions of worthy people and affectionate saints upon earth; but they are as a kingdom within a kingdom, a grain within a husk—it requires a kindred heart and a curious eye to discover them. Evil in man is like evil in the elements; earthquakes, hurricanes, thunders, and lightnings, are conspicuous, noisy, glaring; while goodness, like warmth and moisture, is silent and unperceived, though productive of all the beauties and benefits in nature.

I once told you, my darling, that all the evil which is in you belongs to yourself, and that all the good which is in you belongs to your God; that you cannot in or of yourself so much as think a good thought, or form a good wish, or oppose a single temptation or evil motion of any kind. And what I then said of you may equally be said of all men, and of the highest angels now in bliss.

No creature can be better than a CRAVING AND DARK

DESIRE. No efforts of its own can possibly kindle the smallest portion of light or of love, till God, by giving himself, gives his light and love into it.

Here lies the eternal difference between evil and good, between the creature and the Creator; the spirits who are now in darkness are there for no other reason but for their desire of a proud and impossible independence; for their rejecting the light and love of that God, in whom, however, they live, and move, and have their desolate being.

God is already the fulness of all possible things; he has, therefore, all things to give, but nothing to desire. The creature, while empty of God, is a wanting desire; it has all things to crave, but nothing to bestow. No two things in the universe can be more opposite, more contrasted.

Remember, therefore, this distinction in yourself and all others; remember that, when you feel or see any instance of selfishness, you feel and see the coveting, grudging, and grappling of the creature; but that, when you feel or see any instance of benevolence, you feel and see the informing influence of your God. All possible vice and malignity subsists in the one; all possible virtue, all possible beauty, all possible blessedness, subsists in the other.

As God alone is love, and nothing but love, no arguments of our own can reason love into us, no efforts of our own can possibly attain it. It must spring up within us, from the divine bottom or source wherein our existence stands; and it must break through the dark and narrow womb of self, into sentiments and feelings of good-will for others, before this child of God can be born into the world.

Self is wholly a miser—it contracts what it possesses, and at the same time attracts all that it doth not possess. It at once shuts out others from its own proposed enjoyments, and would draw into its little whirlpool whatever others enjoy.

Love, on the contrary, is a giving, not a craving; an expansion, not a contraction; it breaks in pieces the condensing circle of self, and goes forth in the delightfulness of its desire to bless.

Self is a poor, dark, and miserable avariciousness, incapable of enjoying what it hath, through its grappling and grasping at what it hath not. The impossibility of its holding all things, makes it envious of those who are in possession of any thing; and envy kindles the fire of hell, wrath, and wretchedness, throughout its existence.

Love, on the other hand, is rich, enlightening, and full of delight—the bounteousness of its wishes makes the infinity of its wealth; and, without seeking or requiring, it cannot fail of finding its own enjoyment and blessedness in its desire to communicate and diffuse blessing and enjoyment.

But is it not, sir, a very terrible thing, said Harry, for poor creatures to be evil by the necessity of their nature.

You mistake this matter, my Harry; you take the emptiness, darkness, and desire in the creature, to be the evil of the creature. They are, indeed, the only possible cause of evil in or to any creature; but they are exceedingly far from being an evil in themselves; they are, on the contrary, the only, the necessary, and indispensable foundation whereon any creaturely benefit can be built. It is extremely good for the creature to be poor and weak, and empty, and dark, and desiring; for hereby he becomes a capacity for being supplied with all the riches, power, glories, and blessedness of his God.

As God is every where in and of himself, the fulness of all possible beings and beatitudes, he cannot create any thing independent or out of himself; they cannot be but by being both in him and by him. Could it be otherwise? Could any creature be wise, or powerful, or happy, in and of itself? What a poor and stinted happiness must that have been: its blessedness, in that case, must have been limited like its being; and how infinitely, my child, should we then have fallen short of "that eternal weight of glory" intended for us. But God has been graciously pleased to provide better things. If we humbly and desirously depend upon him, we become entitled to all that he has, and that he is. He will enlighten our darkness with his own illumination; he will inform our ignorance with his own wisdom; his omnipotence will become the strength of our weakness; he himself will be our rectitude and guide from all error; he will purify our pollution; put his own robe on our nakedness; enrich our poverty with the heartfelt treasures of himself; and we shall be as so many mirrors wherein our divine friend and father shall delight to behold the express image of his own person, his own perfections and beatitudes, represented for ever.

Oh, sir! exclaimed Harry, how you gladden, how you transport me! I shall now no longer repine at my own weakness, or blindness, or ignorance, or insufficiency of any kind; since all these are but as so many vessels prepared to contain pearls of infinite price, even the riches, the enjoyment and fulness, of my God. Never will I seek or desire, never will I accept any thing less than himself.

You must, my child, said Mr. Fenton: you are still in the flesh, in a carnal and propertied world; your old man must be fed, though not pampered; it must be mortified, but not slain.

You read in the third chapter of Genesis how our first father lusted after the sensual fruits of this world; how he wilfully brake the sole commandment of his God; how he added to his apostasy the guilt of aspiring at independence; how he trusted to the promise and virtue of creatures for making him equal in godhead to the Creator; how in that day he died the fearfullest of all deaths, a death to the fountain of life, light, and love within him; and how his eyes were opened to perceive the change of his body into grossness, corruption, diseases, and mortality, conformable to the world to which he had turned his faith, and into which he had cast himself.

Now, had man continued in this state, his spirit, which had turned from God into its own creaturely emptiness, darkness, and desire, must have so continued for ever, in its own hell and misery, without the possibility of exciting or acquiring the smallest spark of benevolence or virtue of any kind. But God, in compassion to Adam, and more especially in compassion to his yet unsinning progeny, infused into his undying essence a small embryo or reconception of that lately forfeited image, which, in creation, had borne the perfect likeness of the Creator.

From hence arises the only capacity of any goodness in man. And, according as we suppress, or quench, or encourage and foster, this heavenly seed, or infant offspring of God within us, in such proportion we become either evil, malignant, and reprobate; or benevolent, and replete with divine propensities and affections.

Now, Harry, let us turn our eyes to our gross and outward man; for, as I told you, it must be cared for, and sustained agreeable to its nature: and it is well deserving of our attention, forasmuch as it is the husk, the habitation, and temple of that godlike conception which, when matured, is to break forth into never-ending glory.

Lastly, the same outward man is further to be regarded by us, forasmuch as his infirmities, frailties, distemperatures, afflictions, aches, and anguishes, are so intimately felt by his divine inmate, that they occasionally excite those thousand social charities, relations, and endearments, that with links of golden love connect the brotherhood of man.

It is, therefore, worth while to inquire into the claims and rights of this close though gross companion; at least, so far as may be requisite for his necessary, if not comfortable, subsistence upon earth.

We find that God has intrusted him with life, liberty, and strength to acquire property for his sustenance. It is therefore his duty to preserve all these trusts inviolate; for, as they are wedded to his nature, "what God hath so joined, let no man put asunder."

If these were not, my Harry, the natural, inheritable, and indefeasible rights of all men, there would be no wrong, no injustice, in depriving all you should meet of their liberty, their lives, and properties, at pleasure. For all laws that were ever framed for the good government of men (even with the divine decalogue), are no other than faint transcripts of that eternal LAW OF BENEVOLENCE which was written and again retraced in the bosom of the first man, and which all his posterity ought to observe without further obligation.

The capital apostle, St. Paul, bears testimony also to the impression of this law of rights on the consciences and hearts of all men, where he says, in the second chapter of his epistle to the Romans, "Not the hearers of the law are just before God, but the doers of the law shall be justified. For when the Gentiles, which have not the law, do by nature the things contained in the law, these, having not the law, are a law unto themselves: which shew the work of the law written in their hearts; their consciences also bearing witness, and their thoughts, the meanwhile, accusing or else excusing one another."

But, sir, interrupted Harry, I am quite astonished at the falling off of the father of mankind. So infinitely benefited and obliged as he was, so necessarily dependent also on his omnipotent benefactor; how foolish, how base, how ungrateful, how unpardonable, as I think, was his wonderful apostasy! Wretched creatures that we are! no sound branch, to be sure, could ever spring from so debased, so cankered a stock.

Let us not be prone to judge of others, my Harry. I am confident, as I am of my being, that had you or I been in the case or place of Adam, we should have fallen in like manner. He had an old and a very subtile adversary to deal with. He felt himself powerful, glorious, and happy. He had no notion that his present state could change for the worse. He was yet a novice in existence. He could form no conception of the depravity, pains, and mortality, that afterwards ensued. And he was strongly tempted by sensual objects from without, and by the emotions of his creaturely nature within him. But of this I am assured, Harry, that, if he was the greatest sinner, he was also the greatest and most contrite penitent that ever existed; as the comparison of his first with his latter state must have given him the most poignant and bitter compunctions, and must have caused him, with tenfold energy, to cling to that Rock from which he was hewn, but from whence he had fallen.

I have already shewn you, Harry, that every man has a right in his person and property; and that his right is natural, inheritable, and indefeasible. No consent of parties, no institution, can make any change in this great and fundamental law of right; it is universal, invariable, and inalienable, to any men or system of men. It is only defeasible in particular cases; as where one man, by assailing the safety of another, justly forfeits the title which he had to his own safety.

If human nature had never fallen into a state of inordinate appetence, all laws and legal restraints would have been as needless and impertinent, as the study and practice of physic in a country exempted from mortality and disease. But, forasmuch as all men are tyrants by nature, all prone to covet and grasp at the rights of others, the great LAW OF SAFETY TO ALL can no otherwise be assured, than by THE RESTRAINT OF EACH FROM DOING INJURY TO ANY.

On this lamentable occasion, on this sad necessity of man's calling for help against man, is founded every intention and end of civil government. All laws that do not branch from this stem, are cankered or rotten. All political edifices that are not built and sustained upon this foundation, " of defending the weak against the oppressor," must tumble into a tyranny even worse than that anarchy which is called the state of nature, where individuals are unconnected by any social band. But if such a system could be framed, whereby wrong should not be permitted or dispensed within any man, right would consequently ensue, and be enjoyed by all men, and this would be the perfection of CIVIL LIBERTY.

Sir, says Harry, I have heard some very learned men affirm that God, in whom is the disposal of all lives and all properties, has given to some a right of ruling over others; that governors are his vicegerents and representatives upon earth; and that he hath appointed the descendible and hereditary rights of fathers over families, of patriarchs over tribes, and of kings over nations.

In a qualified sense, my Harry, their affirmation may be just; all the agents and instruments and dispensers of beneficence, whether their sphere be small or great, are God's true representatives and vicegerents upon earth; he hath given authority to the tenderness of parents over their progeny; and he hath invested patriarchs and kings with the rights of protection. But God never gave the vulture a right to govern over the dovecot—never gave up the innocent many for a prey to the tyrannous few. God never can take pleasure in the breaches of the law of his own righteousness and benignity. Arbitrary regents are no further of his appointment than the evils of earthquakes and hurricanes—as, where he is said "to give the wicked a king in his anger, and to set over the nations the basest of men."

The God of all right cannot will wrong to any: "His service is perfect freedom." It is his pleasure to deliver from "the land of slavery and the house of bondage;" he is the God of equity and good-will to all his creatures; he founds his own authority, not in power but beneficence. The law, therefore, of safety and well-being to all, is founded in the nature of God himself—eternal, immutable, and indispensable.

One man may abound in strength, authority, possessions; but no man may have greater right than another. The beggar has as much right to his cloak and his scrip, as the king to his ermines and crown lands.

To fence and establish this divinely inherent right, of *security to the person and property of man*, has been the study and attempt of Hermes, Confucius, Minos, Lycurgus, Solon, Numa, and of all the legislators and systems of civil polity that ever warmed the world with a single ray of freedom.

But so strong is the propensity to usurpation in man; so dangerous is it to tempt trustees with the investiture of power; so difficult to watch the watchers—to restrain the restrainers from injustice—that, whether the government were committed to the One, the Few, or the Many, the parties intrusted have generally proved traitors; and deputed power has almost perpetually been seized upon as property.

Monarchy has ever been found to rush headlong into tyranny—aristocracy into faction and multiplied usurpation—and democracy into tumult, confusion, and violence. And all these, whether distinct or compounded with each other, have ended in the supremacy of some arbitrary tyrant, enabled by a body of military mercenaries to rule, oppress, and spoil the people at pleasure.

How England hath come, after the many wrecks and ruins which you have read of in history, to survive, to recover, to grow sounder from her wounds, and mightier from her discomfitures, and to rise superior, as we trust, to all future external and internal attempts—hath been owing to the peculiarity of her constitution.

Her constitution, it is true, is not yet quit, perhaps never ought to be quit, of some intestine commotions. For, though liberty has no relation to party dissension or cabal against government, there is yet a kind of yeast observable in its nature, which may be necessary to the fermentation and working up of virtue to the degree that is requisite for the production of patriotism and public spirit. But when this yeast of liberty happens to light upon weak or vapid tempers, they are immediately affected like small beer casks, and rave and boil over in abundance of factious sputter and turbulence. Party and faction, therefore, being the scum and ebullition of this animating yeast, are sure signs and proofs of the life of liberty, though they neither partake nor communicate any portion of its beneficence; as rank weeds are the proof of a hot sun and luxuriant soil, though they are the detestable consequence of the one and the other.

" Salus Populi—Public Safety—Security to the Persons and Properties of the People "—constitutes the whole of England's polity. Here empire is " *Imperium legum*, the sway of law ;" it is the dispensation of beneficence, of equal right to all : and this empire rises supreme over king, lords, and commons, and is appointed to rule the rulers to the end of time.

Other states before now have been compounded, like ours, of prince, peers, and people, the one, few, and many united. But the error and failure of their constitution was this :— The People, who are the Fountain of all Power, either retained in their own hands an authority which they never were qualified to wield; or deputed it to trustees without account, without a provident resource, or due reserve of potency, when "those instructed with government should be found to betray their trust."

The people of England, on the contrary, claim no authority in government; neither in the framing, administration, or execution of the laws by which they consent to be governed. They are themselves imaged, and as it were epitomised, in their three several estates. The king represents their majesty; the lords their nobility; and the commons, more immediately, their legislative power. The constitution is the inheritance of them and their posterity; and theirs is the right and duty, at all times, to watch over, assert, and reclaim it. Wherefore, as you find in history, when any of the three estates have usurped upon the others —even when all of them together have dared to violate the frame of this salutary constitution; the people, to whom it belongs, have never failed, as on the other day's revolution, to restore and reinstate it.

England's three estates, of king, lords, and commons, are parts of the people, under covenant with the people, and accountable to the people; but the people, as a people, make not any of the said estates. They are as a perpetual fountain, from whence the three estates arise; or rather as a sea of waters, in which three exalted waves should claim pre-eminence, which yet shall not be able to depart from their fund, but in rotation are dissoluble and resolvable therein.

Thus, however complicated the system of England's polity may be, it is all rooted in, and branches from the *trust of the people*, the trust of powers which they have granted to be returned in protection. And, in truth, it makes little difference whether the powers in such cases be granted or assumed; whoever either receives or assumes such powers, save to the ends of beneficence, is equally guilty of usurpation and tyranny.

Government can have no powers save the powers of the people; to wit, the power of their numbers, strength, and courage, in time of war; and in peace, of their art and industry, and the wealth arising therefrom. Whoever assumes to himself these powers, or any part thereof, without the consent of the proprietors, is a robber, and should at least be divested of the spoil.

On the other hand, if such powers are granted by the people, the people cannot grant them for purposes to which they themselves cannot lawfully apply them. No man, for instance, can arbitrarily dispose of his own life or liberty, neither of the whole product of his own labours; forasmuch as the lives of himself and his family should be first sustained thereby, and his obligations to others fairly and fully discharged. He cannot, therefore, grant an arbitrary disposal of what he hath—not an arbitrary disposal in himself. Much less can any man grant a power over the lives, liberties, or properties of other people, as it would be criminal and highly punishable in himself to assail them.

Hence it follows, as evident as any object at noon, that "no man, or body of men, can rightfully assume, or even accept, what no man or body of men can rightfully grant," to wit, a power that is arbitrary or injurious to others. And hence it necessarily follows, that all usurpations of such powers throughout the earth, with all actual or pretended covenants, trusts, or grants, for the investiture or conveyance of such illicit powers, are null and void on the execution; and that no man, or nations of men, can possibly be bound by any consents or contracts, eversive of the laws of God and their own nature, of common sense and general equity, of eternal reason and truth.

I beg pardon, sir, says Harry, for interrupting you once

more; but you desire that I should always speak my mind with freedom. You have delighted me greatly with the account which you gave of the benefits and sweets of *Liberty*, and of its being equally the claim and birthright of all men; and I wish to heaven that they had an equal enjoyment thereof. But this you know, sir, is very far from being the case; and that this animating fire, which ought to comfort all who come into the world, is now nearly extinguished throughout the earth.

O sir! if this divine, *golden law of liberty* were observed, if *all were restrained from doing injury to any*, what a heaven we should speedily have upon earth! The habit of such a restraint would in time suppress every motion to evil. The weak would have the mightiness of this law for their support; the poor would have the benevolence thereof for their riches. Under the light and delightsome yoke of such a restraint, how would industry be encouraged to plant and to multiply the vine and the fig-tree! how would benignity rejoice to call neighbours and strangers to come and fearlessly partake of the fruits thereof!

How has the sacred name of all-benefiting *Liberty* been perverted and profaned by the mouths of madding demagogues, at the head of their shouting rabble, who mean no other than a licentious unmuzzling from all restraint, that they may ravage and lay desolate the works and fruits of peace!

But liberty, in your system, is a real and essential good; the only source, indeed, whence any good can arise. I see it, I revere it; it shines by its own light in the evidence of your description!

How is it, then, sir, that there are persons so blind or so bigoted against their own interests and those of their fellows, as to declaim with much energy and studied argumentation against this divine, inheritable, and indefeasible right (not of kings, as it should seem), but of human kind?

I lately happened in company with a number of discontented-looking gentlemen, whom I supposed to have been abettors of the late King James, and friends to the arrogating family of the Stewarts. Among them was one of some learning and great cleverness, and he paraded and showed away at a vast rate concerning the divinely inherent right of monarchs, implicit submission, passive obedience, non-resistance, and what not.

Our God, said he, is one God, and the substitutes of his mightiness should resemble himself; their power ought to be absolute, unquestioned, and undivided. The sun is his glorious representative in the heavens; and monarchs are his representatives and mirrors upon earth, in whom he is pleased to behold the reflection of his own majesty.

Accordingly we find, that the monarchs over his chosen people were of his special appointment; and that their persons were rendered sacred and awfully inviolable, by unction, or the shedding of hallowed oil upon them. Many miscarriages and woful defaults are recorded of Saul as a man; yet, as a king, he was held perfect in the eyes of his people. What an unhesitating obedience, what a speechless submission, do they pay to all his behests! Though he massacred their whole priesthood, to a man, in one day, yet no murmur was heard—no one dared to wag a tongue, and much less to lift a finger, against the Lord's anointed.

I own to you, sir, that this last argument staggered me; such an express authority of the sacred writings put me wholly to silence. Say, then, my dearest father, give me the benefit of your enlightening sentiments on this head, that I may know, on all occasions, to give to all men an account of the political faith that is in me.

It is extremely surprising, rejoined Mr. Fenton, that all our lay and ecclesiastical champions for arbitrary power who have raised such a dust, and kept such a coil about the divine, hereditary, and indefeasible right of kings, and the unconditional duty of passive obedience in the subject, have founded their whole pile of argument and oratory on the divine appointment of the regal government of the Jews, as the perfect model and ensample whereby all other states are, in like manner, required to form their respective governments.

Now, if these champions had engaged on the opposite side of the question, and had undertaken the argument against arbitrary power, they could not have done it more effectually, more conclusively, more unanswerably, than by showing that *arbitrary power* was the very *evil* so displeasing to the nature of God, that he exhibited his omnipotence in a series of public and astonishing wonders, in order to deliver this very people from the grievance thereof; and more especially to proclaim to all nations and ages the detestation in which his *eternal justice* holds all lawless dispensations—all acts of *sovereign power* that are not acts of *protection.*

Could these champions, again, have better enforced the argument against arbitrary power, than by showing that this people so miraculously enfranchised, but now fat, and wantonly kicking under the indulgence of their God, had taken a loathing to the righteousness of the dispensations of their deliverer—" had rejected him," as he affirms, " from reigning over them ;" and had required a *King* like to the kings of the neighbouring nations?—the very *evil* from which God had redeemed their forefathers!

Could these champions, further, have better demonstrated the miseries, the iniquities, the abominations of such a government, than by reciting the expostulations, the tender and earnest remonstrances, of God himself, on the sufferings that these rebels were about to bring upon themselves from the enormities of an arbitrary and unlimited sovereignty ? And lastly, could they have better recommended to the free and the virtuous, to stand out to the death against arbitrary oppression, than by showing the obstinacy of these apostate Jews, when they answered to the compassionating expostulations of their God—" Nay, but we will have a king, like all the nations, to rule over us."

Nothing, my Harry, can be more unaccountable, more astonishing, than the perverseness of that stiff-necked nation.

They daily drank the bitterest dregs of slavery; they had been galled by double chains, and had groaned under an unprecedented tyranny and oppression. They cried out to their God, and he miraculously delivered them from the land of their misery, and from the house of their bondage. Yet, on the first cravings of appetite, these soul-sensualized wretches desired to be returned to their chains and their fleshpots, and longed to groan and gormandize in their old sty.

Hereupon God gave them flesh and bread to the full; and he brought them into a land " flowing with milk and honey," and abounding with all the good things of this life. He made them a free and sovereign people; discomfited their enemies before them; and informed their judges with his own spirit for the dispensation of righteousness; insomuch that " every man sat under his own vine, and did what was right in his own eyes." And yet they lasciviously petitioned to be subjected to a state of *absolute despotism ;* and this for no assigned reason, save because it was the fashion : " Make us a king to judge us, like to all the nations around us."

Here God, in the same act, approves his attributes of mercy and reluctant justice to his erring creatures. He punishes their rebellion by no greater severity than the grant of their request.

" And the Lord said unto Samuel, Hearken unto the voice of the people in all that they say unto thee : for they have not rejected thee, but they have rejected me, that I should not reign over them. Howbeit, protest solemnly unto them, and show them the manner of the king that shall reign over them.

"And Samuel told all the words of the Lord unto the people that asked of him a king. And he said, This will be the manner of the king that shall reign over you:

"He will take your sons and appoint them for himself, for his chariots, and to be his horsemen. And some shall run before his chariots. And he will appoint him captains over thousands, and captains over fifties, and will set them to ear his ground and to reap his harvest. And he will take your daughters to be confectioners, and cooks, and bakers, and he will take your fields, and your vineyards, and your oliveyards, even the best of them. And he will take your men-servants, and your maid-servants, and your goodliest young men, and your asses, and put them to his work, and ye shall be his servants. And ye shall cry out in that day, because of your king which ye shall have chosen you; and the Lord will not hear you in that day.

"Nevertheless, the people refused to obey the voice of the Lord and of Samuel; and they said, Nay, but we will have a king over us."

And now, Harry, what do you gather from all these sacred authorities?—I gather, sir, answered Harry, from the express and repeated declarations of holy writ, that whoever he be, whether sovereign or subject, who doth not wish that all men should be limited or restrained from doing injury to any, is a rebel to the will of the *God of Beneficence*, and an enemy to the *well-being of human kind*.

You have, exclaimed Mr. Fenton—you have, in a few words, spoke the whole of the matter. On what you have said hang all the law and the prophets.

Again, my dear, continued Mr. Fenton, it is evident from the history, that the Jews themselves did not pay the smallest regard to the divine hereditary right of kingship. Both

David and Solomon, the second and third in succession, were established on the throne in direct contradiction to such pretended right. And on the succession of Rehoboam, the fourth king, ten of the twelve tribes repented of their submission to an arbitrary monarchy, and required the king to consent to a limitation of his authority, and to enter into a contract with the people.

"And they spake unto Rehoboam, saying—Thy father made our yoke grievous; now, therefore, make thou the grievous service of thy father, and his heavy yoke which he put upon us, lighter, and we will serve thee."

But when Rehoboam, by the advice of his sleek-headed ministry, refused to covenant with the people, the ten tribes cried out—"What portion have we in David? Neither have we inheritance in the son of Jesse; to your tents, O Israel!" And thus the ten tribes revolted from the arbitrary domination of the houses of Saul and David. For as the sacred text says—"*The cause was from the Lord.*"

Now when these ten tribes sent and called Jeroboam, the son of Nebat, and made him king over Israel, it is most evident that they obliged him to limit the regal authority, and to covenant with them for the restoration and re-establishment of their popular rights. For in the sixth succession, when Ahab sat upon the throne, the regal prerogative had not yet so far usurped on the constitutional rights of the people, as to entitle Ahab to deprive his subjects even of a garden for herbs.

"And Ahab said unto Naboth, Give me thy vineyard, that I may have it for a garden for herbs, because it is near unto my house, and I will give thee for it a better vineyard; or, if it seems good to thee, I will give thee the worth of it in money. But Naboth said to Ahab, The Lord forbid that I should give the inheritance of my fathers unto thee. So Ahab came to his house heavy displeased, because Naboth had said I will not give to thee the inheritance of my fathers; and he laid him down upon his bed, and turned away his face, and would eat no bread."

Here we see that the people of Israel had so far recovered their originally inherent and hereditary rights, that the regal estate had not the privilege of wresting from any subject so much as an herb garden.

This was a mortifying circumstance to royal elevation, but power is seldom unfruitful of expedients. A method was found of rending away Naboth's property (without his consent) *under color of the law to which he had consented.* He was falsely impeached, and forfeited his life and inheritance together. But God, by the signal punishment which he inflicted for this breach on the natural rights of his people, evinced to the world how dear they are in the eyes of *eternal justice.*

How deplorable, then, my Harry, is the suppression of these rights, now nearly universal throughout the earth! But when people, from their infancy, and from generation to generation, have been habituated to bondage, oppression and submission, without any tradition or memorial delivered down to them of a happier or more equitable manner of life; they are accustomed to look on themselves, their possessions, and their progeny, as the rightful property of their rulers, to be disposed of at pleasure; and they no more regret the want of Liberty that they never knew, than the blind born regret the want of the light of the sun.

Before I give you this paper that I have in my hand, this epitome or picture, in miniature, of the incomparable beauties of the Britannic constitution, it may be requisite to premise a few matters.

Travellers, when they survey a grand Egyptian pyramid, are apt to inquire by whom the stupendous pile was erected, and how long it hath stood the assaults of time. But when nothing of this can be developed, imagination runs back through antiquity without bounds; and thence contemplates an object with peculiar veneration, that appears as it were to have had no beginning.

Such a structure is the constitution of Great Britain! No records discover when it had a commencement; neither can any annals specify the time at which it was not.

William the Norman, above seven hundred years ago, on his entering into the original contract with the people, engaged to govern them according to the *bonæ et approbatæ antiquæ regni leges*, the good, well-approved, and ancient laws of the kingdom; this constitution was therefore ancient, even in ancient times.

More than eighteen hundred years are now elapsed since Julius Cæsar, in the sixth book of his commentaries, bore testimony as well to the antiquity as excellency of the system of the laws of Britain. He tells us that the venerable order of the Druids, who then administered justice throughout Gaul, derived their system of government from Britain; and that it was customary for those who were desirous of being versed in the said ancient institutions to go over to Britain for that purpose.

Cæsar seems to recommend, while he specifies, one of the laws that was then peculiar to the constitution of Britain. He tells you that, if a woman was suspected of the death of her husband, she was questioned thereupon with severity " by her neighbours;" and that, if she was found guilty, she was tied alive to a stake, and burned to death. The very trial used in Britain, " by a jury of neighbours," to this day.

It is hence very obvious that our Gothic ancestors either adopted what they judged excellent in the British constitution, or rather superadded what was deemed to be excellent in their own.

The people who went under the general name of Goths,

were of many different nations, who, from the northern, poured down on the more southern parts of Europe.

Their kings were originally chiefs or generals, appointed to lead voluntary armies, or colonies, for the forming of new settlements in foreign lands; and they were followed by a free and independent multitude, who had previously stipulated that they should share and enjoy the possessions which their valour should conquer.

Next to the general in order, the officers or principal men of the army were attended, on such expeditions, by their kinsfolk, friends, and dependents, who chose to attach themselves to their persons and fortunes respectively; and such attachments gave these officers great power and consideration.

On their conquest or seizure of any tract of country, a certain portion thereof was allotted to the general for the maintenance of his person and household. The general then divided the remainder among his officers, to hold of him in fief, at the certain service of so many horse or foot, well armed and provided, etc., and proportioned to the value and extent of the land assigned. And the said officers again parcelled out the greatest part of the said possessions among their respective followers, to hold of themselves in like manner and service as they held of their general.

On the conquest of a country, they seldom chose to exterminate the natives or old inhabitants, but allotted to them also separate remnants of the land; and admitted them to the common and equal participation of such laws or usages as they brought from their own country, or chose to adopt.

Independent of the military services above reserved, the prince, or chief, further reserved the civil services of personal attendance of his feudatory officers at certain times, and for certain terms, at his general or national court. This court was composed of three estates, the prince, the nobles, and such of the priesthood, whether Pagan or Christian, as held in fief from the prince; and from this *national council* our *parliament* took its origin.

The feudal officers also, on their part, reserved the like service and personal attendance of their proper tenants and vassals, at their respective courts of judicature. And for as much as, in such courts, no civil or criminal sentence could take place till the voice of the judge was affirmed by the court, which consisted of such as were peers or equals to the party accused; from thence we derive our free, ancient, and sacred institution of *juries*.

If we look back upon one of those fief or feudal kings, seated high on his throne, and encircled with all the ensigns of royalty; when we find him entitled the sole proprietor of all the lands within his dominions; when we hear his subjects acknowledge that he alone is the fountain from whence are derived all possessions, rights, titles, distinctions, and dignities; when we see his most potent prefects and nobles, with lifted hands and bended knees, swearing fealty at his feet—who would not take him for an arbitrary and most absolute prince?

Such a judgment, however, would have been very premature. No prince could be more limited. He had not the licence of doing hurt to the person or property of the meanest vassal throughout his dominions. But was he the less powerful, think you, for being less absolute? quite the contrary. While he acted within the sphere of his compact with the people, he acted in all the persons and powers of the people. Though prescribed with respect to evil, the extent of his beneficence was wholly unconfined. He was not dreaded indeed, but on that account he was the more revered and beloved by his subjects. He was a part of themselves; the principal member of their body. In him they beheld, with delight, their own dignity and strength so gloriously represented; and, by being the proprietor of all their hearts, he became the master of all their hands.

O! exclaimed Harry, who would wish, after this, to be unrestrained from any kind of evil? how frightful, how detestable is that power, which is not exercised in acts of benevolence alone! and all who please may be infinite in the stretch of a good-will.

True, my dear, said Mr. Fenton—I have now, continued he, given you the rough and unformed rudiments of our Britannic constitution. And here I deliver to you my little model of the finished construction thereof, as it now stands on the revolution just achieved by his present glorious majesty, King William.

Your reading has informed you, and may further inform you, of the several steps and struggles whereby this great business was finally effected. It was not suddenly brought to pass; it was the work of many ages; while Britain, like Antæus, though often defeated, rose more vigorous and reinforced from every soil. Of times long passed, what stupendous characters! what sacred names! what watchful councils! what bloody effusions! what a people of heroes! what senates of sages! How hath the invention of nature been stretched, how have the veins of the valiant been exhausted, to form, support, reform, and bring to maturity, this unexampled constitution, this coalescence and grand effort of every human virtue, *British liberty!*

[Here follows Mr. Fenton's short system of the beauties and benefits of our constitution. But, if the reader loves amusement preferable to instruction, he is at liberty to pass it over, and proceed in the story.]

THE REGAL ESTATE.

THE king, in the constitution of Great Britain, is more properly the king of, than a king over the people, united to them, one of them, and contained in them. At the same time that he is acknowledged the head of their body, he is their principal servant or minister, being the deputee of their executive power.

His claim to the throne is not a claim as of some matter of property or personal right; he doth not claim, but is claimed by the people in their parliament; and he is claimed or called upon, not to the investiture of possessions, but the performance of duties. He is called upon to govern the people according to the laws by which they themselves have consented to be governed; to cause justice and mercy to be dispensed throughout the realm; and to his utmost to execute, protect, and maintain the laws of the gospel of God, and the rights and liberties of all the people without distinction; and this he swears on the gospel of God to perform. And thus, as all others owe allegiance to the king, *the king himself oweth allegiance to the constitution.*

The existence of a king, as one of the three estates, is immutable, indispensable, and indefeasible; the constitution cannot subsist without a king. But then his personal claim of possession, and of hereditary succession to the throne, is in several instances precarious and defeasible; as in case of any natural incapacity to govern, or of an open avowal of principles incompatible with the constitution; or in case of overt acts demonstrative of such principles; or of any attempt to sap or overthrow a fundamental part of that system which he was called in, and constituted, and has sworn to maintain.

Though the claim of all kings to the throne of Great

Britain is a limited and defeasible claim; yet the world can afford no rival in power or glory, to *a constitutional sovereign* of these free dominions.

For the honour of their own body, they have invested this their head with all possible illustration; he concentrates the rays of many nations. They have clothed him in royal robes, and circled his head with a diadem, and enthroned him on high; and they bow down before the mirror of their own majesty.

Neither are his the mere ensigns or external shows of regency; he is invested also with powers much more real than if they were absolute.

There are three capital prerogatives with which the king is intrusted, which, at first sight, appear of fearful and dangerous tendency, and which must infallibly and quickly end in arbitrary dominion if they were not counterpoised and counteracted.

His principal prerogative is to make war or peace, as also treaties, leagues, and alliances with foreign potentates.

His second prerogative is to nominate and appoint all ministers and servants of state, all judges and administrators of justice, and all officers, civil or military, throughout these realms.

His third capital prerogative is, that he should have the whole executive power of the government of these nations by his said ministers and officers, both civil and military.

I might here also have added a fourth prerogative, which must have been capitally eversive of the constitution, had it not been limited in the original trust—I mean a power of granting pardon to criminals. Had this power been unrestrained, all obligations to justice might be absolved at the king's pleasure. An evil king might even encourage the breach of law; he must, unquestionably, have dispensed with all illicit acts that were perpetrated by his own orders; and this assurance of pardon must, as unquestionably, have encouraged all his ministers and officers to execute his will as the only rule of their obedience.

But God and our glorious ancestors be praised! He is restrained from protecting his best-beloved ministers when they have effected, or even imagined, the damage of the constitution. He is also limited in appeals brought by the subject for murder or robbery. But on indictments in his own name, for offences against his proper person and government, such as rebellion, insurrection, riot, and breaches of the peace by murder, maim, or robbery, etc., here he is at liberty to extend the arm of his mercy; forasmuch as there are many cases so circumstanced, so admissive of pitiable and palliating considerations, that *summum jus*, or strict justice, might prove *summa injuria*, or extreme injustice.

All pardonable offences are distinguished by the title of "crimina læsæ majestatis—sins against the king:" all unpardonable offences are distinguished by the title of "crimina læsæ libertatis—sins against the constitution." In the first case, the injury is presumed to extend no further than to one or a few individuals; in the second, it is charged as a sin against the public, against the collective body of the whole people. Of the latter kind are nuisances that may endanger the lives of travellers on the highway; but more capitally, any imagination, proven by overt act or evil advice, tending to change the nature or form of any one of the three estates; or tending to vest the government, or the administration thereof, in any one or any two of the said estates, independent of the other; or tending to raise standing armies, or to continue them in time of peace without the consent of parliament; or tending to give any foreign state an advantage over these realms by sea or by land, etc.

The king hath also annexed to his dignity many further

very important powers and prerogatives, though they do not so intimately interfere with the constitution as the capital prerogatives above recited.

He is first considered as the original proprietor of all the lands in these kingdoms; and he founds this claim, as well on the conquest by William the Norman, as by the limited kings or leaders of our Gothic ancestors.

Hence it comes to pass, that all lands to which no subject can prove a title, are supposed to be in their original owner, and are therefore, by the constitution, vested in the crown. On the same principle, also, the king is entitled to the lands of all persons who die without heirs; as also to the possessions of all who are convicted of crimes subversive of the constitution or public weal.

His person, while he is king or inclusive of the first estate, is constitutionally sacred, and exempted from all acts of violence or constraint. As one of the estates, also, he is constituted a corporation, and his Teste-Meipso, or written testimony, amounts to a matter of record. He also exercises, at present, the independent province of supplying members to the second estate by new creation, a very large accession to his original powers. Bishops also are now appointed and nominated by the king, another considerable addition to the royal prerogative. His is the sole prerogative to coin or impress money, and to specify, change, or determine the current value thereof; and for this purpose he is supposed to have reserved, from his original grants of lands, a property in mines of gold and silver, which are therefore called royalties.

As he is one of the three constitutional estates, no action can lie against him in any court, neither can he be barred of his title by length of time or entry. And these illustrations of his dignity cast rays of answerable privileges on his royal consort, heir-apparent, and eldest daughter.

The king hath also some other inferior and conditional powers, such as of instituting fairs and markets, and of issuing patents for special or personal purposes, provided they shall not be found to infringe on the rights of others. He is also intrusted with the guardianship of the persons and possessions of idiots and lunatics, without account.

I leave his majesty's prerogative of a negative voice in the legislature, as also his prerogative (or rather duty) frequently to call the two other estates to parliament, and duly to continue, prorogue, and dissolve the same, till I come to speak of the three estates when in such parliament assembled.

Here then we find, that a King of Great Britain is constitutionally invested with every power that can possibly be exerted in acts of beneficence; and that, while he continues to move within the sphere of his benign appointment, he continues to be constituted the most worthy, most mighty, and most glorious representative of Omnipotence upon earth.

In treating of the second and third estate, I come naturally to consider what those restraints are, which, while they are preserved inviolate, have so happy a tendency to the mutual prosperity of prince and people.

THE ARISTOCRATICAL OR SECOND ESTATE.

THE nobility, or second estate in the constitution of Great Britain, is originally representative. The members were ennobled by tenure, and not by writ or patent; and they were holden in service to the crown and kingdom for the respective provinces, counties, or baronies, whose name they bore, and which they represented.

A title to be a member of this second estate was from the beginning hereditary: the king could not anciently either create or defeat a title to nobility. Their titles were not forfeitable save by the judgments of their peers upon legal trial; and when any were so deprived, or happened to die without heirs, the succession was deemed too important to be otherwise filled than by the concurrence of the three estates, by the joint and solemn act of the *Parliament*, or *Commune Concilium Regni.*

These truths are attested by many ancient records and parliamentary acts. And although this most highly ennobling custom was, at particular times, infringed by particular tyrants, it was inviolably adhered to by the best of our English kings, and was observed even by the worst, excepting a few instances, till the reign of Henry VII., who wished to give consequence to the third estate by deducting from the honours and powers of the second.

In truth, it is not to be wondered that any kings, who were ambitious of extending their own power, should wish to break and weaken that of the nobility, who had distinguished themselves by so many glorious stands for the maintenance of liberty and the constitution; more particularly during the reigns of John, Henry III., the second Edward, and second Richard.

Till Harry VII. the nobles were looked upon as so many pillars whereon the people rested their rights. Accordingly we find that, in the coalition or grand compact between John and the collective body of the nation, the king and people jointly agree to confide to the nobles the superintendence of the execution of the great charter, with authority to them and their successors to enforce the due performance of the covenants therein comprised.

What an illustrating distinction must it have been, when patriot-excellence alone (approved before the country in the field or the council) could give a claim to nobility, and compel, as it were, the united estates of kings, lords, and commons, to call a man up to a second seat in the government and steerage of the nation.

Such a preference must have proved an unremitting incitement to the cultivation and exercise of every virtue; and to such exertions, achievements, and acts of public beneficence, as should draw a man forth to so shining a point of light, and set him like a gem in the gold of the constitution.

The crown did not, at once, assume the independent right of conferring nobility. Henry III. first omitted to call some of the barons to parliament who were personally obnoxious to him, and he issued his writs or written letters to some others who were not barons, but from whom he expected greater conformity to arbitrary measures. These writs, however, did not ennoble the party till he was admitted by the second estate to a seat in parliament; neither was such nobility by writ hereditary.

To supply these defects, the arbitrary ministry of Richard II. invented the method of ennobling by letters patent at the king's pleasure, whether for years or for life, or in special or general tail, or in fee-simple to a man and his heirs at large. This prerogative, however, was thereafter in many instances declined and discontinued, more particularly by the constitutional king Harry the Fifth, till, meeting with no opposition from the other two estates, it has successively descended from Harry VII., on nine crowned heads, through a prescription of near a century and a half.

Next to the king, the people have allowed to their peerage several privileges of the most uncommon and illustrious distinction. Their Christian names, and the names that descended to them from their ancestors, are absorbed by the name from whence they take their title of honour, and by this they make their signature in all letters and deeds. Every temporal peer of the realm is deemed a kinsman to the crown. Their deposition on their honour is admitted in place of their oath, save where they personally present themselves as witnesses of the facts, and saving their oaths of allegiance, supremacy, and abjuration. Their persons are at all times exempted from arrest, except in criminal cases. A defamation of their character is highly punishable, however true the facts may be, and deserving of censure. During session of parliament, all actions and suits at law against peers are suspended. In presentments or indictments by grand juries, and on impeachments by the house of commons, peers are to be tried by their peers alone; for in all criminal cases they are privileged from the jurisdiction of inferior courts, excepting on appeals for murder or robbery. Peers are also exempted from serving on inquests. And in all civil cases, where a peer is plaintiff, there must be two or more knights empannelled on the jury.

The bishops, or spiritual lords, have privilege of parlia-. ment, but have not the above privileges of personal nobility. In all criminal cases, saving attainder and impeachment, they are to be tried by a petit jury. Moreover, bishops do not vote, in the house of lords, on the trial of any person for a capital crime.

All the temporal and spiritual nobles that compose the house of lords, however different in their titles and degrees of nobility, are called peers (pares), or equals; because their voices are admitted as of equal value, and that the vote of a bishop or baron shall be equivalent to that of an archbishop or duke.

The capital privilege (or rather prerogative) of the house of peers consists in their being the supreme court of judicature, to whom the final decision of all civil causes are confided and referred in the last resort.

This constitutional privilege is a weighty counterpoise to his majesty's second prerogative of appointing the administrators of justice throughout the nation; forasmuch as judges (who are immediately under the influence of the crown) are yet intimidated from infringing, by any sentence, on the laws or constitution of these realms, while a judgment so highly superior to their own impends.

The second great privilege of the house of peers consists in their having the sole judicature of all impeachments commenced and prosecuted by the commons. And this, again, is a very weighty counterpoise to his majesty's third prerogative of the executive government of these nations by his ministers; since no minister can be so great as not justly to dread the coming under a judgment from which the mightiness of his royal master cannot protect him.

The third capital privilege of the house of peers subsists in their share, or particular department of rights, in the legislature. This extends to the framing of any bills, at their pleasure, for the purposes of good government; saving always to the commons their incommunicable right of granting taxes or subsidies to be levied on their constituents. But on such bills, as on all others, the house of lords have a negative—a happy counterpoise to the power both of king and commons, should demands on the one part, or bounties on the other, exceed what is requisite.

The change of the ancient modus in conferring nobility, has not hitherto, as I trust, been of any considerable detriment to the weal of the people. But should some future majesty, or rather some future ministry, entitle folk to a voice in the second estate on any consideration save that of eminent virtue and patriotic service, might it be possible that such ministers should take a further stride, and confer nobility for actions deserving of infamy; should they even covenant to grant such honours and dignities in lieu of services subversive of the constitution; a majority of such a peerage must either prove too light to effect any public benefit, or heavy enough to effect the public perdition.

THE DEMOCRATICAL OR THIRD ESTATE.

THE election of commoners to be immediate trustees and apt representatives of the people in parliament, is the hereditary and indefeasible privilege of the people. It is the privilege which they accepted, and which they retain, in exchange of their original inherent and hereditary right of sitting with the king and peers IN PERSON, for the guardianship of their own liberties, and the institution of their own laws.

Such representatives, therefore, can never have it in their power to give, delegate, or extinguish the whole or any part of the people's inseparable and unextinguishable share in the legislative power; neither to impart the same to any one of the other estates, or to any persons or person whatever, either in or out of parliament. Where plenipotentiaries take upon them to abolish the authority of their own principles, or where any secondary agents attempt to defeat the power of their primaries, such agents and plenipotentiaries defeat their own commission, and all the powers of the trust necessarily revert to the constituents.

The persons of these temporary trustees of the people, during their session, and for fourteen days before and after every meeting, adjournment, prorogation, and dissolution of parliament, are equally exempted, with the persons of peers, from arrests and duress of every sort.

They are also, during their session, to have ready access to the king or house of lords, and to address or confer with them on all occasions.

No member of the house of commons, no more than of the house of peers, shall suffer, or be questioned, or compelled to witness or answer, in any court or place whatsoever, touching any thing said or done by himself or others in parliament, in order that perfect freedom of speech and action may leave nothing undone for the public weal.

They have also, during session, an equal power with the house of lords, to punish any who shall presume to traduce their dignity, or detract from the rights or privileges of any member of the house. .

The commons form a court of judicature distinct from the judicature of the house of lords. Theirs is the peculiar privilege to try and adjudge the legality of the election of their own members. They may fine and confine their own members, as well as others, for delinquency or offence against the honour of their house; but in all other matters of judicature, they are merely a court of inquisition and presentment, and not a tribunal of definitive judgment.

In this respect, however, they are extremely formidable. They constitute the grand inquest of the nation; for which great and good purpose they are supposed to be perfectly qualified by a personal knowledge of what hath been transacted throughout the several shires, cities, and boroughs from whence they assemble, and which they represent.

Over and above their inquiry into all public grievances, wicked ministers, transgressing magistrates, corrupt judges and judiciaries, who sell, deny, or delay justice; evil counsellors of the crown, who attempt or devise the subversion or alteration of any part of the constitution; with all such overgrown malefactors as are deemed above the reach of inferior courts—all come under the particular cognizance of the commons, to be by them impeached, and presented for trial at the bar of the house of lords. And these inquisitory and judicial powers of the two houses, from which no man under the crown can be exempted, are deemed a sufficient allay and counterpoise to the whole executive power of the king, by his ministers.

The legislative department of the power of the commons

is in all respects coequal with that of the peers. They frame any bills at pleasure for the purposes of good government. They exercise a right, as the lords also do, to propose and bring in bills for the amendment or repeal of old laws, as well as for the ordaining or institution of new ones. And each house, alike, hath a negative on all bills that are framed and passed by the other.

But the capital, the incommunicable privilege of the house of commons, arises from that holy trust which their constituents repose in them; whereby they are empowered to borrow from the people a small portion of their property, in order to restore it threefold in the advantages of peace, equal government and the encouragement of trade, industry, and manufactures.

To impart any of this trust would be a breach of the constitution; and even to abuse it would be a felonious breach of common honesty.

By this fundamental trust, and incommunicable privilege, the commons have the sole power over the money of the people; to grant or deny aids, according as they shall judge them either requisite or unnecessary to the public service. Theirs is the province, and theirs alone, to inquire and judge of the several occasions for which such aids may be required, and to measure and appropriate the sums to their respective uses. Theirs also is the sole province of framing all bills or laws for the imposing of any taxes, and of appointing the means of levying the same upon the people. Neither may the first or second estate, either king or peerage, propound or do any thing relating to these matters that may any way interfere with the proceedings of the commons; save in their negative or assent to such bills when presented to them, without addition, deduction, or alteration of any kind.

After such like aids and taxes have been levied and disposed of, the commons have the further right of inquiring and examining into the application of such aids; of ordering all accounts relative thereto to be laid before them; and of censuring the abuse or misapplication thereof.

The royal assent to all other bills is expressed by the terms, "Le roy le veut—the king wills it;" but when the commons present their bills of aid to his majesty, it is answered—"Le roy remercie ses loyal sujets, et ainsi le veut —the king thanks his loyal subjects, and so willeth." An express acknowledgment, that the right of granting or levying monies for public purposes lies solely, inherently, and incommunicably, in the people and their representatives.

This capital privilege of the commons constitutes the grand counterpoise to the king's principal prerogative of making peace or war; for how impotent must a warlike enterprise prove without money, which makes the sinews thereof! And thus the people and their representatives still retain in their hands the *grand momentum* of the constitution, and of all human affairs.

Distinguished representatives! Happy people! immutably happy while *worthily represented!*

As the fathers of the several families throughout the kingdom, nearly and tenderly comprise and represent the persons, cares, and concerns, of their respective households, so these adopted fathers immediately represent, and intimately concentrate, the persons and concerns of their respective constituents, and in them the collective body or sum of the nation. And while these fathers continue true to their adopting children, a single stone cannot lapse from the *great fabric of the constitution.*

THE THREE ESTATES IN PARLIAMENT.

WITH the king, lords, and commons, in parliament assembled, the people have deposited their legislative or absolute power, *in trust*, for their whole body; the said king, lords, and commons, when so assembled, being the great representative of the whole nation, as if all the people were then convened in one general assembly.

As the institution, repeal, and amendment of laws, together with the redress of public grievances and offences, are not within the capacity of any of the three estates distinct from the others; the *frequent holding of parliaments* is the vital food, without which the constitution cannot subsist.

The three estates originally, when assembled in parliament, sat together consulting in the open field. Accordingly, at Running Mead, five hundred years ago, King John passed the great charter (as therein is expressed) by the advice of the lords spiritual and temporal, by the advice of several commoners (by name recited), *et aliorum fidelium*, and of others his faithful people. And, in the twenty-first clause of the said charter, he covenants that, "for having the common council of the kingdom to assess aids, he will cause the lords spiritual and temporal to be summoned by his writs; and moreover, that he will cause the principal commoners, or those who held from him in chief, to be generally summoned to said parliaments by his sheriffs and bailiffs."

In the said assemblies, however, the concourse became so great and disorderly, and the contests frequently so high, between the several estates, in assertion of their respective prerogatives and privileges, that they judged it more expedient to sit apart, and separately to exercise the offices of their respective departments.

As there is no man or set of men, no class or corporation, no village or city throughout the kingdom, that is not represented by these their delegates in parliament; this great body-politic, or representative of the nation, consists, like the body-natural, of a head and several members, which, being endowed with different powers for the exercise of different offices, are yet connected by one main and common interest, and actuated by *one life or spirit of public reason,* called the *laws.*

In all steps of national import the king is to be conducted by the direction of the parliament, his great national council—a council on whom it is equally incumbent to consult for the king with whom they are connected, and for the people by whom they are delegated, and whom they represent. Thus the king is, constitutionally, to be guided by the sense of the parliament, and the parliament alike is, constitutionally, to be guided by the general sense of the people. The two estates in parliament are the constituents of the king; and the people, mediately or immediately, are the constituents of the two estates in parliament.

Now, while the three estates act distinctly within their respective departments, they affect, and are reciprocally affected by each other. This action and reaction produces that general and systematic control which, like *conscience*, pervades and superintends the whole, checking and prohibiting evil from every part of the constitution. And from this confinement of every part to the rule of *right reason*, ariseth the great *law of liberty to all.*

For instance:—the king has the sole prerogative of making war, etc.; but then the means are in the hands of the people and their representatives.

Again—To the king is committed the whole executive power; but then the ministers of that power are accountable to a tribunal from which a criminal has no appeal or deliverance to look for.

Again—To the king is committed the cognisance of all causes; but should his judges or justiciaries pervert the rule of righteousness, an inquisition, impeachment, and trial impends, from whose judgment the judges cannot be exempted.

Again—The king hath a negative upon all bills, whereby his own prerogatives are guarded from invasion; but should he refuse the royal assent to bills tending to the general good of the subject, the commons can also withhold their bills of assessment, or annex the rejected bills to their bills of aids, and they never failed to pass in such agreeable company.

Lastly—To the king is committed the right of calling the two estates to parliament; but should he refuse so to call them, such a refusal would be deemed "an abdication of the constitution;" and no one need be told at this day, that "an abdication of the constitution is *an abdication of the throne.*"

Thus, while the king acts in consent with the parliament and his people, he is limitless, irresistible, omnipotent upon earth; he is the free wielder of all the powers of a free and noble people—a king throned over all the kings of the children of men. But should he attempt to break bounds—should he cast for independence—he finds himself hedged in and straitened on every side—he finds himself abandoned by all his powers, and justly left to a state of utter impotence and inaction.

Hence is imputed to the sovereign head, in the constitution of Great Britain, the high and divine attribute—*the king can do no wrong;* for he is so circumscribed from the possibility of transgression, that no wrong can be permitted to any king in the constitution.

While the king is thus controlled by the lords and the commons—while the lords are thus controlled by the commons and the king—and while the commons are thus controlled by the other two estates from attempting any thing to the prejudice of the general welfare; the three estates may be aptly compared to three pillars, divided below at equidistant angles, but united and supported at top, merely by the bearing of each pillar against the others. Take but any one of these pillars away, and the other two must inevitably tumble. But while all act on each other, all are equally counteracted, and thereby affirm and establish the general frame.

How deplorable then would it be, should this elaborate structure of our happy constitution, within the short period of a thousand years hence—possibly in half the time—fall a prey to effeminacy, pusillanimity, venality, and seduction; like some ancient oak, the lord of the forest, to a pack of vile worms that lie gnawing at the root; or, like Egypt, be contemptibly destroyed by "lice and locusts!"

Should the morals of our constituents ever come to be debauched, consent, which is the salt of liberty, would then be corrupted, and no salt might be found wherewith it could be seasoned. Those who are inwardly the servants of sin, must be outwardly the servants of influence. Each man would then be as the Trojan horse of old, and carry the enemies of his country within his bosom. Our own appetites would then induce us to betray our own interests, and state policy would seize us by the hand of our lusts, and lead us "a willing sacrifice to our own perdition."

Should it ever come to pass that corruption, like a dark and low-hung mist, should spread from man to man, and cover these lands—should a general dissolution of manners prevail—should vice be countenanced and communicated by the leaders of fashion—should it come to be propagated by ministers among legislators, and by the legislators among their constituents—should guilt lift up its head without fear of reproach, and avow itself in the face of the sun, and laugh virtue out of countenance by force of numbers—should public duty turn public strumpet—should shops come to be advertised where men may dispose of their honour and honesty at so much per ell—should public markets be opened for the purchase of consciences, with an "O yes! We bid most to those who set themselves, their trust, and their country, to sale." If such a day, I say, should ever arrive, it would be doomsday indeed to the virtue, to the liberty, and constitution of these kingdoms! It would be the same to Great Britain as it would happen to the universe should the laws of cohesion cease to operate, and all the parts be dissipated, whose orderly connection now forms the beauty and common wealth of nature. Want of sanity in the materials can never be supplied by any art in the building. A constitution of public freemen can never consist of private constitutes.

CHAPTER IV.

In little more than a month, Harry made himself perfect master of the system of the British constitution, and wrote comments upon it much more voluminous than the text. As he had lost his friend Ned, little Dicky Clement became the principal companion of his hours of amusement, and Dicky, with his good-will, would never be from his heels.

One morning as they strolled up the road, some distance from the town, Harry observed a crowd gathering fast on the way, and hastened like others to see what was the matter.

As soon as he arrived, he perceived Mr. Gripe the constable at the head of the posse, with his painted staff of authority exalted in his hand. Pray, what are you about Mr. Constable? says Harry.—I am going, sir, to seize a robber who has taken shelter in yonder waste hovel.—And whom did he rob?—He robbed Mr. Niggards here, that is to say, his boy here, of a sixpenny loaf.—Perhaps the man was hungry, said Harry, and had not wherewithal to buy one. Pray tell me, my lad, how the affair was.

Why, master, you must know as how Mr. Niggards, my master here, sent me this morning to the town with a shilling to buy two sixpenny loaves. So, as I was coming back, I met an able-looking man, who made me afraid with his pale and meagre face.—My good boy, says he, will you give me one of those loaves in charity?—I dare not, sir, says I; they are none of my own.—Here, says he, I will give you my hat for one of them; but this I refused, as his hat, to my thinking, was not worth a groat.—Nay, says he, I must have one of the loaves, that is certain, for I have a wife and seven children all starving in yonder hovel, and while there is bread in the world I cannot but snatch a morsel for them. So, as I told you, I was frighted. I gave him one of the loaves without any more words, and away he run as fast as his legs could carry him; but I followed him with my eye till I saw him safe lodged.

Here Harry wiped his eye, and mused awhile. Tell me truly now, my good boy, continued he, if both those loaves had been your own, would you willingly have given one of them to keep the poor man and his family from perishing?

I would, sir, said the lad, with a very good will. And, had I a sixpence of my own, I would have gone back with all my heart and have bought another loaf. But my master is a hard man, and so I was forced to tell him the truth.

Here, my lad, says Harry; here is a crown. Go back, buy two loaves for your master in place of the one he has lost, and keep the remaining four shillings to yourself for your trouble. You see, Mr. Constable, continued he, you never can make anything like felony of this matter. The boy confesses that he gave the bread with a very good will, and that he would not have informed had it not been for fear of his master.

It is very true, please your honour, replied Mr. Gripe; I myself do pity the poor man from my heart, and will have nothing more to say in this business. .

Stay a while, says Harry, perhaps we may find some further employment for you. I think I should know the face of yonder man. Is not that the Niggards whom you had in custody the other day, and for whose deliverance I paid five-and-twenty pounds to his creditors?—The very man, sir, says Gripe.

Harry then put his hand in his pocket, and taking out a small scrip of parchment, exclaimed—I am glad of what you tell me, with all my heart! Indeed, I did not like the looks of the man at the time, and that made me accept an assignment of this action. Here, Mr. Gripe, take your prisoner again into custody in my name. Away with him to jail directly! As the holy gospel has it: "He shall not depart thence till he has paid the utmost farthing." No, no, Mr. Niggards! I will not hear a word. Go and learn henceforward to be merciful yourself, if you would look for any mercy from God or man.

Dicky, my dear, go back again, says Harry; our neighbour Joseph here will see you safe home. I will not suffer any one to go in my company, for fear of putting the poor man or his family to shame.

Harry had not advanced fifty paces towards the hovel, when his ears were struck with the sound of sudden and joint lamentation; and turning, he perceived that the inquisitive crowd had gathered at his heels.—My friends, says he, I entreat, I beseech you to leave me for the present. I would not choose any witnesses to what I am about. Pray, oblige me so far as to depart on your own occasions.

Hereupon, being loth to offend him, they retired a few steps, and stood together aloof, attentive to the event of this uncommon adventure.

Meanwhile the cry continued with a bitterness that thrilled through every nerve of our hero; and, as he now approached the place, he did his utmost to restrain himself, and quell the feelings within him, and he drew his hat over his eyes to prevent the parties from seeing the emotion that they caused.

The hovel was of mud walls, without any roofing; but,

as there was an opening where a door had once been, Harry stole to the entrance, casting an under eye of observation about him.

Hereupon a 'woman turned. She had been fearfully peering over the wall at the crowd which had not yet dispersed; but, having notice of Harry's entrance, she looked towards him, and dropped on her knees.

O sir! she cried, if you are the gentleman who owned the loaf, for Christ his sake I pray you to have mercy upon us! Money, indeed, we have not; but we have these shreds remaining, and we will strip ourselves of our covering to make you a recompense. Alas! alas! could we have guessed how my husband came by it, we would have famished a thousand times rather than touch a morsel. But he, dear good man, did it all for our sakes, for the sake of the heavy burden with which he is overladen. Ah, I would to heaven we were all dead, hanged, or drowned, out of his way! He might then walk the world at large, and be happy, as he deserves.

Here again she set up her wailing, which was accompanied by her seven children, in such a woful concert as the heart of Harry could not sustain, neither suffer him for a season to interrupt or appease.

At length he said with a faltering voice—Pray, be not alarmed, madam, for I discern that you are a gentlewoman, though in a very unhappy disguise. The affair of the loaf is settled to your satisfaction; and here are ten guineas, it is all that I have about me, and it is only to shew you for the present that you are not quite so friendless in the world as you thought. Mean time I request that you will all come with me to Hampstead, where we will try to do something better for you.

Here the woman looked with an earnest and eager rapture at him. May Jesus Christ, she cried, be your portion, fair angel! and he is already your portion; he is seen in your sweet face, and breaks out at your eyes in pity to poor sinners.

Harry was now stepping forth, and the rest prepared to follow him; when the poor man, who for shame had not yet uttered a syllable, gently stayed him at the opening. —Turn, generous master, said he; pray turn, and hear a small apology for my transgression. I am a very unhappy man, I have seen better times; but I am driven by cruel usage from house, and home, and maintenance. I was going to London to apply to the law for relief, when my youngest child, who was on the breast, fell desperately sick about four days ago. As we had no money to hire lodging, and had begged the means of life for the two foregoing days, we were compelled to take up with this shelterless hovel. From hence I frequented the road, and for the three last days begged as much as sustained us in coarse bread and water. But this morning my boy died, and his brothers and I, with our sticks and our hands, dug his grave that you see yonder, and I placed that flag over him to preserve his tender limbs from the pigs and the hounds, till it may please heaven to allow me means to bury him according to the holy rites of our church. This melancholy office, sir, detained me so long, and exercise had made the appetites of my children so outrageous, that I was in a manner compelled to do what I did. As I had no coffin nor winding-sheet, I took the waistcoat from my body, and wrapped it about my babe, and would willingly have wrapped him with my flesh and my bones, that we might quietly have lain in one grave together.

Harry answered not a word, but walking onward before his company, plentifully watered the ground with his tears as he passed; while the poor man took his youngest son in his arms, and the woman her youngest daughter on her back, and thus, with a leisurely pace, they all arrived at Mr. Fenton's.

The door being opened, Harry led his nine guests to the back parlour, where he instantly ordered plenty of bread and butter and milk for the children, with cold meat, ale, and cakes, for the father and mother: and this was a matter too customary in this house to be any cause of wonder to any member of the family.

As soon as they were refreshed, he took them all to his wardrobe, where he constrained the parents to take of the very best things for themselves and their children; and having so done he walked out, and left them to dress.

Mr. Fenton was in his study, and had just finished a letter as Harry entered with a smiling countenance. I have been very lucky this morning, sir, says he; I think I have got the prettiest family of boys and girls that is to be found within five shires.—Do you know any thing about them, Harry?—Nothing further as yet, sir, than that they and their parents are exceeding poor, and have fallen, as they say, into great misfortunes. The mother is a very handsome and genteel young woman, and the father a portly and very comely man, save that he has a large purple mark on the left side of his face.—A purple mark! cried Mr. Fenton, and started. Go, my dear, and bring that man to me directly.—Why, pray, sir, do you know him?—No, my love, I should not know him though he stood before me; but I would give a thousand pounds that he may prove the man I mean, and that I shall discover on short examination.

By this time the father of our new family was dressed, and Harry, taking him by the hand, bade him be of good courage, and led him to his uncle. He bowed twice, and with an awful and timid respect, while Mr. Fenton rose and looked earnestly at him. I rejoice, sir, says he, to find that my son here has been of some little matter of use to you and your family. Pray, take a seat nearer to me, sir, if you please. He tells me you have met with misfortunes; I also have had my share. I think myself nearly of kin to the unhappy; and you will singularly oblige me by as much of your story as you shall please to communicate. I am interested in it.

I have nothing to conceal from your honour, answered the stranger. And I shall willingly give you an open and faithful narrative of my short but sad history.

My name is Giffard Homely. My father was a farmer in easy circumstances near Stratford. He bound me apprentice to a tanner, and, when my time was out, gave me a hundred and twenty pounds to set me up in my business. But, dying soon after, he bequeathed the bulk of his substance to my elder brother.

Though my brother was a spendthrift, yet I loved him dearly, and, when his creditors fell upon him, I became his bail for two hundred pounds. Within a few months after he suddenly disappeared, and I never could learn further tidings concerning him.

A writ was thereupon marked against me, and put into the hands of bailiffs. But liberty was precious. I left all my substance to the possession of my pursuers, and, passing at a great rate, I escaped into Lincolnshire.

There I joined myself to Anthony Granger, the tanner. Independent of his trade, he held a very beautiful and well-parked farm under Sir Spranger Thornhill, the lord of the manor. And as I served him with great zeal, affection, and application, his affairs prospered under my hands.

He had an only child, a very lovely girl, of about ten years of age; her manners, like her countenance, were extremely engaging, and I took vast delight, at all leisure hours, in teaching her to read and write, and in diverting her with a variety of little plays and amusements.

I had no intention, at that time, of gaining her young heart, but that happened to prove the miserable consequence; and a heavy price it is that my poor déar girl has since paid for her affection.

Year after year she now grew in stature, but much more in loveliness, at least in my eyes; and yet I flattered myself that I affected her merely for her own sake. I used to please myself with the prospect of her being advanced to high fortune: and I thought that I would willingly have given her up at the altar to some lord of the land.

One twelfth night a parcel of young folks of us were diverting ourselves about the fire with several pastimes, and among the rest the play was introduced of, *I love my love with an A, because she is amiable*, and so on through the alphabet.

When it came to my Peggy's turn, she said—I love my love with an *H*, because he is very *honest*, and I never will hate him for his being *homely*. And this might have passed without any observation, had she not cast a glance at me, and blushed exceedingly, which threw me also into equal confusion.

As this was the first discovery that I made of her affection, it also served to open my eyes to the strength of my own passion, and this cost me many a sleepless night and aching heart. I did not look upon myself as a sufficient match for her; I reflected that it would be very ungenerous to lessen the fortune or happiness of the girl that I loved; and I resolved a hundred times to quit the country, that my absence might cure both her and myself of our foolish fondness for each other. But though this was what my reason still prompted and approved, my heart still held me back, as it were, for a while longer when I was on the brink of departure.

Peggy was just arrived to her fifteenth year on the 24th

of April, and was elected by the neighbours to be queen of the following May, and to deliver the prizes to the victors at the wake.

I had made a vow within myself to forsake her and the country the very day after her regency; but in the meanwhile, I could not resist the temptation of showing my address before the queen of my wishes.

Accordingly, on that day I entered the lists among the other young candidates. But I will not burden your honour with a particular detail of our insignificant contests. You have unquestionably been witness to the like on several occasions. It will be sufficient to inform you, that as I had the fortune to get the better at the race and at wrestling, when I successively went to receive the respective prizes my Peggy's eyes danced, and her feet went pit-a-pat with joy, as I approached her.

Cudgels came next in play, and a little stage of boards was erected for the purpose, that the spectators might see with the better advantage. I had long learned this art from a famous master in Stratford; and, as I was confident of my superiority, I hurt my rivals as little as possible, only just sufficient to make them acknowledge that they were foiled.

At length one Hector Pluck, a butcher, mounted the stage. He had, it seems, been quite an adept at this sport, and for ten foregoing years had carried off the prize in several neighbouring shires; but he was now come to settle near Lincoln, and was to have been married the following day to a farmer's daughter, who was one of the fair spectators at the wake.

The moment he assailed me, I perceived that his passions were up, and that his eye was a plain interpreter of the deadliness of his heart. He fought cautiously, however, and kept on a watchful reserve; and we had long attacked and defended, without any advantage on either part, when, with a motion and fury quick as lightning, he made a side stroke at me, and aimed to cut me across the face with the point of his stick. This was a blow which I had not time to intercept, or even to see. The villain, however, happily missed of his intention; for his cudgel, being something advanced, only bruised my cheek, when instantly I gave him an exasperated stroke on the head, and, cutting him in the skull, laid him sprawling on the stage, whereat all who knew me gave a great shout.

After some time he rose, and advancing a little toward me, he stretched out his left hand as if in token of reconciliation; while, pulling out his butcher's knife from a sheath in his side-pocket, he with his right hand made a stab at my heart, and, suddenly leaping off the stage, attempted to escape.

Immediately the blood poured from me in a stream, and ran along the boards. I found myself growing weak, and, sitting down on the stage, I had the presence of mind to open my bosom, and, taking out my handkerchief, I held it to the wound.

In the mean time the whole concourse was in an uproar. The cry went about that Giffard Homely was murdered! Giffard Homely was killed! My poor dear Peggy fell senseless from her throne, and was carried home in a fit. Several horsemen hasted away, of their own accord, for a surgeon; and the butcher was pursued, knocked down, hard pinioned, and conveyed with following curses to the jail of Lincoln.

Among others who came to condole with me, little Master Billy Thornhill, our landlord's son and heir, came running, and desired to be lifted upon the stage.

As soon as he saw the blood, and how weak and pale I looked, he broke out into a passionate fit of tears—O Giffard, my Giffard, my poor Giffard! he cried; I fear you are a dead man! You will no more be my holiday-companion, Giffard! Never more will you go a-birding with me, or set gins for the rabbits, or catch little fishes for me, or carry me on your back through the water, or in your arms over the mire. Alack! alack! what shall I do if I lose you, my poor Giffard!

The surgeon came at full gallop. As soon as he had seen the greatness of the gash—Say your last prayer, my friend, he cried; in a very few minutes you must be a dead man. But when he had probed the wound, his face turned to cheerfulness. A most wonderful escape, he cried: the weapon has missed your vitals, and only glanced along the rib. Be of good courage; I engage, in a few weeks, to set you once more upon your legs.

Mean time my loving neighbours made a litter and bed for me of the tents and tent-poles, all striving who should carry me, and all escorting me home.

The good Mr. Granger had been that day confined by a sprain in his ankle, and now sat weeping by his child, who fell out of one fainting fit into another, till she was told that I was brought home, and that the doctor had pronounced me out of danger.

As soon as I was put to bed, and my kind attendants withdrawn, Mr. Granger on a crutch came limping, and sat down by me. He had endeavoured to restrain his tears before the crowd; but as soon as he was seated they broke out anew.

O Giffard, Giffard! he cried; my dear Peggy is very ill, and you are very ill; and to lose you both at once would be hard upon me, indeed!

Notwithstanding a short fever, the doctor happened to keep his promise, with the assistance of youth and a good habit, and I began to gather strength and recover apace.

As soon as I was up and about, I observed that Miss Peggy seemed no longer desirous of restraining her kind looks or her kind offices; and this gave me some concern, till I also observed that her father took no umbrage or no notice of it.

One evening, as we sat over a tankard of October—Giffard, says he bluntly, what would you think of my Peggy for a wife?—Nothing at all, sir, says I. I would not marry your daughter if she would have me to-morrow.—Pray, why so, Giffard? Peggy is very pretty, and deserving, as I think, of as good a man as you.—Her deservings, sir, said I, are my very objection; I scarce know a man in the land who is deserving of her.—If that is the case, Giffard, her hand is at your service, with all my heart.—Oh, sir! I replied, I have no suitable fortune; but know you are pleased to banter; I am no match for her.—You are an industrious and a making young man, said he; and such a one is richer in my eye than a spender with thousands. Beside, you are loving and good-natured, my son; and I shall not lose my child by you, but gain another child in you as dear to me as herself.

Here I was so transported, so overpowered by the kindness of the dear good man, that I could not get out a syllable; but, sinking before him, I eagerly grasped his legs, and then his knees, and rising went out to vent my passion.

In about a month after, Sir Spranger Thornhill and my young friend, Master William, honoured our nuptials with their presence; and all our kind neighbours came crowding to the solemnity, and, by their joy, appeared to be parties to our union.

For eight following years never was known a happier family. And about that time Sir Spranger Thornhill sickened and died, and was attended to the dark mansion of the bodies of his ancestors, by the greatest concourse of true mourners that ever was seen in the shire, all lamenting that goodness was not exempted from mortality.

Our dear father could never be said to hold up his head from that day. He silently pined after his old friend and patron, Sir Spranger; and all our cares and caresses were not able to withhold him from following the same appointed track.

Never, sure, was grief like mine and my Peggy's. In looking at each other we saw the loss that we had sustained; and while we lay arm in arm, often, often have we watered the good man's memory with our tears.

Time, however, who has many severe sorrows in prospect, helps to soften and lessen those that he brings in his train. An increasing family of children, sweetly tempered like their mother, called for all my concern; and our young landlord, Sir William, whenever he came from college, used to make our house his home, and take me with him wherever he went, till Lord Lechmore, his guardian, took him from the university, and sent him abroad, with a tutor and servants, on his travels.

As I had made considerable savings, and now looked to have a number of children to provide for, I resolved to realize all that I could for the poor things; so I built a malthouse and windmill, and planted a large orchard, with other profitable improvements, that cost me to the amount of about eight hundred pounds.

Whilst these things were in agitation, Sir Freestone Hardgrave, one of the knights of our shire, came into that part of the country. He had lately purchased a fine estate adjoining to the west side of my concern; and was a man of vast opulence, but a stranger among us at that time.

Though Sir Freestone was an old bachelor, and had one of the most remorseless hearts that ever informed the shape of man, he had yet a pleasing aspect and insinuating address, and always applied those qualities to the purpose of betraying. Alas! I was informed, but too late, of his character—that his avarice outgrew even the growth of his wealth; and that his desires increased in exact proportion as age happened to deduct from his ability to gratify them.

Unhappily he cast a greedy eye at my little farm. Like another lordly Ahab, he coveted the vineyard of poor Naboth; and at length compassed his ends by means equally iniquitous.

When he proposed to give me more than value for it, I answered that I myself had taken a fancy to it, for the sake of the dear man who had given it to me in trust for his child and her posterity, and that I would not part with it for twenty times an equivalent. With this, however, he did not appear in the least disconcerted; but said that he esteemed and affected me the more for my gratitude to the memory of my old benefactor.

I was afterwards told, and learned by dear experience, that he never pardoned an offence, nor even a disappointment; but nothing of this appeared for the present. He visited—made it his business to meet me in several places—sought and seemed quite desirous of cultivating an acquaintance with me—did me many little friendly offices with my richer neighbours—condescended to toy with my little ones—appeared to take a huge liking to my two eldest boys—stood godfather to my little girl that is now in her mother's arms—said he wondered how I contrived to maintain so numerous a family upon such slender means—and promised to procure me a beneficial post in the collection of the customs.

After a course of such specious kindnesses, and while my heart glowed with gratitude, in the recollection of his favours both passed and proposed, he came to my house in a mighty hurry. My dear Homely, says he, I have just struck up a most advantageous bargain with our neighbour Squire Spendall. But he wants the money immediately—I have not the whole about me; and yet, if I do not pay him down directly, some cursed disappointment may intervene. Do run and bring me all that you have quickly. I will repay you within two or three days at farthest.

Here I hasted with joy to the corner where I had deposited my cash, as well for payment of rent as another little matter that I had in my eye; and, bringing out a leathern bag, I laid it on the table. There, sir, said I, are two hundred and thirty guineas; take but the trouble to count them out, and give me a short acknowledgment. No, said he, my dear Homely, never heed it for the present, I will be back with you the moment I have made the purchase; and so saying, he caught up the bag and huddled away as fast as his old legs could scamper, while I sat still through astonishment, my heart misgiving me at the time, as if it foreboded the mischiefs that were to follow.

I waited with great anxiety for his return till evening, when, hastening to his lodge, I was there informed that he had set out for London five hours before. This threw me into a panic, though not altogether without a mixture of hope, and so I waited till the three days of his promise should expire. Mr. Snack then came to me and demanded the rent. He was a Lincoln attorney, whom Lord Lechmore had lately preferred to the care of my landlord's concerns, upon the death of Mr. Kindly, the good old agent. I told him ingenuously how matters had happened, and said I would hurry to London and bring back the money directly.

Accordingly I posted away, and rested not till I arrived at the great city. There, for seven days successively, I besieged the doors of Sir Freestone, hourly knocking and requesting to 'be admitted to his presence; but he was either not up, or just gone out, or had company with him, or was just then very busy, and not to be spoken to, and so forth.

At length, when he found that I would not quit his house without an answer, he ordered me before him. His chariot waited at the gate, and he stood dressed in the hall. As I approached, and bowed with the respect and mortified air of a petitioner, he put on a look of the most strange and audacious effrontery I ever beheld.—Who are you, friend, said he, and what may your business be with me?—I am come, and it please your honour, humbly to tell you that I am called upon for my rent; and to beseech your honour to restore me the two hundred and thirty pieces you had from me the other day.—Here, says he to his servants, this must be some desperado who is come to rob me in broad day, and in the middle of my own people. The fellow says I owe him money: I know not that I ever saw his face before. I desire that you will not suffer such a dangerous villain to enter my doors any more. And so saying, out he stepped, and away he drove.

O, sirs, how I was struck to the heart at that instant! I sneaked out, scarce half alive, not remembering where I was, or whither I was to go. Alas! I was far from making the speed back again that I had done in going. I knew not how to shew my face to my Peggy or her dear little ones, whom I had plundered and stripped of their substance, by stupidly surrendering it without witnesses, or a single line whereby I might reclaim it. At length I got home, if home it might be called, that had then nothing in it, or at least nothing for me.

Mr. Snack had taken the advantage of my absence to possess himself of my farm, and of all that I was worth. Under colour of distraining for rent, he had seized every thing, even the beds whereon my wife and children lay, with

7*

all their wearing apparel, save what they had on their backs. The bill of appraisement, which I have here, comes to upwards of six hundred pounds; but when the cattle and other effects were set up for sale, the auctioneer and bidders proved of Mr. Snack's providing; all were intimidated from offering any thing save those who offered in trust for this charitable agent, and the whole of my substance went off within the value of one year's rent, being one hundred and eighty-five pounds.

Never! exclaimed Mr. Fenton; never did I hear of so bare-faced and daring a violation of all laws, divine and human, and that too under sanction of the most perfect system of law that ever was framed. But what will not power effect, when unrestrained by conscience, when prompted by avarice, and abetted by cunning?—And is there no remedy, sir? cried out our hero.—None that I know of, my Harry, save where power opposes power in favour of weakness, or wealth opposes wealth in favour of poverty.

But we will see what may be done. Meanwhile let Mr. Homely proceed in his narrative.

When my family, continued Homely, were thus turned out of doors, an old follower made way for them in his own cottage, and retired with his wife and daughter to a cow-house hard by. Meanwhile my loving neighbours supplied them with sufficient bedding, and daily kept them in victuals, even more than they could eat.

While I went slowly to see them, stopping and turning every minute towards our old habitation, all the horrors of our situation flew upbraidingly in my face, and I accused myself as the robber and murderer of eight persons, for any one of whom I would have spent my life.

When I stooped to enter their lowly roof, all trembling and sick at heart, I expected to meet nothing but faces of aversion and expressions of reproach; but when they all set up a shout of joy at my appearance, when they all crowded clasping and clinging about me, the violence and distraction of my inward emotion deprived me of sensation, and I swooned away.

When I revived, I cast a look about me, and perceived that their grief had been as extreme as their joy was at my arrival. Ah, my Peggy! I cried, how have I undone you! By you I got all my possessions, and, in return, I have deprived you of all that you possessed. You were every blessing to me, and I have repaid you with nothing but misery and ruin.

Do not be concerned, my love, said she, nor repine at the consequences of your own goodness and honesty. You are not as God to see into all hearts; the wisest may be deceived; and the best, as I believe, are the most subject to be imposed upon. Common charity must have supposed that there could not be such a soul as Sir Freestone upon earth. But be of good courage, my husband, I have good news for you; I dreamed that our dear father appeared to me last night. Do not be disheartened, my child, says he; bear the cross that is laid upon you with a cheerful and free will, and all shall be restored to you sevenfold upon earth, and seventy-seven fold in the life that has no ending.

When I found that my Peggy, instead of distaste and upbraiding, had nothing but love in her looks, and consolation in her expressions, I folded her to my bosom, and to my soul that went to meet her, and I would willingly have made her one with my own being.

My neighbours were not as birds of the season; they neither despised nor forsook me because of my poverty. They came crowding to condole with me; they advised me to apply to the law against Sir Freestone and attorney Snack; and they offered to contribute towards my journey. They also joined in this written testimony of my character, and prosperous circumstances, before Snack made the seizure; and two of them have witnessed, in this bit of paper, that when the alarm came of Mr. Kindly's death, and of a strange agent being put in his room, they heard me say that I did not matter the worst he could do, and saw me count down twenty pieces over and above my year's rent.

The late frights and fatigues which Peggy underwent during Snack's operations, together with her extremes of joy on my return, and of grief at the fit into which I had fallen, hastened on her labour, and she was delivered before her time of that weakly little babe whom I buried this morning.

Within six weeks after her childbirth we prepared for our journey. Our neighbours, like the good Samaritan, had compassion upon him who fell among the thieves. They made me up a purse of thirty-five pounds, and promised to contribute further towards the carrying on of my suit.

We travelled happily, by easy journeys of a few miles a day, till, nine days ago, we reached a small village the other side of St. Alban's; there we took up our rest for the night at a house that had no sign, but let occasional lodgings, and sold bread and small beer.

As I desired a separate apartment for ourselves, we were put into a kind of waste room, that had no fastening to the door except a latch. After a slender supper, we lay down to sleep, and I stuffed my breeches close under my head with all possible caution. We had made an extraordinary journey that day, and I was particularly fatigued by carrying several of my tired children successively in my arms, so that we all slept but too soundly; and, when I awoke in the morning, neither money nor breeches were to be found.

Such a loss, at another time, would have been as nothing to me; but in our present circumstances, it was a repetition and doubling of all that we had lost before. I instantly summoned the people of the house, and in a good deal of warmth charged our landlord with the felony, telling him that I had been robbed of about thirty-three pounds. Why, master, says he, I know nothing to the contrary; but it would be very hard indeed if I was to be answerable for the honesty of every one who goes this road. If you had given your money in charge to me, I would have been accountable for it. I believe, by the grief you are in, that you must have been losers: I will therefore forgive you your reckoning, and give you a pair of breeches of my own into the bargain; but this is all I will do till the law forces me.

As there was no remedy, at least for the present, I accepted his overture, and set out. But, O sir! it is impossible to describe the horrors of my soul as I silently stepped along, casting an eye of mingled pity and despair upon my children. I cursed in secret my own existence, and wished for some sudden thunderbolt to crush me into nothing. All trust in God, or his providence, had now wholly forsaken me, and I looked upon him as neglecting all other objects of his wrath, and exerting his omnipotence against me and mine alone.

Peggy, as I suppose, perceived how it was with me, and kept behind a while, that she might give way to the present tumult and distemper of my mind. At length, hoping to administer some matter of comfort to me, she came up, and silently put a few shillings into my hand, saying—Courage, my dear husband, all cannot be lost while we have a God who is infinitely rich to depend upon.—Ah! said I, these are the fruits of your dreams, these are your promised blessings that heaven had in store for us.—And still has in store, she replied; the same hand that holds the rod, holds the comforting staff also.—Tell me not of comfort, I cried; I see that the face of God is set in blackness and blasting against me. But for me it matters not, had he not taken me at an advantage. He sees that I have eight lives, all dearer than my own, and he is determined to kill me in every one of them.

Do not cast from you, my love, she said, the only crutch that the world and the wretched have to rest upon. God is pleased, perhaps, to take all human means from us, that he may shew forth the wonders of his power in our relief. While any other hope is left, we are apt to trust to that hope, and we look not towards the secret hand by which we are fed and supported; but when all is lost, all gone, when no other stay is left, should sudden mercy come upon us, our comforter them becomes visible, he stands revealed in his greatness and glory before us, and we are compelled to cry out, with unbelieving Thomas—My Lord and my God!

Though these pious expostulations of my dearly beloved preacher had little influence at the time for appeasing my own passions, I was yet pleased that my Peggy had her secret consolations, but little imagined that her prophecy approached so near to its completion.

For two days we held on, living on such bread and milk as we could purchase at the cottages that had the charity to receive us. But my boy who was on the breast grew exceedingly sick; so we were obliged to shorten our journeys for the two succeeding days, partly begging, and partly paying for such victuals as we could procure. Towards evening we came within sight of this town. Our little money was quite exhausted, and our child grown too ill to bear further travel; so I looked about, and perceived some roofless walls that stood off from the highway, and thither we turned and took up our bleak abode.

For the three following days, I frequented the road, and by begging procured what scantily kept my family from perishing! Meantime my spirit was tamed and subdued by the habit of mortification, and I looked up to heaven, and cried—Pardon, pardon, O my God! the offences and blasphemies of my murmurings against you! You formerly blessed me with an over-abundance of blessings, and that, too, for a long season; and, as Job justly says, Shall we receive good at the hand of God, and shall we not receive evil? O Friend and Saviour of sinners! if thou lovest whom thou chastenest, and receivest those whom thou dost scourge, when death shall have put a period to the sufferings of mortality, may I not humbly look to find grace at the footstool of the throne of thy mercy?

At length our child died this morning, and we buried him in our hovel, and watered his grave with the tears that we shed for him, and for each other. The rest, sir, you know, till this angel of God was sent to accomplish the prediction of my Peggy in all its fulness.

Here Homely concluded; and after a pause and a deep sigh Mr. Fenton demanded:—Have you told me the whole of your history, Mr. Homely?—I have so, please your honour, through every particular of any signification.—I am sorry for it. Pray think again. Did you never meet with any adventure that is yet unrecited? Did you never save any person at your own peril?—No, sir. O, now I recollect!

Some two or three and twenty years ago, as I fled from the bailiffs who pursued me, as I told you, for the bail of my brother, I came to the river Avon; the flood was great and rapid after the late rains, and I thought of looking for a place of smoother water for my passage, when a gentleman and lady, attended by a train of servants, came riding along the banks. As they road, chatting and laughing, a fowler, who was concealed in a copse just at hand, let fly at a bird, whereupon the fiery horse that the gentleman was on took fright, and, with a bound, suddenly plunged into the current, whereat the lady gave a loud shriek, and fell senseless to the ground. The horse rose without his rider, and swam down the stream. Soon after the rider appeared, and the attendants were divided between their care of the lady and their lamentations for their master on the edge of the bank. Then, seeing no other help, my heart smote me, and I cast myself in without reflection. I kept aloof, however, for fear he should grapple at me, and sink us both together; so I supported and shoved him before me towards land, till, having reached the bank, I laid hold on it with one hand, and with the other raised him up within the reach of his servants, who had stretched themselves flat upon the brink to receive him; then, being already drenched, and having nothing further to do, I turned and swam over, and so made my escape.

Did you ask the name of the party whom you saved in the manner you say?—No, truly, sir, there was no leisure for such an inquiry.—Why did you not wait for the recompense that was so justly your due for so great a deliverance?—Recompense! Please your honour, I could have done no less for the beggar that begs at the corner.

Noble, noble fellow! exclaimed Mr. Fenton; I am he—I am he whom you saved that day, my brother! And so saying, he arose and caught Homely in his arms, and pressed and pressed him over again to his bosom; while Harry, all impatient, seized hold of Homely also, and struggled hard to get him to himself from his father.

When they were something composed, and all again seated —Ah, Homely! says Mr. Fenton, I have sent and made many inquiries after you, but not for many years after the day in which you saved me. I hated, I loathed you, for having prolonged my life to such a misery as no other man ever endured. Oh, that lady! that lady!—But no matter for the present (and, so saying, he wiped the swelling tear from his eye). Tell me, Homely—that devil, Sir Freestone—I am not of a malicious temper, and yet I wish for nothing more than full vengeance on his head. Don't you believe that he went to you with a felonious intention of defrauding you of your property?—Believe it, sir! I can swear it. The circumstances, and their consequences, are full evidence thereof.

Very well, said Mr. Fenton, though we may not be able to carry a civil action against him, we may assail him with better advantage in a criminal way. I will draw up and take your deposition myself; and, to-morrow, I will send you with a note to Lord Portland, where more may be done for you, my Homely, than you think.

In the mean time, you and your family shall take up your abode in the back part of my house, and from thence you shall not depart till, as your Peggy's dream has it, all your losses shall be restored to you sevenfold upon earth; what your portion may be in heaven must be your own care, and may the Spirit of grace guide you in the way you should go!

Early the next morning Mr. Fenton sent Homely to London with his deposition and several papers, accompanied by a letter from himself to Lord Portland. In the evening Homely returned, and, entering with a face of triumph, he seized Mr. Fenton's hand, and eagerly kissing it—Blessed, blessed be the hand, he cried, that hath the power of God among men for good works. When I sent in your honour's letter I was not detained a moment. His lordship made me sit down, perused my papers with attention, questioned me on the particulars, grew inflamed against Sir Freestone, and gave him two or three hearty curses for an execrable villain. He then called a gentleman to him who was in waiting, and ordered an attachment to be instantly issued against the knight. It was accordingly executed upon him, and he now lies in Newgate.—God be praised! said Mr. Fenton; so far there is equity still extant upon earth.

It is not unnatural to suppose that Mr. Fenton's family were immoderately fond of those whose father had saved the life of their most dear master. Mr. Clement, in particular, took pains and pleasure in forwarding the boys in their letters; and Mrs. Clement passed most of her time very happily with Peggy and her little girls.

Frank, the butler, had been abroad upon an expedition at the time that Mr. Homely's family arrived, and did not return till Homely had come back from Lord Portland's. He was then informed, with joy, of the guests they had got; and he waited with impatience till the man he longed to see should come out from his master. As soon as he appeared, he catched one of his hands in both of his, and looking lovingly at him, cried—Do I once more behold that happy face, Mr. Homely? I was the man to whose hands you delivered my precious lord from the devouring of the floods. Gladly, Heaven knows! would I have sacrificed my own life for the salvation of his. But, alas! I had no skill in contending with the waters, and the sure loss of my own life would not have given the smallest chance for the recovery of my master. You are the person, Mr. Homely, to whom God committed that blessed task and trust: and Mr. James, and I, and all of us, have agreed to make up a hundred pounds apiece for your children, in acknowledgment of the benefit you did us on that day.

Here Homely took Frank very affectionately into his arms, and with a faltering voice said—Your offer, sir, is dear, very dear indeed, unto me, as it is a proof of that love which you all so warmly bear to our common lord and master. If there is any occasion, I will not refuse this extraordinary instance of your benevolence; but our master's influence and bounty are doing much in my behalf. And, in the mean time, I will take it as a very particular favour, if you will be pleased to introduce me to my fellow-servants of this house.

Within the following fortnight, a servant in a rich livery came on a foaming horse, and, delivering a letter at the door, rode away directly. The letter ran thus:—

"To HENRY FENTON, ESQ.

"Dear Sir,—The trial of our recreant knight is at hand; and, if you insist upon it, shall be prosecuted to the utmost extent of our laws. The wretch, indeed, deserves to be gibbeted. But he has relations of worth and consideration among us. They have besought me to shield them from shame on this occasion; and I join them in requesting you to accept the enclosed order for three thousand pounds in favour of your client, together with his farm and effects, which attorney Snack shall immediately restore.

"Let me have your answer within three days; and believe me—Your true, as well as obliged servant,

"PORTLAND."

The day following Mr. Fenton sent Harry in his chariot, attended by Mr. James and two servants in livery, to return his acknowledgments to the favourite of the king.

Lord Portland received our hero with pleasure and surprise equally evident in his countenance. As he piqued himself on being one of the finest personages in the nation, he secretly respected his own resemblance in another.

After a few mutual compliments, and some occasional discourse, the earl told Harry that he must take a private dinner with him.—We are quite alone, says he, only two viscounts, a baronet, and four or five gentlemen of the ministerial quill. —Pray, my lord, said Harry smiling, is a dinner the whole of their pension?—Not so, sir, I confess; they are the Swiss of the lettered world, and fight for pay. They were formerly of the opposite junto, but they have changed their opinions along with their party; and our honour obliges us to give them at least as much in the cause of the crown, as they formerly got in the cause of the populace.—I doubt, my lord, returned Harry, that their silence would answer your ends full as well as their oratory, unless your treasury could hold out in bribing people to read also.—Very pleasantly severe, indeed, replied the laughing earl. But come, the bell calls us to dinner.

When dinner was over, and cheerfulness circulated with the bottle—I would give a good deal to know, Mr. Harry, said the earl, what you and your father think of his majesty and his ministers?—Should I speak my downright sentiments, my lord, answered Harry, in some things I might offend, and in others appear to flatter.—O, you cannot offend in the least, cried the earl; we are daily accustomed to be told of all the faults whereof we are, or may be, or might have been guilty; and, as to flattery, you know it is the food of us courtiers.—Why, my lord, you want no champion for the present, said Harry: you are all, as I perceive, on one side of the question, and if some one does not appear, however impotent, to oppose you, the shuttlecock of conversation may fall to the ground.—Right, very right, my sweet fellow, rejoined his lordship; proceed, you shall have nothing but fair-play, I promise you.

To be serious, then, said Harry, my father thinks, in the first place (for I have no manner of skill in such matters)—he thinks, I say, that his majesty is one of the greatest warriors and one of the wisest statesmen that ever existed. He thinks, however, that he has attachments and views that look something further than the mere interests of the people by whom he has been elected; but he says that those views ought, in a measure, to be indulged in return for the very great benefits that he has done us. He is therefore grieved to find, that his majesty has met with so much reluctance and coldness from a nation so obliged.

You are a darling of a politician! exclaimed the earl; but we will not thank you for your compliments till we know what you have further to object against us.

My father admits, my lord, that his majesty and his ministers have re-established and exhibited, in a fair and open light, the most glorious constitution that ever was constructed. But then he apprehends that you are beginning to sap the foundations of the pile that you yourselves erected.

As how, my dear young mentor?—By being over bounteous in paying former friends, and by being still more profuse in procuring new adherents.—Child of honour, cried the earl, another less elegant than yourself would have said, that we are sapping the constitution by *bribery* and *corruption*. You have indeed, my Harry, delicately tempered with your admonitions—even like the cup of life—the sweets the bitters. But what say you, gentlemen, shall a babe lately from the breast bear away the whole palm from people grown grey in politics?

The young gentleman, says Mr. Veer (the principal of the court writers), talks wonderfully for one not versed in the subject of which he treats. The people of England are stupidly proud and licentiously ungovernable; they are the most ignorant, and yet most obstinate, of any people upon earth. It is only by their being selfish that they become in any degree manageable. If their voices were not bought, they would either give them to persons of their own stupid cast, unknowing in our laws or our constitution, or to men of antimonarchal and republican spirit, who would be perpetually putting rubs before the wheels of good government.

I never knew till now, sir, returned Harry, that, in order to make people true to their country and their king—that is, in order to make men honest—it was necessary to corrupt them. But I have still good hopes that the picture which you have drawn of our governors is not altogether a just one.

Governors! cries Veer, I spoke not a word of governors. —You spoke of the people, sir, says Harry, and they, as I take it, are our governors.—The people our governors! this is the most wonderful and the newest doctrine that ever I heard.—A doctrine even as old as the constitution, rejoins Harry. They are not only our governors, but more absolutely so than any so styled. His lordship is the only man in company whose person, in some instances, is exempt from their jurisdiction; but his property remains still subjected to their decision.

No law can be made in Britain but by the people in their proxies; and, when those laws are made, the people are again constituted the judges thereof on their *jury-tribunals*, through their respective shires; as also judges of facts and rights, whether civil or criminal, throughout the realm.

Thus their privilege of making laws for themselves in PARLIAMENT, and of judging of the said laws (when made) on JURIES, composes, as it were, a rudder, whereby the people are admitted (gloriously) to steer the vessel of their own commonwealth.

Would it not be a pity, then, that so great a people should be no other than such as Mr. Veer has described them—a parcel of ignorant, licentious, selfish, base, venal prostitutes, unenlightened by reason, and uninfluenced by conscience?

If they should be reduced—if it is possible, I say, that they should ever be reduced—to so very vile and deplorable a state, it can only be by the very measures that Mr. Veer has recommended. The character, as ye know, of a certain old tempter, is not over amiable, and I should be sorry that any whom I love and respect should follow in his steps.

And now, gentlemen, take the argument home to yourselves. The people have the disposal of our lives, liberties, and properties. Which of you, then, would like to have life itself, and all that is valuable in it, at the arbitration of a pack of wretches, who, being wholly selfish, can have no kindred feelings or compassion for you? who, being themselves devoid of honour and equity, cannot judge according to the one or the other; who, being already accustomed to influence and prostitution, have their ears and hands open to all who would whisper or bribe them to your prejudice?

I, as a fool, gentlemen, utter the dictates of wisdom; for I speak the sentiments of a much wiser and much better man than myself. Should a general corruption take place in the land, adieu to all virtue; adieu to humanity, and all social connections!—all reason and law, all conscience and magistracy, all public and private weal, must vanish or be confounded in one chaos together. And from hence it is self-evident, that he who debauches the morals of the least of his majesty's subjects, is an enemy to his king, to his country, and mankind.

I protest, said his lordship, with some little confusion, I never beheld this matter in the same light before; but I shall take care to inspect and examine it at better leisure.

Here the company rose to separate, when Harry, stepping towards Veer with an affectionate pleasantry in his countenance—Mr. Veer, says he, I fear I have misbehaved a little to-day; I am naturally warm, and am apt to be too much so on particular subjects.—O, sir, says Veer, I am an old prize-fighter, and accustomed to cuts; but I now know my man, and shall hereafter avoid engaging, or keep barely on the defensive; do me the honour, however, as old combatants were wont, to shake hands at parting, in token of hearts free from malice.—In the contest of love, Mr. Veer, you never shall foil me, cried Harry.

Now, my lord, if you have any commands for my father,

pray, let me have the pleasure of being your messenger.—Upon my honour, my dear boy—and that is the oath of a lord—you shall not part from me for this night at least.—My father, sir, will be uneasy.—I will despatch one to him directly. I have particular designs upon you; you must go with me to the levee. I cannot refuse myself the pleasure of introducing you to his majesty; I expect to get credit by you.—I rather fear, my lord, that I may do you some disgrace.

O! cried the earl, you think you are not fine enough! Why, truly, you will see folks there of much more illustrious attire. But let others disgrace their ornaments; be you humbly content, my child, with adorning your dress. Harry blushed and bowed.

When they arrived at court, the earl left his young friend a while in the levee-room, and went to impart some matters to the king in his closet.

While our hero stood in the crowd, some one came and pinned a paper to his back, whereon was written in capital letters—THE FOOL.

However, it did not remain long enough to do him much disgrace. A young gentleman, of a graceful figure and very amiable aspect, pressed close behind Harry, and gently stole the writing away; then, taking him by the hand, requested to speak with him apart.

I wonder, sir, said the stranger, who it was that could be so malicious, or so base, as to fasten this title on your back; I am certain he must never have seen your face.—O, sir! said Harry, blushing and smiling together, this must have been the office of some old acquaintance; it is the title to which I have been accustomed from my infancy, and I am well contented to carry it with me to the grave. I am much affected, sir, however, by this uncommon instance of humanity to an unknown; pray, add to the obligation, by letting me know to whom it is that I am so endearingly bound.

My name, sir, is Thornhill. I am just arrived from my travels; and I would willingly go my long journey over again to become just such another fool as you are.

Harry seized him by the hand, and gave him at once the squeeze and the look of love.—Sir William Thornhill, I presume?—The same, my dear sir.—I have been enamoured of your character before I saw you, Sir William.—My name is Harry Fenton; I live on Hampstead-hill; I see that your pleasure lies in communicating pleasure. I am therefore persuaded you will indulge me with a call at some leisure hour. —I will not defer that advantage a single day.—I shall have the longings of a lover till you arrive.

Here the king entered, and all converse was broken off. Lord Portland, looking about, discovered Harry, and, taking him by the hand, led him up, and left him standing before his majesty. Then approaching the royal ear—May it please you, sire, says he; this is the son of the gentleman who advanced us two hundred thousand pounds on our expedition from Holland.

The King turned to Harry with a solemn and piercing look; and, having eyed him for some time, he again turned to the earl, and cried—Ay, Portland, this is something; this, indeed, is a gem fit to set in the crown of a monarch. He then reached forth his hand, and, while our hero stooped to kiss it, he pressed Harry's shoulder with his other hand.

My dear child, said the king, we are much obliged to your father. You, by inheritance, are attached to our crown, and you may justly demand whatever we can bestow.—We humbly thank your majesty, answered Harry; we only claim the privilege of serving you with all our hearts and all our powers.

Which would you choose, the army or the court? Indeed,

VOL. II.—8

I should best like to have you about my own person.—That is the pitch to which I aspire, answered Harry, as soon as I am capable of so high a duty.

But why have you been such a stranger? said the king, had we seen you before, I think we should not have forgot you.—O sire! said Harry, I am but as a bird from the nest, and this is the first of my unfledged excursions.—If a bird, cried the king, it must be a young eagle.—Not so, sire, answered Harry; I should then better support the brightness of the sun that is now before me.—I would give one of my kingdoms that you were my son!—I am already one of the millions of happy sons and daughters who have the glory of calling you their royal father.

So saying, our hero bowed twice, and drew back; while the king looked towards him in silence and wonder.

After some talk with his courtiers, his majesty retired. And Lord Portland took Harry, and was followed by a number of the young gentry, to the ball-room.

There the queen, at the upper end, was seated under a canopy, her maids of honour attending, and two brilliant ranges of foreign and British ladies were seated on either hand.

The earl gave a whisper to the master of the ceremonies, and he immediately led Harry up to the presence, where he had the honour of kissing Queen Mary's fair hand.

After some whispering chat between her majesty and Lord Portland, the ball was ordered to be opened by our hero and the lovely young Princess of Hesse.

All eyes were fixed upon them with attention still as night, while they moved like Homer's gods, without seeming to press the ground; or like a mist before the breeze along the side of some stately hill.

As soon as the minuet was closed, the princess said softly to Harry, in French, *The Louvre*, sir, if you please.

This was a dance of the newest fashion, and was calculated to show forth and exhibit a graceful person in all the possible elegances of movement and attitude. As soon as they had finished, the whole assembly could scarce refrain from breaking forth in loud plaudits, as at the public theatre; and a humming of mixed voices and patting feet was heard throughout.

When Harry had led the princess to her seat, and left her with a bow of the most expressive respect, he happened to see Lady Louisa, and, hinting to the lord chamberlain his desire to dance with her, his lordship readily indulged him.

When Harry had finished, the lord chamberlain honoured Sir William Thornhill with Lady Louisa's hand; and, after four or five more minutes, the country dances began, in which all the younger part of the company joined, except Lord Bottom, who refused to step forth, and sat apart ruminating and feeding on his own cogitations.

The princess and our hero led up the dance, and Louisa and Sir William were appointed the next in course, in order to do the principal honours to the two young strangers.

In the intervals of dancing, Lady Louisa took occasion to say to Harry—You are a great stranger, sir; but we desire you should be so, since we did not treat you with the respect that your merit should have commanded.—That, madam, answered Harry, is not wholly the cause of my distance; but there are persons whose loveliness is more formidable to me, than a whole regiment of sabred hussars with their fierce-looking moustaches.

Harry had no sooner said this than his heart smote him with remorse; for, though Louisa was indeed lovely, and he felt for her the propensities and tenderness of a brother, yet she was not of that species of beauty that was formed to fix his heart; and he secretly reproached himself for having attempted to raise the vanity or draw the affections of an innocent girl, with no other view than of making a parade of his own talents—a measure, he justly adjudged, unbecoming a man of a spark of honour or integrity.

As soon as the dances were ended, and that all had mixed, and chatted, and roved about a while, Harry observed Sir William coming towards him in a little fluster. What is the matter, my friend, says Harry; pray, what has discomposed you?—Tell me, my dear Harry, that jackanapes in the blue and gold, do you know who he is? I protest, had it not been for the respect I owe the presence, I would have chastised him on the spot. The dance was no sooner done than he came up with a most provoking sauciness in his looks. I wonder, sir, said he, at the insolence of one of your rank; you ought to have had more modesty than to suffer yourself to be paired with a lady so far above you.

O! cried Harry, taking Sir William very lovingly under the arm, pass this matter over, my sweet friend, I beseech you. That is young Lord Bottom, the very person who, I am pretty confident, contrived the honour of the *pasquinade* on my back this day. But he is brother to the sweet girl with whom you danced. For her sake, for my sake, forgive him, I entreat you; but, above all, forgive him for the sake of his dear father, the Earl of Mansfield, one of the noblest nobles, and one of the worthiest men that ever stepped on English ground. He has been these two years past abroad upon an embassy; and, while he is promoting the interests of the public, has left his own household unchastened and unguided.

Here the converse of the friends was suddenly broken off. The lord chamberlain came, and, tapping Harry on the shoulder, told him that the queen desired to speak with him.

When he had with a lowly reverence advanced to the

throne—You are, said the queen, the most accomplished cavalier that ever I beheld; and, had I sufficient youth and beauty, I would choose you for my knight, to bear my fame through the world.—I would rather, said Harry, that your majesty would employ me on some more dangerous enterprise. —How is that? said the queen.—Why, answered Harry, your majesty's champion could have little or nothing to do, as all would willingly acknowledge the justice of his cause.

You are, cried the queen, the loveliest and the sweetest fellow I ever knew. My eye has followed you all along, and marked you for my own, and I must either beg or steal you from our good friend your father. I therefore want no token to put me in mind of you, but you may want some token to keep your friends in your memory. Here are two pictures —the one is the portrait of our master and sovereign lord, the other is the picture of the woman who sits before you, lowly, simple, unadorned; choose which you please.

Give me the plain picture, cried Harry, with a kind of rapture; it shall henceforth become my riches and my ornament.

So saying, he bent his knee, and taking the little portrait, he pressed it to his lips, with the ardour of an ancient lover in romance. Then, putting it into his bosom, he gracefully arose and retired from the presence.

O the fool! the egregious fool! muttered some.—Nobly, most nobly done! cried others.

As Harry was following the Earl of Portland down-stairs, Lord Bottom came up in the crowd, and in a half whisper said—You are too great a man to-day, sir, to acknowledge your old acquaintance.—But not so great a fool, retorted Harry, as not to be taught my distance with those who, like Lord Bottom, have a right to look down upon me.

After a short but sound sleep, Harry hurried home to prepare for the reception of his new friend. He told Mr. Fenton that Sir William was returned; how he had been obligingly made known to him in the forementioned instance of his humanity to a stranger; and that he had promised to be with them that morning. But pray, sir, don't tell Homely a word of the coming of his landlord, till we place them, as it were by surprise, face to face.

In about an hour after, a chaise and four came rapidly to the door; and Harry instantly sprung and caught his friend in his arms before he came to the ground.

The two friends entered the parlour, caressing and caressed, and casting looks of cordial love and delight on each other. My father, sir, said Harry, and led Sir William by the hand to Mr. Fenton, who received him with a countenance of that heart-speaking complaisance which never fails to attach the soul of the person to whom it is directed. Ah, my Harry! cried Sir William, I no longer wonder at you, I see that you are all that you are by inheritance.

But, sir, continued he, you had like to have lost your son last night. Their majesties were most unwilling to quit their hold of him, and I believe in my soul, would willingly have adopted him the heir of their crown.—I should be very sorry, Sir William, replied Mr. Fenton, to see a circle about his head that would give him an aching heart. I am sure that is the case with the present royal proprietors. In a limited monarchy like ours, the station of the prince is looked upon with a malignant eye by the envious, and, at the same time, rendered uneasy by the perpetual contests between rights and privileges on the one part, and prerogative on the other.

Moreover, Sir William, I shall never wish to see one of my child's disposition on the throne of Great Britain. I should be jealous of such a person in behalf of my country. No people could be more tenacious of their liberties than the Swedes, till Gustavus the son of Eric ascended the throne.

His manners were so amiable, his virtues so conspicuous, his government so just, and he made so popular an use of all his powers, that his subjects thought they could never commit enough into his hands. But what was the consequence? His successors made his power a precedent for their own, without attending to the precedent of his administration.

Thus you see that a prince of qualities, eminently popular, might prove of dangerous tendency to a free people, forasmuch as he might charm the eyes of their jealousy to sleep, and so seduce them from that guard which is ever necessary to preclude the encroachments of ambition.

But, Sir William, may we not order your horses up? You must not think of going till you take a plain dinner with us. —A supper, too, sir, most joyfully answered the knight. I leave London in the morning on a certain expedition, and shall not have the pleasure of embracing you again for some time.

Mr. Fenton then addressing the baronet with a smile— Our Harry here, Sir William, never saw a court before; it is natural, therefore, to think that he must have been greatly amused, and his young heart deceived by the splendor and parade. But you have seen and observed upon many courts of late; pray what do you think of the entertainment they afford?

As of the dullest of all dull farces, answered the knight. All the courts that I have seen are nearly of the same cast. Conceive to yourself, sir, a stage or theatre of comedians without auditors or spectators. They are all actors, and all act nearly the same part of solemn complaisance and nauseous grimace. Each intends to impose, and yet no one is imposed upon; where professions are taken to imply the very reverse of what they express.

What do you say to this, Harry? said Mr. Fenton.—I

have very little to say, sir, in favor of the actors; but the actresses, as I take it, afford better entertainment. Here Sir William and Mr. Fenton laughed; and Harry, upon a wink, stepped out to bring in Homely, as it were by accident.

Sir William, said Mr. Fenton, there is a man come to this house who once saved my life at the risk of his own. It is a great many years ago, and I have not seen him since the action till very lately. I have sent Harry for him, that you may learn the particulars, and advise with me what recompense he ought to receive.

If the recompense is to be proportioned to the value of the life he saved, my honoured sir, I should not know where to fix the bounds of retribution. And in truth, Mr. Fenton, from my knowledge of you this day, I also hold myself very highly his debtor.

At this instant Harry led in Homely by the hand, and left him standing directly opposite to the baronet.

Homely gazed with all his eyes, and stood mute through astonishment. At length he exclaimed—Bless me! mercy upon me—as sure as I hope for heaven—it is—I think it is—my dear young master!

Sir William, at the voice, lifted up his eyes to Homely, and, remembering his marked man, rose quickly, and, springing forward, embraced him with much familiar affection; while Mr. Fenton sat, and his Harry stood beside him, both wrapped in their own delicious sensibilities.

My dear Homely, my old companion and brother sportsman! cried Sir William, how in the world comes this about? so joyfully, so unexpectedly, to meet you here! How is your wife and pretty babes? I hope you left all well at home.

Yes, please your honour, they are all well—wonderfully well in this house, I assure you; for, indeed, your Homely has no other home upon earth.

What you tell me is quite astonishing, replied the knight; no home for you within the manor or demesne of your friend? What misfortunes, what revolutions, could bring this wonder to pass?

Sit down, said Mr. Fenton; pray be seated, Mr. Homely, and give your lord a succinct but deliberate account of the inimitable pair, Sir Freestone and his coadjutor.

As soon as Homely had told his tale from the commencement of his distresses to his arrival at the hovel, he stopped short, and said—I have something more to impart; but I hope your honour will pardon me. I am loth to deprive your friends of your company; but then my Peggy and my boys will be so transported to see your dear face again, that I cannot but beseech you to indulge them, a minute or two, with that blessing.

Sir William rose with a troubled humanity in his countenance, and followed to a back apartment, where Homely again stopped him short; and, before he would take him to his Peggy, he gave him a minute detail of all his obligations to what he called this wonderful family. But pray, sir, continued he, let them know very little of what I have told you; for nothing puts them to so much pain as any kind of acknowledgments.

After a short visit to Peggy and her children, Sir William returned to his friends, with such an inward awe and veneration for their characters, as for a while sunk his spirits, and solemnized his features. This poor man, sir, said he, has been miserably treated; but God has been exceedingly gracious to him, in casting the shipwrecked wretch on such a happy shore as this. But this makes no discharge of any part of my duty towards him.

Mark me, Homely, I am now of age, and Lord Lechmore has no further authority in my affairs; wherefore, before I leave this house, I will give you a letter of attorney for the whole agency of the manor.—Thank your honour, thank your honour! cried Homely in a kind of transport; if I do not prove as faithful to you as another, I will do you justice on myself with the first rope I can lay hold on.

As for that reprobate Snack, continued the knight, I will take care to be up with him. He owes the executors of my father six hundred and seventy pounds. I will have that matter put directly in suit, and, as soon as it is recovered, it shall be laid out on a commission for your son, my friend Tom; as I do not choose yet to ask any favour from the ministry. Lastly, that you may no more be distressed for rent, I will never accept a penny of it till you are decently and competently provided for.

O, sir! exclaimed Homely, I shall be too rich, quite overburdened; I shall not know where to lay my treasures.—Not so fast, my good friend, replied Sir William smiling; you have not heard of the drawback that I propose to have upon you. Whenever I reside in the country, you are to have a hot dish—ay, and a cool hogshead, too—ready for me and my company.—Agreed, sir, cried Homely, provided I may have the liberty, during your absence, to drink your honour's health out of that same hogshead.—A just reserve, said Harry, laughing.—And full as grateful as it is jovial, cried Mr. Fenton.—Why, gentlemen, rejoined Homely, a man of spirit would scorn to accept such benefits without making conditions.

After twelve o'clock at night, and an affectionate and tender adieu, Sir William set out by moonlight for London.

The two following days were employed in preparing for Homely's departure; and a coach and four, with a chaise, were provided for the conveyance of him and his family.

The night before their parting, Mr. Fenton desired that Homely and his wife should be sent to him to his closet. As soon as they entered, he closed the door. My dear friends, said he, as I may not be up in the morning, to take a timely leave of you, it might do as well to go through that melancholy office to-night. Here, Mrs. Homely, here is some little matter apiece towards beginning a fortune for your three pretty daughters. Pray, Homely, take care to have it disposed of for them upon good securities. Here he put three orders upon his banker, for five hundred pounds each, into Peggy's hand; then, turning to Homely, and taking him straitly in his arms—God be with you and your dear Peggy, my Homely, he cried, and give us all a blessed meeting where friends shall part no more!

The distressed Homely was past utterance; but disengaging, and flinging himself at the feet of his patron, while Peggy kept on her knees weeping and sobbing beside him; O, he cried, at length, next to my God! O, next to my Lord and my God!—My lord and my master, my master and my lord!

The next morning before sunrise Harry was up, and, going to Homely's apartment, embraced him and his wife. He then kissed and caressed all the girls and boys round, and gave to each of them a gold medal to keep him in their remembrance; when Homely and his Peggy, with open arms, trembling lips, and swelling eyes, began to take their leave. God be with you! God be with you! sobbed Homely aloud; never, never till I get to heaven, shall I meet with such another dear assembly!

Mr. Fenton now judged it time to forward his Harry's education, especially with respect to his knowledge of the world, of the views, pleasures, manners, bent, employments, and characters of mankind.

For this purpose, he proposed to leave Arabella sole regent of his family, and, for a few weeks, to stay with Clement and Harry in London, there to shew him whatever might gratify his curiosity, or merit his inspection

While the coach was in waiting, and they all stood on the hill, the great city being extended in ample view beneath them, Mr. Fenton exclaimed—Oh, London! London! thou mausoleum of dead souls, how pleasant art thou to the eye, how beautiful in outward prospect; but within, how full of rottenness and recking abominations! Thy dealers are all students in the mystery of iniquity, of fraud and imposition on ignorance and credulity. Thy public officers are hourly exercised in exactions and extortion. Thy courts of judicature are busied in the sale, the delay, or perversion of justice; they are shut to the injured and indigent, but open to the wealthy pleas of the invader and oppressor. Thy magistracy is often employed in secretly countenancing and abetting the breach of those laws it was instituted to maintain. Thy charities subscribed for the support of the poor, are lavished by the trustees in pampering the rich, where drunkenness swallows till it wallows, gluttony stuffs till it pants, and unbuttons and stuffs again. Even the great ones of thy court have audaciously smiled away the gloom and horrors of guilt, and refined, as it were, all the grossness thereof, by inverting terms and palliating phrases. While the millions that crowd and hurry through thy streets are universally occupied in striving and struggling to rise by the fall, to fatten by the leanness, and to thrive by the ruin of their fellows. Thy offences are rank; they steam and cloud the face of heaven. The gulf also is hollow beneath that is one day to receive thee. But the measure of thy abominations is not yet full; and the number of thy righteous hath hitherto exceeded the proportion that was found in the first Sodom.

That evening they went to the opera, where Harry was so captivated by the sentimental meltings and varied harmony of the airs, that he requested Mr. Fenton to permit him to be instructed on some instrument. Not by my advice, my dear, answered Mr. Fenton; I would not wish you to attempt any thing in which you may not excel. Music is a science that requires the application of a man's whole life in order to arrive at any eminence. As it is enchanting in the hand of a master, it is also discordant and grating in its inferior degrees. Your labours have been employed to much more valuable purposes; and I would not, as they say, give my child's time for a song. Harry instantly acquiesced with the best temper imaginable, as the will of his beloved patron was, truly speaking, his own will; and that he only wanted to know it, to be at all times, and on all occasions, conformable thereto.

A few following days were employed in visiting the Tower, in surveying the armoury, regalia, etc., in viewing the Monument and Exchange; and lastly, in contemplating the solemnity of Westminster Abbey, with the marbled effigies and monumental deposits of the renowned in death— the place, as Mr. Fenton affectingly observed, to which all the living must finally adjourn.

The next night they went to the theatre, to see the feats of Signor Volanti, the celebrated Italian posture-master, rope-dancer, and equilibrist. Such wonders are now so common as to be scarce entertaining; but at that time, they were received with bursts and roars of applause.

Our hero felt himself attached by the similar excellences of his own activity in another; and, going behind the scenes, he accosted Volanti in French. Signor, said he, I have been highly entertained by your performance this night, and here are five guineas in return of the pleasure you have given me. The foreigner looked at Harry, and then at the money, with a kind of astonishment.—I thank you, noble sir, he cried; my poor endeavours are seldom so liberally rewarded.— Pray, how long do you stay with us?—In about a fortnight, so please your nobleness, I intend to leave London; but, before I go, I would do something to leave a name behind me. A day or two before my departure, I will fly from the spire of Saint Clement's church, in the sight of all the people; and this I will do *gratis*, or rather in acknowledgment of the favours I have received in this kingdom.—But is it possible to execute what you propose?—With all ease and safety, sir; I have done nearly as much three times in Germany, and once at Madrid.

Here an arch thought struck Harry, and musing a moment —Will you permit me, said he, to be the conductor of this affair? Allow me only to appoint the day, and draw up your advertisement, and I will make you a present of twenty pieces.—Agreed, sir, cried Volanti, and twenty thousand thanks to confirm the bargain.—Accept these five guineas, then, in earnest of my engagement; my servant here will tell or shew you where I am to be found. That night at supper, Mr. Fenton remarked an unusual pleasantry in the muscles of his darling's sweetly sober countenance.—My Harry, I find, said he, does not always impart all his secrets to his friends; he has certainly some roguish matter in cogitation.—*Magicum calles*, sir, cried Harry; you are a conjurer, that is certain. Why, the public, as you know, sir, have put the fool on me from my birth; Homer says, that revenge is sweet as honey to the taste; and so I am meditating in turn how to put the fool upon the public.—And how do you contrive it, Harry? Only by acting the old proverb, That *one fool makes many*. But pray ask me not about the manner, till I bring the business to some bearing.

The next day being Thursday, they all went in Mr. Fenton's coach to Smithfield, where numbers of tents were set up, and several drolls and pantomimes, etc., prepared, in imitation of the humours of Bartholomew fair. The weather was fair and calm, and they let down all the glasses, that they might see, without interruption, whatever was to be seen. Their coach stopped just opposite to an itinerant stage, where a genius, who comprised within his single person the two important functions of a tumbler and merry-andrew, by his successive action and oratory, extorted plaudits and huzzas from all the spectators.

Among the rest a countryman, who rode upon a mule, sat gaping and grinning by intervals, in all the ecstatic rapture that can be ascribed to enthusiasm. While his attention was thus riveted, two knavish wags came, and, ungirthing his saddle, supported it on either hand till a third of the fraternity led his mule away from under him, and a fourth came with a three-legged horse, such as housewives dry their linen on, and, having jammed it under the saddle, they all retreated in peace.

The populace were so delighted at this humorous act of felony, that, instead of interrupting it, it only served to redouble their joys and clamours. Harry, too, greatly chuckled and laughed at the joke. But, when he saw the beast led off, and that the amazed proprietor, on stooping to take the bridle, had fallen precipitately to the ground, his heart twitched him with a kind of compunction, and throwing himself out of the coach, he made all the speed that the press would admit, and, recovering the mule, brought it back to its owner.

Here, friend, said he, here is your beast again; take care the next time that they do not steal your teeth.—Thank you, master, said the clown; since you have been so honest as to give him to me back, I will never be the one to bring you to the assizes or sessions.—I am much obliged to your clemency, answered Harry; but pray let me have the pleasure of seeing you safe mounted. So saying, he held the stirrup, while the booby got up and said—Well, my lad, very well; if we happen to meet at Croydon, we may take a pot together.

In the evening they adjourned from coffee to David's Harp in Fleet Street, in order to hear Marmulet, the famed Genoese musician, who performed on the psaletry, the viol d'amor, and some other instruments not known till then in England.

They took Mr. James with them to partake of the entertainment, and were shewn to a large room, where each paid half a crown at the door.

The room was divided into a number of boxes, where each company sat apart, while they were jointly gratified and charmed by the inimitable execution of the musician.

A flask of burgundy was set before Mr. Fenton and his friends, while Mr. Hardy and Mr. Hilton, who sat in the next box, were regaling themselves with a glass of rosa solis.

All was silence and attention till there was a pause in the performance. Then, said Mr. Hardy—Do you know, Jack, that the Earl of Albemarle is to have a mask on Monday night?—I am sorry to hear it, said Mr. Hilton, as I am obliged to be out of town.—I may happen to save something by that, said Hardy; you must lend me your *domino*.— Indeed I cannot; it was torn to fritters in a scuffle, as I came out from the last masquerade.—Lend me your mask, then.— That, too, was lost at the same time; but what occasion can you have for a mask, Hardy? I'm sure no one will take that for a natural face.—Mine is the face of Mars, Hilton; yours that of Adonis, with which no modern Venus will ever be smitten, I promise you. I will engage to out-rival an army of such jackanapes in an assault on the fair.—If impudence may compensate for the want of other artillery, I believe you may do wonders, Hardy.—And it does compensate, my friend. Women, take my word and experience for it, love nothing of their own resemblance except in the glass. They detest any thing that looks like an ambiguity in the sex. While what you are pleased to call impudence, Jack, spares their modesty, saves them the appearance of an advance on their part, and gives them the pleasure of piquing themselves on their extraordinary virtue, in case they should happen to make a defence. However, since you have complimented me on my assurance, I will put it to the test on this occasion, and go to his excellency's ball, without any other vizard save this which nature, in her great bounty, hath bestowed.

When our company were on the return to their lodgings —Harry, said Mr. Fenton, would you not like to go to this masquerade?—Why, sir, as I have not yet seen one, perhaps it might not be amiss to satisfy my curiosity for once in my life.—In truth, said Mr. Fenton, I wish they never had been introduced into this kingdom, as they are inlets to intrigue, and give countenance to licentiousness. However, for once in your life, as you say, you shall be gratified, my Harry.— Be pleased to tell me, sir, are they very entertaining?—They would be extremely diverting, my dear, if people acted up to the characters that they pretend to represent. But, on the contrary, they have sailors who don't know a point in the compass, or the name of a rope in the ship; shepherds and shepherdesses who never eloped from the Cockney dialect of the city; Indian queens who can say nothing as to their subjects or their sovereignty; gods and goddesses totally ignorant of their own history in the mythology; and Italian cardinals, who will swear you in the phrase of a Yorkshire fox-hunter.

But what shall we do for tickets, Harry? I don't care to apply to my friends, for fear of discovering that we are in town. O, sir! said Mr. James, I am acquainted with his excellency's major-domo, and can procure you as many tickets as you please.

Mr. Fenton assumed to himself, for the present, the appointment of Harry's character and dress.—As the plainness of your garb has hitherto, said he, been a mask and disguise to your internal ornaments, the brilliancy of your dress shall now, on the other hand, disguise and conceal the simplicity of your manners.

About two hours before the opening of the ball, Harry wrapped himself in a black *domino*, and stepped into a hackney coach with Mr. James, who had promised to introduce him to his friend, in order for him to reconnoitre the several scenes of operation before the action began.

The major-domo rèceived Harry with the utmost complacence, for he held his mask in his hand, and the loveliness of his aspect shone with peculiar lustre through the blackness of his attire.

After surveying several apartments, they passed through the long room, and entered by an arched gateway into a kind of saloon, at the upper end of which was a pedestal of about five feet in height, whereon a celebrated statue of the Hercules Farnese had formerly stood.

Harry eyed it attentively, and, conceiving a sudden frolic, he instantly cast away his cloak, clapped on his mask and winged helmet, grasped his caduceus with his right hand, and, laying his left on the top of the pedestal, sprung lightly up, and threw himself into that attitude to which the statuaries have formed their Mercury when just preparing for flight.

His headpiece was of thinly-plated but polished gold, buckled together at the joining by four burning carbuncles. His silk jacket exceeded the tint of an Egyptian sky. It was braced close to his body with emerald clasps, that showed the fitness of his proportion to inimitable advantage; and over the whole, in celestial confusion, were sown stars of different magnitudes, all powdered with diamonds.

The moment that Harry cast himself into his posture, the major-domo started back seven or eight paces, and, raising his hands, with staring eyes and a mouth of open amazement, at length he exclaimed—Stay a little, my dear sweet master! do now; do but stay just as you are for a minute, and you will oblige me past expression; I will be your own for ever.

So saying, he turned off, and running to an adjacent apartment, where their majesties, with the Princess of Denmark, the Princess of Hesse, and the chief of the court, were gathered, he told his master aloud that he had the greatest curiosity to shew him that human eye ever beheld.

All rose with precipitation and crowded after the earl and the royal pair, as close as decency would admit, till they came to the saloon, and beheld, with astonishment, the person, shape, attitude, and attire, of our hero.

Some doubted, but most believed, that he was a real statue, placed there by his excellency on purpose for a surprise. Mr. Fielding, who was the acknowledged connoisseur of the age, and was, in fact, what the people of taste call an *elegans formarum spectator*, exclaimed with some vehemency—Never, never did I behold such beauty of symmetry, such roundings of angles; where, where, my lord, could you get this inestimable acquisition? Others cried—Phidias, Phidias never executed the like; all the works of Praxiteles were nothing to it!

The earl, however, was well apprised of the deception, and knew that our Mercury was no part of his property. Son of Maia, said he aloud, what tidings from heaven?—A message, answered Harry, from my father, Jupiter, to their majesties.—And, pray, what may your errand intend?—Matters of highest importance; that they are the favourite representatives of my father upon earth; and that, while their majesties continue the monarchs of a free and willing people, they are greater than if they were regents of an universe of slaves. All buzzed their applause and admiration.—It must be he, whispered the king.—It can be no other, cried the queen.—Albemarle, whispered his majesty, we have marked this youth for our own; keep your eye upon him, and do your best endeavours to engage and bind him to us.

In the mean time, Harry, on delivering his celestial message, flew like a feather from his post, and, casting his cloak about him, vanished into an adjoining closet.

The company now began to gather fast, and Harry, stealing from his retreat, kept his cloud about his sky, and mingled in the crowd. Mr. Clement had accompanied Mr. Fenton in *dominoes*. They soon discovered Harry, and were highly diverted by the account which he gave them of his metamorphosis into a statue.

While the assembly was dividing into pairs and chatty parties, a phenomenon entered that drew all their attention. The Honourable Major Gromley, the lustiest and fattest young man in the kingdom, advanced without a mask, in petticoats, a slobbering bib and apron. He carried a large round of bread and butter in one hand, while Lady Betsy Minit, an elderly miss of about three feet high, held his leading-strings with her left hand, and in her right brandished a birch rod of lengthened authority. His governante pressed him forward, and seemed to threaten chastisement for his delay; while the jolly, broad, foolish, humorous, half-laughing, half-crying, baby-face of the major, extorted peals of laughter from all who were present. And this is sufficient to convince us, that the performers of the ancient drama could not possibly in masks excite the passions of nature. No excellence of voice or gesture, of action or emphasis, could compensate for the exclusion of the immediate interpreters of the soul, the living speech of the eye, and varied expression of the countenance.

After the major had leisurely traversed the full length of

the room, and inimitably executed the whole of his part, he retired to undress and assume a new appearance.

Meanwhile, two females entered in very unusual habits. The first was dressed in a choice collection of old English and Scotch ballads, from Chevy-Chace and the fragment of Hardi-Canute, down to Barbara Allan and the Babes in the Wood. The other was all hung from top to bottom with looking-glasses.

Immediately the crowd gathered about them. All who were fond of their own history, preferable to that of others, paid their homage in a circling throng, to the queen of the looking-glasses; while the few who preferred instruction, were intent in perusing the fair covered with knowledge. But the lady of the mirrors did not long retain her votaries; her glasses were all emblems of her own disposition—they were the glasses of scandal and calumny, and represented the human species in the most distorted view; some lengthened and some widened their objects beyond measure, while others wholly inverted and turned them topsy-turvy. All slunk away in disgust from such prospects of their own persons, and the reflecting lady was justly left to glitter apart from society.

The next rho entered was a Goliath, all sheathed in complete steel. He advanced with slow and majestic steps to the sideboard, and asking for a flask of champagne, turned it down without taking it once from his head. He then demanded another, and another, and so on, till the provedore, who had looked and longed in vain to see him drop, ran panic-struck to his master, and, in a half whisper, said— My lord your cellars will scarcely suffice to quench the thirst of one man here; he has already turned down fifteen flasks of champagne, and still is unsatisfied, and calls for more.— Then give him fifteen hogsheads, replied the earl, laughing; and, if that will not answer, send out for more.

In the mean time, the mailed champion had withdrawn from the sideboard, and, with a large drinking-glass in his hand, advanced till he got into the midst of the assembly. He then turned a little instrument that was fixed in a certain part of his double-cased armour, and filling the glass to the brim, he unclasped the lower part of his beaver, and accosting a Peruvian princess who stood just opposite—Permit me the honour, madam, says he, of drinking your highness's health; so saying, the liquor was out of sight in a twinkling. Will your royal highness, continued he, be pleased to try how you relish our European wines?—I am obliged to you, sir, said she, I am actually athirst; then, raising her mask below, she pledged him to the bottom. Her companion, a shining Arcadian, advanced and requested the same favour. Then another and another lady, and several others in succession, all of whom he graciously gratified till he was nearly exhausted. Some of the men then pressed to him, and entreated for a glass.—No, no, gentlemen, said he, go and be served elsewhere; I am a merchant for ladies alone; I import no liquors for vile male animals.

Our former acquaintance, Mr. Hardy, had adventured, according to promise, without a mask. After looking about a while for some object of his gallantry, he fixed upon a lady of a very elegant shape and sprightly appearance.

When they had bandied between them some occasional chat, of more smartness than humour, and more wit than meaning, he called for a favourite air, and led the fair one a minuet, in which they both performed *assez bien*.

He now began to grow more warm in his addresses. If your face, madam, said he, should happen to be answerable to the enchantments of your form, and the siren in your voice, I beseech you to keep that mask on for ever; the safety of mankind is interested in my request.—But suppose, said she, that my face should happen to prove an antidote to the danger of my other charms?—Then, madam, let me see it by all means; and make haste, I pray you, before I am past remedy.—I see, said she, tittering, I see that you are already more than half a dying man; poor wretch, I pity you, and have taken it into my head to slay you outright, in order to put you out of pain!

So saying, she drew her mask on one side, and showed him indeed a very lovely countenance. But while his flood of complimentary eloquence was just upon breaking forth—Hush sir! cried the lady, I will not hear a syllable till you first return the compliment that I have paid you, and let me see what you have got under that vizard of yours. Here Hardy, in spite of impudence, stood mute with astonishment. The lady burst into a laugh—the joke was caught and spread like wildfire—the laugh grew universal—all eyes were on poor Hardy, and a hundred tongues cried at once—Your mask, sir, your mask, sir!—take off your mask for the lady! This was something more than human assurance could stand. Hardy retired with precipitate confusion, and justly suffered for the presumption of his boasted facility of conquests over the fair.

Our hero had hitherto kept himself concealed, being secretly ashamed of the lustre of his apparel; but, at Mr. Fenton's desire, he laid his cloak aside, and instantly all the eyes of the assembly were upon him. In order to avoid their gaze, he advanced into the throng, where a parcel of circling females asked him a number of insignificant questions, to which he returned in kind answers pretty nearly as insignificant.

At length a Diana approached, whose diamond crescent was of the value of a princely ransom. She took him carelessly by the hand and said—Come, brother Mercury, let us give these mortals a sample of what we celestials can perform.—Lead where you please, madam, said Harry, I cannot miss my way while I tread in the light of so fair a moon.

The lady called to the orchestra for a saraband, and all made ample room, attentive to the motions of the shining pair.

The dance began, and the spectators in a manner suppressed their breathing for fear of giving or receiving the smallest interruption. The performers stepped music, their action was grace, and they seemed with difficulty retained to the floor over which they moved. They ended, and the assembly was still mute with astonishment, till they broke out into a general murmur of praise.

Mr. Mercury, said Diana, the story of Argus tells us, that you were formerly accustomed to set folks to sleep; but, for the present, you have opened all eyes to observation.—Ah, madam! answered Harry, could I have guessed at the moon that was to shine this night, I should have assumed a very different character.—What character, I pray you?—That of Endymion, madam.—I wish, she whispered, that you were a prince, or that I were a peasant; and so saying, she turned from him and mixed in the crowd.

Harry was next addressed by a shepherdess, and again by a nun. But he declined as honourably as he could to tend the flock of the one, or to be the cause of any breach of vows in the other, observing to her that she had already taken the veil. The boy is a FOOL! said she;—I know it, said Harry.

A gipsy then accosted, and taking him by the hand—Will you be pleased, sir, to be told your fortune? said she. —By no means, my sweet-voiced Cassandra, answered Harry; I would avoid, above all things, prying into futurity. —Knowledge, sir, is surely desirable, and above all, foreknowledge.—Not so, said Harry, foreknowledge of evil would but double the misery; and foreknowledge of good would deprive me of hope by certainty; and hope is a blessing perhaps preferable to possession.—Tell me, sir, and tell me truly, did you ever yet see the girl that you could like?—Yes, madam, two or three, for whom I have conceived a very tender friendship, but no one yet for whom I have conceived a passion.—Ah, then, Mr. Mercury! said the gentle prophetess, I have only to desire the last cast of your office; when I am dead, be so grateful as to waft my friendly spirit to the shades of Elysium, there to join Dido and other unfortunate lovers.

So saying, she turned and retired with a sigh that entered and sunk into the heart of our hero.

The company now began to depart, when the Earl of Albemarle, coming up to Harry, took him a little apart, and throwing his arm over his shoulder, pressed him to him and said—My dear fellow, you have done me singular honour this night; pray, double the favour to me by letting me see you again speedily and as often as you can. For the present, you must not go till their majesties have spoken with you.— Not to-night, so please your excellency, answered Harry; at all other times I shall be ready to attend and serve their majesties without any mask.

The next morning Mr. Fenton was much surprised by a visit from the great man. During breakfast the earl pressed eagerly for Harry's attendance at court, and promised every advantage and honour that the crown could bestow. You must pardon me, my lord, said Mr. Fenton; I am willing to advance to you two hundred thousand pounds more towards his majesty's present expedition against the French, whom I look upon to be our natural and salutary enemies. They are as Carthage was to Rome; they hold us in exercise, and keep a quarrelsome people from falling out among themselves. Indeed, my lord, I am desirous of gratifying my royal master with anything except the sacrifice of my child. I cannot part with him till his education is completed; and then, if he answers my expectations, I doubt I may be more unwilling to part with him than ever.

In the afternoon our company went again to the Tower, to see as well as to hear the recent story of the great lion and the little dog.

They found the place thronged, and all were obliged to pay treble prices, on account of the unprecedented novelty of the show, so that the keeper in a short space acquired a little fortune.

The great cage in the front was occupied by a beast who, by way of pre-eminence, was called the king's lion; and, while he traversed the limits of his straitened dominions, he was attended by a small and very beautiful black spaniel, who frisked and gamboled about him, and at times would pretend to snarl and bite at him; and again the noble animal, with an air of fond complacence, would hold down his head, while the little creature licked his formidable chops. Their history, as the keeper related, was this:—

It was customary for all who were unable or unwilling to pay their sixpence, to bring a dog or a cat as an oblation to the beast in lieu of money to the keeper. Among others, a fellow had caught up this pretty black spaniel in the streets, and he was accordingly thrown into the cage of the great lion. Immediately the little animal trembled and shivered, and crouched and threw itself on its back, and put forth its tongue, and held up its paws, in supplicatory attitudes, as an acknowledgment of superior power, and praying for mercy. In the mean time, the lordly brute, instead of devouring it, beheld it with an eye of philosophic inspection. He turned it over with one paw, and then turned it with the other; and smelled to it, and seemed desirous of courting a further acquaintance.

The keeper, on seeing this, brought a large mess of his

own family-dinner; but the lion kept aloof, and refused to eat, keeping his eye on the dog, and inviting him as it were to be his taster. At length, the little animal's fears being something abated, and his appetite quickened by the smell of the victuals, he approached slowly, and, with trembling, ventured to eat. The lion then advanced gently and began to partake, and they finished their meal very lovingly together.

From this day the strictest friendship commenced between them—a friendship consisting of all possible affection and tenderness on the part of the lion, and of the utmost confidence and boldness on the part of the dog; insomuch that he would lay himself down to sleep within the fangs and under the jaws of his terrible patron.

A gentleman who had lost the spaniel, and had advertised a reward of two guineas to the finder, at length heard of the adventure, and went to reclaim his dog. You see, sir, said the keeper, it would be a great pity to part such loving friends. However, if you insist upon your property, you must even be pleased to take him yourself; it is a task that I would not engage in for five hundred guineas. The gentleman rose into great wrath, but finally chose to acquiesce rather than have a personal dispute with the lion.

As Mr. Fenton had a curiosity to see the two friends eat together, he sent for twenty pounds of beef, which was accordingly cut in pieces, and given into the cage; when immediately the little brute, whose appetite happened to be eager at the time, was desirous of making a monopoly of the whole, and putting his paws upon the meat, and grumbling and barking, he audaciously flew in the face of the lion. But the generous creature, instead of being offended by his impotent companion, started back, and seemed terrified at the fury of his attack; neither attempted to eat a bit till his favourite had tacitly given permission.

When they were both gorged, the lion stretched and turned himself, and lay down in an evident posture for repose, but this his sportive companion would not admit. He frisked and gamboled about him, barked at him, would now scrape and tear at his head with his claws, and again seize him by the ear, and bite and pull away; while the noble beast appeared affected by no other sentiment save that of pleasure and complacence.

But let us proceed to the tragic catastrophe of this extraordinary story, still known to many, as delivered down by tradition from father to son.

In about twelve months the spaniel sickened and died, and left his loving patron the most desolate of creatures. For a time, the lion did not appear to conceive otherwise than that his favourite was asleep. He would continue to smell to him, and then would stir him with his nose, and turn him over with his paw; but, finding that all his efforts to awake him were vain, he would traverse his cage from end to end at a swift and uneasy pace, then stop and look down upon him with a fixed and drooping regard; and again lift his head on high, and open his horrible throat, and prolong a roar as of distant thunder, for several minutes together.

They attempted, but in vain, to convey the carcase from him; he watched it perpetually, and would suffer nothing to touch it. The keeper then endeavoured to tempt him with variety of victuals, but he turned from all that was offered with loathing. They then put several living dogs into his cage, and these he instantly tore piecemeal, but left their members on the floor. His passion being thus inflamed, he would dart his fangs into the boards, and pluck away large splinters, and again grapple at the bars of his cage, and seem enraged at his restraint from tearing the world in pieces.

Again, as quite spent, he would stretch himself by the remains of his beloved associate, and gather him in with his paws, and put him to his bosom; and then utter under roars of such terrible melancholy as seemed to threaten all around, for the loss of his little playfellow, the only friend, the only companion, that he had upon earth.

For five days he thus languished, and gradually declined, without taking any sustenance, or admitting any comfort; till one morning, he was found dead, with his head lovingly reclined on the carcase of his little friend. They were both interred together, and their grave plentifully watered by the tears of the keeper, and his loudly lamenting family.—But to return.

When our company were on their way from the Tower to their lodgings—Sir, said Harry, what we have just seen reminds me of the opinion of my friend Peter Patience, that one who is fearless cannot be provoked. You saw how that little, teasing, petulant wretch had the insolence to fly in the face of his benefactor, without offending or exciting in him any kind of resentment.—True, Harry, for the lion was sensible that his testy companion was little and impotent, and depended upon him, and had confidence in his clemency, and therefore he loved him with all his faults. Anger, however, in some cases, is not only allowable, but becomes a duty. The scripture says—"Be angry, but sin not." We ought to feel and fear for others; and lust, violence, and oppression of every sort, will excite the indignation of a generous and benevolent person, though he may not fear for himself.

After supper, Harry appeared to ruminate, and said— How comes it, sir, that creatures not endued with reason or conscience, shall yet, in the affections that are peculiarly called humane, exceed even most of the human species? You have seen that it was the case between the lion and little dog.

It was the opinion, my Harry, of an ancient philosopher,

that God was the soul and spirit of brutes; and this he judged from observing that what we call instinct was incomparably wiser, more sagacious, and more accomplishing for attaining its ends, throughout its sphere of action, than the most perfect human reason. Now had this philosopher, instead of saying that God was the soul of brutes, barely alleged that he ruled and dictated within them, he would not have gone a tittle wide of the truth.

God, indeed, is himself the beauty and the benefit of all his works. As they cannot exist but in him and by him, so his impression is upon them, and his impregnation is through them.

Though the elements, and all that we know of nature and creature, have a mixture of natural and physical evil, God is, however, throughout, an internal, though often a hidden principle of good, and never wholly departs from his right of dominion and operation in his creatures; but is, and is alone, the beauty and beneficence, the whole glory and graciousness that can possibly be in them.

As the apostle says, "The invisible things of God are made manifest by the things that are seen." He is the secret and central light that kindles up the sun, his dazzling representative; and he lives, enlightens, and comforts in the diffusion of his beams.

His spirit inspires and actuates the air, and is in it a breath of life to all his creatures. He blooms in the blossom, and unfolds in the rose. He is fragrance in flowers, and flavour in fruits. He holds infinitude in the hollow of his hand, and opens his world of wonders in the minims of nature. He is the virtue of every heart that is softened by a sense of pity or touch of benevolence. He coos in the turtle and bleats in the lamb; and, through the paps of the stern bear and implacable tigress, he yields forth the milk of loving-kindness to their little ones. Even, my Harry, when we hear the delicious enchantment of music, it is but an external sketch and faint echo of those sentimental and rapturous tunings that rise up, throughout the immensity of our God, from eternity to eternity.

Thus all things are secretly pregnant with their God. And the lover of sinners, the universal Redeemer, is a principle of good within them, that contends with the malignity of their lapsed state. And thus, as the apostle speaks—" All nature is in travail, and groaneth" to be delivered from the evil ; till the breath of the love of God shall kindle upon the final fire, out of which the new heavens and new earth shall come forth, as gold seven times refined, to shine for ever and ever!

Harry, agreeable to his covenant with Signor Volanti, had penned the following advertisement, and inserted it in all the public papers, to wit:—On Saturday next, between the hours of ten and twelve in the forenoon, the celebrated Dominico Jachimo Tonino Volanti will take his flight from the spire of Clement's steeple, and alight at the distance of two bows shot, on the Strand; and this he will perform before the eyes of all people."

On the impatiently-expected morning, Harry took Mr. Clement with him in a hackney chaise, and found an innumerable concourse, as well of the gentry in their carriages as of the populace on foot. London had poured forth its numbers to behold this astonishing flight. The windows were all eyes on every side, and the house-tops were hung with clusters of people as of bees.

After Harry had surveyed the crowd with inward titillation, he whispered to Clement, and said—You shall see now what a sudden discomfiture I will make of this huge army.

He then put forth his head and said to all around—Do not ye perceive, my friends, what fools we are all made ? do not ye remember that this is the *first of April?*

He had scarce spoken the words when they spread from man to man, and soon were muttered throughout the assembly. And then louder, and more loud, the *first of April! the first of April!* was repeated all about.

The company now began to be in motion. All heads were instantly withdrawn from the late thronged windows, and the house-tops began to be cleared with a shameful caution.

Immediately was heard the rolling of many wheels, and the lashing of many whips, while every coachman pressed through the crowd, impatient to deliver his honourable freight from public shame. But the public now began to relish a joke that was so much against their betters; and in peals of laughter, and united shouts of triumph, they echoed and re-echoed after them, *April fools! April fools!*

Among others, Lord Bottom had come with his friend Rakely, in an elevated phaeton, of which his lordship was charioteer. As they happened to brush close by Harry's carriage, swearing and puffing, and lashing and cursing at the crowd, Harry cried to his old enemy—You need not be in so violent a hurry, my lord; perhaps you are not so great a Fool as you imagine.

The fools of fashion were scarce withdrawn, when a long and strong rope was let down from the top of the steeple, to which it was fastened at the upper end. A man then, laying hold on it below, dragged it along through the crowd, and braced it, at a great distance, to an iron ring that was stapled into a post, purposely sunk on a level with the pavement. They then brought a large and well stuffed feather-bed, and fixed it under the cord where it joined the ring.

In the mean time Volanti appeared on the top of the steeple, and bending cautiously forward, and getting the cord within an iron groove that was braced to his bosom he pushed himself onward, and with a kindling rapidity flew over the heads of the shouting multitude, poising himself with expanded legs and arms as he passed, till he was landed without damage on his yielding receiver. And in the very next papers Harry published the following advertisement, to wit:—

"Before the first of April next, Signor Dominico Jachimo Tonino Volanti, by the help of canvass wings contrived for the purpose, purposes to fly over-sea from Dover to Calais, and invites all his London friends to come and see him set out."

Harry had now seen whatever London could exhibit of elegant, curious, or pleasing; and Mr. Fenton judged it time to hold up to him the melancholy reverse of this picture— to shew him the *house of mourning* the *end of all men*—to shew him the dreary shades and frightful passages of mortality, which humanity shudders to think of, but through which human nature of necessity must go.

For this purpose he took him to the GENERAL HOSPITAL, where death opened all his gates, and shewed himself in all his forms. But the great poet, on this occasion, has anticipated all description:—

> Immediately a place
> Before his eyes appear'd—sad, noisome, dark.
> A lazar-house it seem'd, wherein were laid
> Numbers of all diseased, all maladies
> Of ghastly spasm, of racking torture, qualms
> Of heart-sick agony—all fev'rous kinds,
> Convulsions, epilepsies, fierce catarrhs,
> Intestine stone and ulcer; cholic pangs,
> Demoniac frenzy, moping melancholy,
> And moonstruck madness; pining atrophy,
> Dropsies, and asthmas, and joint-racking rheums.
> Dire was the tossing, deep the groan—Despair
> Tended the sick, busiest from couch to couch,
> And over them triumphant Death his dart
> Shook, but delay'd to strike, though oft invoked
> With vows as their chief good.   MILTON.

While Mr. Fenton led his pupil through groaning galleries, and the chambers of death and disease, Harry let down the leaf of his hat, and drew it over his eyes to conceal his emotions. All that day he was silent, and his countenance downcast; and at night he hastened to bed, where he wept a large tribute to the mournfully inevitable condition of man's miserable state upon earth.

The next day Mr. Fenton took him to the Bethlehem Hospital for idiots and lunatics. But when Harry beheld and contemplated objects so shocking to thought, so terrible to sight—when he had contemplated, I say, the ruin above all ruins, human intelligence and human reason so fearfully overthrown; where the ideas of the soul, though distorted and misplaced, are quick and all alive to horror and agony; he grew sick and turned pale, and suddenly catching his uncle by the arm—Come, sir, let us go, said he, I can stand this no longer.

When they had reached home, and that Harry was more composed:—Are all the miseries, sir, said he, that we have witnessed these two days, the consequences of sin?—Even so, indeed, my Harry; all these, and thousands more, equally pitiable and disgusting, are the natural progeny of that woe-begetting parent. Nor are those miseries confined to hospitals alone; every house, nay every bosom, is a certain though secret lazar-house, where the sick couch is preparing, with all the dismal apparatus, for tears and lamentations, for agonies and death.—Since that is the case, sir, who would laugh any more? Is it not like feasting in the midst of famine, and dancing amidst the tombs?

All things in their season, my dear, provided that those who laugh be as though they laughed not, remembering that they must weep; and provided that those who weep be as though they wept not, having joy in their knowledge that the fashion of this world quickly passeth away.

On the following day, Mr. Fenton returned to Hampstead, leaving Harry and Mr. Clement ability to indulge the benevolence of their hearts.

One evening, as our companions were drinking tea in the Temple Exchange Coffee-house, a man, advanced in years but of a very respectable appearance, got up and addressed the assembly:—

Gentlemen, said he, among the several hospitals and other charitable foundations that have done honour to the humanity of the inhabitants of this city, there is one still wanting, which, as I conceive above all others, would give distinction to the beneficence of its founders; it is a house for repenting prostitutes, an asylum for unhappy wretches who have no other home—to whom all doors are shut, to whom no haven is open, no habitation or hole for rest upon the face of the earth.

Most of them have been seduced from native innocence and modesty by the arts of cruel men. Many have been deceived under promise and vows of marriage; some under the appearance of the actual ceremony, and afterwards abandoned or turned forth to infamy by their barbarous and base undoers. Shall no place, then, be left for repentance, even to those who do repent? Forbid it, charity; forbid it, manhood! Man is born the natural protector of the weakness of woman; and, if he has not been able to guard her innocence from invasion, he ought at least to provide a reception for her return to virtue.

I have the plan of this charitable foundation in my pocket; and if any of you gentlemen approve my proposal, and are willing to subscribe, or to solicit your friends to so beneficent a purpose, I request your company to the tavern over the way.

Here the speaker walked towards the door, and was followed by Harry and Clement, and thirteen or fourteen more of the assembly.

When the company was seated round a large table, the gentleman produced his plan, with a summary of the rules and institutes for the conduct of the house, which he proposed to call the Magdalene House: a plan which hath since been espoused and happily executed by others, without ascribing any of the merit to the first projector.

As all present applauded the manner of the scheme, and intention of the charity, each of them subscribed from a hundred to twenty pounds, till it came to Harry's turn, who subscribed a thousand pounds in Mr. Fenton's name.

I suppose, sir, said one of the company, that your largest contributions will arise from the ladies, as the whole is intended for the benefit of the sex.—I shall not, answered the gentleman, apply to a single lady on this occasion. Not one of them will dare to contribute a penny, lest it should be thought that they partly allow in themselves the vices that they can pardon or patronize in others. It is this that makes the case of the wretches whom we are about to befriend, deplorable beyond measure. They are first betrayed by our sex, and then driven out to irretrievable infamy and misery by their own. For women to women are as turkeys to turkeys; do but cast a little dirt upon the head of any one of them, and the rest of the flock combine in an instant to pick out her eyes, and to tear her to pieces.

Mr. Mole, a learned philosopher, and a man of principal figure in the present company, then addressed the projector, and said—If you will admit me, sir, into partnership in the conduct of your scheme, I will engage to levy contributions to the amount of some thousands over and above the hundred I have subscribed.—You are heartily welcome, sir, replied the gentleman, either to join or take the conduct of the whole upon yourself; provided the good is done, I care not by what means. All my ends will be answered; I wish to be nameless.—That is not fair, neither, said another of the company; you, Mr. Goodville, had the trouble of contriving this business, and you ought at least to have the honour, if not the conduct, of your own plan.

Mr. Goodville! Mr. Goodville! exclaimed Clement in a surprise, eagerly staring at him, and recollecting, as from a dream, the altered features of his quondam friend and benefactor. Pray, sir, do you remember any thing of one Clement, a worthless young fellow, whom once in your goodness you condescended to patronize?—Clement! Clement! cried Mr. Goodville, getting up and hastening to him, and catching him in his arms. My dear, my dear Clement, my man of merit and misfortunes, how rejoiced am I to find you! God be praised! God be praised! it is at length in my power to do something material for you! But come with me to another room, I have something to say to you; we will leave these gentlemen the while to think further of the plan that lies before them.

When Mr. Goodville and Clement had withdrawn—Mr. Mole, said one of the company, you are concerned in a number of these public benefactions.—Yes, gentlemen, answered Mole, I believe there is no charitable institution of any note in London in which I am not a trustee, and to which I am not a contributor. For, though I do not set up for sanctification by faith, yet I think I may pretend to some justification by charity. Let the vulgar herd pay their priesthood for cheating them out of their senses—I give nothing to the fat impostors, or their lucrative fable; my substance is little enough for myself and the poor.—Why, pray, sir, said Harry, are you not a Christian?—No, indeed, master, answered Mole, nor any man who has sense enough to think for himself.—Be pleased then, cried Harry, to hand me that paper a moment; here, sir, I dash my name and contribution from the list of the subscribers. He who denies *glory to God in the highest*, can never have *peace or good will towards men;*

and so, sir, you shall never be the almoner of a penny of my money.

You talk as you look, my dear, cried Mole; like one just eloped from the nursery, where you were affrighted by tales of ghosts and hobgoblins. I acknowledge, gentlemen, the benefit and beauty of morality in its fullest extent; and had Jesus, the Christian Prophet, confined himself to his system of moral precepts, I think he would justly have been esteemed the greatest philosopher and legislator that ever breathed; but when he, or rather his disciples in his name, in order to enhance the authority of their mission, pretended to divinity in their master, the low-bred and ignorant wretches pulled together against the grain, and compounded such a strange medley of fighting inconsistencies, and self-evident absurdities, as are wholly eversive of every principle of right reason and common-sense. They taught that God was made a man—that, in order to expiate the sins of the world, the innocent was appointed to suffer for the guilty—that the sins of all offenders were to be imputed to one who had never offended, and that the righteousness of him who had never offended was to be imputed to criminals of the deepest dye—that the Creator submitted himself to the malignity of his creatures, and that God himself died a shameful death on the cross. And this, gentlemen, makes such a heap of ridiculous incoherences—such contradictions in sense and terms—as exceeds even the worship of apes and serpents, leeks and onions, and the other garbage of Egypt.

You are a villain, and a thief, and a liar, cried Harry, altogether inflamed with choler. Mole, on hearing these terms of highest affront and reproach, instantly caught up a bottle and threw it at our hero's head; but it happily missed him, and only bruised the fleshy part of the shoulder of the gentleman who sat next. Harry instantly sprung up and made at Mole, while the company rose also and attempted to interfere; but some he cast on one hand and some on the other, and overturning such as directly opposed him, he reached Mole, and with one blow of his fist on the temple, he laid him motionless along the floor. Then, looking down on his adversary—I should be sorry, said he, that the wretch would die in his present state of reprobacy; here, drawer, run quickly and bring me a surgeon. Then, returning to his place, he sat down with great composure.

After a pause, he looked round—I hope, gentlemen, said he, that none of you are hurt. Indeed, I am much concerned for having in any degree contributed to your disturbance. But, had any one of you a dear benefactor and patron, to whom you were bound beyond measure, whom you loved and honoured above all things, could you bear to hear him defamed and vilified to your face?—No, certainly, answered one man.—No man could bear it, cried another.— But pray, asked a third, how came you to call the gentleman a thief?—Because, replied our hero, he attempted to rob me of my whole estate. He endeavoured to thieve from me the only friend I had in the universe—the friend of my heart— the peace and rest of my bosom—my infinite treasure—my never-ending delight—the friend without whom I would not choose to be—without whom existence would become a curse and an abhorrence unto me.—Happy young creature! exclaimed an elderly gentleman, I understand you; you mean your Christ and my Christ—the friend who has already opened his early heaven within you.

By this time Mr. Mole began to move; whereupon Harry rose, and putting his hand in his pocket—Here, gentlemen, said he, is one guinea for the surgeon and another for the reckoning. When my companion returns be pleased to tell him I am gone to our lodgings; for I will not stay to hold further converse or altercation with that bane of society—

that pest, which the rulers in darkness have commissioned to spread contagion, distemper, and death among men.

Harry went early to bed, but lay restless and much disturbed in his spirit all night. Mr. Clement had heard the particulars of our hero's behaviour, which he partly disapproved; but, as he saw him already dejected, he did not choose to expostulate with him for the present.

The next day they returned to Hampstead, where Mr. Fenton, notwithstanding the constrained smiles of his Harry, observed an unusual cloud and uneasiness in his countenance. I want to speak with you, my love, said he; and beckoning him into his closet, he took him affectionately by the hand and made him sit beside him. What is the matter, my dear, said he, looking concernedly in his face; what is it that has disturbed the peace of the bosom of my beloved?

Ah, sir! cried Harry, I am indeed very unhappy. I doubt that I am partly losing my faith, and the fear of that has given me inexpressible horror. It is like tearing me from a fort, out of which there is no home or rest for me in the universe.

Here Harry made a recital of the late affair to his patron, and having closed his narrative—Is not this very wonderful, sir, said he, how or where in the world could this Mole have mustered together such arguments against reason—such appearances against truth? How must the vulgar and illiterate be staggered by such objections, when even I, who have been bred, as I may say, at the feet of Gamaliel, have not been able to answer them otherwise than by the chastisement which the blasphemer received at my hand?

Here Mr. Fenton smiled, and said—Do not be alarmed, my love. We shall quickly dispel the thin mists of infidelity that were collected to shut the sun of righteousness from your eye. I confess, indeed, that this spawn of Antichrist has compiled a summary of all that has ever been uttered against "the Lamb who was slain from the foundation of the world;" yet he is but a Mole in nature as well as name; and he with his brother moles know no more, and see no further, than the little heap of dirt and rubbish that the working of their own purblind and floundering reason hath cast about them.

Sacred depths and stupendous mysteries belong to this matter, and, when you are able to bear them, they shall be clearly and fully unfolded to you, my Harry; in the mean space, a few simple observations will suffice to re-establish the peace of your sweet and pious heart.

As Christianity was instituted for the salvation of the vulgar, the principal truths thereof are very obvious and plain, and want no learning, no letters, to inculcate or teach them. They speak the language of nature, and all nature is expressive of the sense and the sound thereof. Whatever is within you, whatever is without you, cries aloud for a Saviour. For sin hath been as the Mezentius, of whom you read in Virgil, who bound the bodies of the dead to the persons of the living. Thus it is that the sin of fallen angels, and of fallen man, hath bound change and corruption, distemperature and death, to the elements, to the vegetables, to animals, and even to the immortal image of God himself in the humanity; so that all things cry out with the apostle St. Paul—"Who shall deliver me from the body of this death?" so that all things cry out with the apostle St. Peter—"Save, Lord, or I perish!"

These are inevitable truths, my Harry, which all men, at some time, must feel throughout their existence, whether they read them or not. And he alone, who never experienced, nor never shall experience, frailty, error, or sickness, pain, anguish, or dissolution, is exempt from our solar system of salvation from sin.

But what sort of a Saviour is it for whom all things cry

so loudly? Is it a dry moralist, a legislator of bare and external precepts, such as your Mole philosopher required our Christ to be? No, my darling, no! The influence and existence of the Redeemer of nature must, at least, be as extensive as nature herself.

Things are defiled and corrupted throughout; they are distempered and devoted to death from the inmost essence of their being; and nothing under him, in whom they live, and move, and have their being, can redeem them, can restore them.

"O, sir! exclaimed Harry—his countenance brightening up—why could I not think of this? I should then have been able to foil my malignant adversary even at his own weapons.

Our Jesus himself, continued Mr. Fenton, appeals to the truth I have told you, where he says to the sick of the palsy —" Son, be of good cheer, thy sins are forgiven thee." But when the Pharisees thereupon concluded that he blasphemed, he demonstrated his influence in and over the soul, by the sensible evidence of his operation and influence in and over the body. "What reason ye in your hearts?" said Jesus; "Whether is it easier to say, 'Thy sins be forgiven thee;' or to say, 'Rise up and walk?'" Then said he to the sick of the palsy, "Arise and take up thy couch, and go to thine house." And immediately he rose up before them, and took up that whereon he had been carried, and departed to his own house, glorifying God.

Here it was necessary, for the performance of this wonderful and instantaneous cure, that Jesus should instantly operate in and through every member, nerve, and fiber, of the sick of the palsy. And it was equally necessary, for that purpose, that the sick of the palsy should have lived, and have had his being, in Jesus. In like manner, also, his sins must have been pardoned by an inward salvation, by imparting to the will of the sinner a new and rectified will, and by informing his spirit with a detestation of evil, and a love of goodness and virtue.

But pray, sir, if it is not too profound a mystery for me, be pleased to inform me how God could be made man? For this was one of the principal objections of Mole.

God was never made man, my Harry. God cannot be debased. He could not degrade himself by any change into manhood, though he could exalt and assume humanity into God. Neither could God die or suffer. To this, Christ himself, who was God and man, bears testimony, where he cries out, in the agonies of his suffering humanity, "My God! my God! why hast thou forsaken me?" And again, where, crying with a loud voice, he said, "Father into thy hands I commend my spirit." But you are leading me something deeper than I choose to go for the present.

From eternity, God saw that, should he produce any creatures in his own image, to be glorious by his likeness, and happy by his communication, he must of necessity create them intelligent and free: and that consequently as creatures, they must be finite; and that, as creatures who were free, they should also be fallible.

He therefore saw that all might fall, and he also foresaw that some would fall. But his graciousness had provided *two infallible remedies* for this evil of fallibility. He had provided a *Saviour*, and he had also provided *suffering*. The *Saviour* was to restore them by an inward redemption, by a reinfusion and new birth of his own nature in their essence; and *suffering* was to prepare and open his way, by humbling their pride, by mortifying their lust, and thus compelling them to unfold their hearts to their own happiness.

Indeed, had no creature ever fallen, God could not have been duly glorified to all eternity. Millions of his infinitely amiable qualities must have lain an inscrutable secret to worlds upon worlds. While all his creatures were happy in him, and participated of him, no distinction could be duly made between them and their Creator. Had evil never been, goodness would have sunk unspeakably in the sense of its value, which is now infinitely heightened and glorified by the contrast. Free grace and free mercy on the part of our God, and penitence and thanksgiving on the part of humbled sinners, would have been prevented of their thousand endearing connections. And all the amities and charities throughout the brotherhood of man; all the melting and fond relations which the vine Christ infuses throughout his ingrafted branches, bearing blossoms and fruits of divine fragrance and flavour, must ever have remained unblessing, and as dead, from eternity to eternity.

But our God, my child, is as powerful as he is gracious and wise, to bring light out of darkness, and life out of death, and infinite and ever-enduring good out of the limited and short state of transitory evil.

To prove that no beings beneath himself could stand of their own sufficiency, God permitted his two principal creatures—the most immediate and most glorious representatives of his divine perfections—to fall off from their allegiance, and consequently from their happiness, with all their progeny. The first was the angel Lucifer who fell through *pride*, and the second was the man Adam who fell through *lust*. These two capital sins of *pride* and of *lust*, are the genuine parents of all moral and natural evil, of all the guilt or misery that ever did, or ever can, rise throughout duration; and our heavenly Father, in his love, hath appointed intense suffering to abate and abase the *one*, to mortify and slay the *other*, that transgressors may finally be capable of his mercy, through the salvation and grace of his Christ.

The first of these arch-felons deemed himself worthy of Deity, and being inexperienced in the power with whom he had to contend, he attempted to arrogate all worship to himself, and to rob his divine benefactor of glory and godhead.

The second of these felons was tempted by the first to aspire, through his own merits, as a godlike independence; to cast off his allegiance to the author of his being; and to expect intelligence and knowledge from the sensual fruits of this world, after which he lusted. He accordingly took and eat of the tree that was pregnant with all the goods and all the evils of this external, elementary, and transient system; "according to his faith it was done unto him;" according to his lust his desire was accomplished; his nature became a partaker of temporary nature; and he fell, with his progeny, into all the depravity and evils that the sin of fallen Lucifer had introduced into these vast regions, now made more exceedingly corrupt and sinful by the sin of fallen Adam.

Why, pray, sir, demanded Harry, had Lucifer any concern in this world before the fall of our first parents?

Yes, my dear; all the space that is now occupied by this earth and these elements, with the sun, moon, and stars, to an inconceivable extent, was once the heaven and dominion of Lucifer and his angels. But when, by their apostasy from the light, and love, and goodness of God, they had caused darkness and malignity, envy, rage, and uproar, and every species of evil and horror, to be predominant throughout their kingdom, God determined, by a new creation, to take it out of their hands. Accordingly he compacted it into the present system of temporary nature, whose duration is to be measured by the revolution of our luminaries, until the appointed period of the great consummation, when all the malignity that remains and is compacted therein, shall be finally done away.

To this truth Moses bears testimony, where he tells you that, at the commencement of the creation, darkness was upon the face of the great deep. And again, where he tells you, that the tree of the knowledge of the goods and evils of this world sprung up even in the midst of the paradise of God. But it is altogether impious and blasphemous to suppose that God would create evil, or infuse a tendency thereto into any of his works. Again, the same truth is attested by many passages of the sacred writings, where Lucifer, or Satan, tells Christ to his face, that this world, with all its glories, are his portion and property; that they were delivered unto him; and that he giveth them to whomever he will. And again, where Christ calls him " the prince of air ;" and again, where he says, " The prince of this world cometh, and hath no part in me."

Now when God, by this new creation, had delivered this system of things from the influence and dominion of evil spirits, they became altogether prisoners in their own darkness. But when Adam, the second lord of this vast domain, by a second apostasy had brought additional sin and evil into temporary nature, the paradise of God, that was over all, vanished; and the new guilt of Adam opened a new and wide gate for the re-admission of Lucifer into his ancient possessions. And he remains a prince and a ruler in the elements and hearts of men unto this evil day.

These two capital apostates, Lucifer and Adam, who had thus robbed their kind God of their affections and allegiance, were thereafter represented by the two thieves who suffered in company with Christ, who reached out to each of them a bleeding arm of his mercy. The one accepted his grace, and on that day entered paradise along with his Lord. The other rejected *the Christ* with contempt and reproach, and therefore, if ever reclaimable, must be constrained.by suffering to open his heart to redemption; when, after a process of many agonizing ages, blaspheming and indignantly spurning at the power of his punisher, he may be compelled to cry out—O seed of the woman! heal, heal the head thou hast crushed, and admit me also, though last, to some, the least portion of thy pardoning salvation!

These two, my Harry, even Lucifer and Adam, were also the thieves among whom the traveller fell, going from Jerusalem to Jericho, from the city and place of peace to the place of destruction. He represented the wretched race of fallen man, whom Lucifer, and their first father, had robbed of all their substance, and stripped of their robe of righteousness, and wounded and left half dead in trespasses and sins. Neither did the law or the priesthood avail anything for their cure, till JESUS, the good SAMARITAN, had compassion upon them, and bound up their wounds, pouring therein the oil of his grace and the wine of his gladness; and expended twopence, even the two precious pence of his own body and blood, for perfecting their recovery.

But, my dearest sir, said Harry, if my question does not intrude, pray, how was it consistent with justice that the sufferings of the innocent should atone both for, and instead of, the guilty? For this also was one of Mole's cardinal objections.

Your question, said Mr. Fenton, falls aptly in its place. When Adam, as I have told you, apostatized from his God, and lusted after the gross and sensual fruits of this world, and fed upon them, and thereupon became a partaker of their nature and malignity; he fell from his paradise and sovereignty together, and he became a poor subject, and miserable slave, to all the evils and inclemencies of that temporary nature, over which he had been constituted a throned lord and controller.

Here was a deep and woful fall, my Harry, from sovereignty to slavery, from eternity into time, from immortality into corruption, from bliss into misery, and from life into death! The very state in which the wretched heirs of his fallen nature find themselves at this day. How then was he to rise, if ever to rise again? Could this be effected by any powers of his own? If he did not stand in the state of his strength, how shall he recover and be able to re-ascend in the state of his weakness? How think you, my Harry?—A self-evident impossibility, answered Harry.

Here then, continued Mr. Fenton, we find the universe of man depraved, fallen and sunk into the darkness of sin and error, into the dungeon of gross and corruptible flesh, and circled about and closed in by the barriers and gates of death. And these prisons were to be broken through, these gates were to burst open, before he could re-enter upon light and immortality. All the enemies who had conquered man, *sin*, *Satan*, and *temptation*, were also to be conquered.

But how was this to be done? A world lay at stake, and the great question was, Whether the whole race of man should continue in endless guilt and misery, or be restored to ever-enduring purity and blessedness? Wherefore, what all the powers of creation were not able to attempt, Jesus, in the humanity, undertook to accomplish.

Here you see, my child, that justice had little to do in the case. It was not the *justice of punishment*, but the *mercy of deliverance*, that the love of our heavenly Father required. Justice indeed affirmed that suffering was due to sin, and was the necessary attendant and consequence thereof; and this also the love of our Christ willingly took upon himself. He conquered *suffering* through *sufferings*, and was thereby made the perfect and accomplished captain of our salvation. He entered into our flesh, he went through all the passages of this vale of tears and region of misery into which we are fallen; through poverty, contempt, rejection, reproach; through all the rage and rancour of men and devils could inflict, his bloody sweat and horrors of hell, bonds, buffetings, spittings, scourgings, the bloody mockery of a thorny crown, and all the soul-rending tortures of an agonizing crucifixion, till at last he triumphantly cried—"It is finished!" and gave up the ghost. From the cross he descended into the grave; from the grave again he rose in glory, and ascended into heaven, where he led captivity captive, and shewed the powers of darkness bound; that he might lead all the followers of his beatific cross, in his own divine process, to conquest through sufferings, to glory through abasement, to exaltation through humiliation, through death into life, and through the calamities of time to a never-ending, ever-blessing, ever-joyful, eternity!

But, sir, said Harry; was the humanity of our blessed Saviour the same as ours is? for so the scripture seems to intimate, where it says—"He was made man, like unto us in all things, sin only excepted.'

This was only spoken, answered Mr. Fenton, with respect to his outward humanity. His creaturely soul indeed, and the flesh which he derived from his mortal mother, were even as ours are, sin only excepted. But these were only as the husk or case of his internal and divine humanity, which was conceived from the essence of the FATHER, by the operation of the HOLY SPIRIT in the womb of a pure virgin. It was this humanity to which JESUS was intimately united, and that became one with the ever-blessed TRINITY. And it was of the ubiquity of this humanity that Christ speaketh, when he says to Nicodemus, "No man hath ascended up to heaven but he that came down from heaven, even the son of man which is in heaven." But when the external humanity of Jesus was, by sufferings and death, prepared to be swallowed up in glory, the whole CHRIST was then assumed up into Godhead. He saw all things in Jesus, as they were and shall be from eternity to eternity. And, though the glory of his personal appearance may be visible in certain places, yet he is invisibly present in all places and in all hearts, begetting in them a new birth of his own divine humanity; that their bodies may also be fashioned like unto his glorious body; and that, when our corruptible shall have put on incorruption, and when that our mortal shall have put on immortality, "we all may be made one, as he is in the Father, and the Father in him, that we also may be one in them." An elevation, sure, well worth the hardest striving, the highest ambition.

Thus I have shewn you, my Harry, the inevitable necessity of the sufferings of our innocent Christ for the salvation of guilty sinners. And this also shews you the equal necessity of his taking upon himself the external imputation of the sins for which he suffered; that he might thereby be inwardly imputed to us, and become to us, and in us, the LORD OUR RIGHTEOUSNESS; and be to us a better Adam, a second and divine father, regenerating us to a birth of his own heavenly nature. And thus, as the first Adam died unto God, and lived to fallen nature, there was a necessity that Christ, as well in his own person as his redeemed progeny, should die to the fallen nature, that through him they might live again unto God.

I thank you, thank you, sir, cried Harry; I shall henceforth be enabled to give an account, to all who ask, of the faith that is in me. But, pray, did the divine humanity of our Christ suffer in the crucifixion?

I believe it did, Harry, even as our souls are found to suffer in our bodies, though of a nature so very different from them. It was the suffering of this divine humanity that caused such violent repugnance and convulsions in nature; that shut up the world from light even at mid-day; that rent the rocks; that opened the graves, and gave up the dead to attend their Lord, and revive in the life of his resurrection.

Will you be pleased, sir, to indulge me in one question

more? Could not God, in his omnipotence, have effected the salvation of man by some other means than the suffering of our dear Christ? I think, were it to be done again, I would rather forfeit my salvation than that he should endure such agony on my account.

I will not pretend, my Harry, to give limits or directions to the measures of my God, neither to say what he might or might not do within his own world, and with regard to his own creatures. But it is certain that he chose the most effectual method for compassing his great and eternal purpose that infinite love could dictate, infinite wisdom contrive, and infinite power execute. O, my Harry! how unutterably endeared must this measure make our God to the universe of his creatures, and that to all eternity; it is herein that the nature of our God is revealed; it is hereby alone that he could ever have been duly known—known to be the God of love—to be nothing but love, in this his wonderful work of mercy, transcending mercy; and of grace, transcending grace, that he might bring us to glory—transcending glory.

In this stupendous work of redemption, I say Jesus makes himself as it were little, that we may become great; he stoops into manhood, that he may exalt us into God. He came not arrayed in the fool's coat of the lustre of this despicable world, nor in the weakness of its power, nor in the meanness of its dignity; but over his immensity he threw the appearance of limitation, and with time he invested his eternity; and his omnipotence put on frailty; and his supremacy put on subjection; and with the veil of mortality he shrouded his beauty, that he might become familiar to us, that we might behold and converse with him face to face, as man converses with man, and grows fond of his fellow.

Before the incarnation, God was feared in his thunders, and adored in the majesty and magnificence of his works. But it is in the meek and lowly Jesus that he becomes the object of affection; in the bleeding, the suffering, the dying Jesus, we behold him with weeping gratitude, we love him with a love of passion and burning, a love that languishes for him, that cannot bear to exist without him.

How could that perverse people shut their eyes to the divinity of their gracious Messiah, while he gave such hourly and ocular proofs of the power and extent of his godhead in and over all things? while he went about doing good, carrying healing in his breath, in his touch, in his garments; while the lame sprung up as a bounding roe at his bidding; while the tempest heard his voice and was still, and the sea spread itself as a carpet beneath the foot of its creator; while the deaf ear was opened, and the dumb tongue loosed to utterance; while he poured the beams of his light upon the new opening eyes of the blind-born gazer; and while in death, and amidst the tombs, his word was life and resurrection?

Thus, my Harry, you find yourself united to your Saviour by many endearing and intimate connections, by creation, by redemption, by brotherhood, by fatherhood in the flesh, in the spirit; by his being bone of your bone, and spirit of your spirit; by being the "first-born of many brethren," and by being the divine father of a new and celestial progeny.

But what need we further? the world from the beginning is fraught with him, and speaks of him. The world is, in itself, no other than a history of the two capital and eternally important truths—the greatness of the fall in *Lucifer* and *Adam*, and the greatness of the redemption in *Jesus Christ*. These truths are engraven in the rocks as deep as the centre; they are written on both sides of every leaf in nature. All that is within us, all that is without us, utters forth the same language, proclaims the same tidings aloud. All ceremonials, all institutions of divine authority, all ancient predictions and prophecies, were pregnant with, and in travail of the great deliverance to be achieved by the *Shiloh* who was to come. They give us a previous history of his whole process upon earth, from his birth to his resurrection, as circumstantially, as minutely as though it were a bare transcript of what had recently passed before their eyes. But I shall only dwell a minute on three principal articles—first, that Messiah was to be God; secondly, that he was, however, to be a suffering Messiah; and, thirdly, that he was to give himself to death for the salvation of sinners.

First, With respect to his divinity, Daniel says—" I saw in the night-visions, and behold, one like unto the Son of Man came with the clouds of heaven, and came to the Ancient of Days, and they brought him near before him. And there was given him dominion, and glory, and a kingdom, that all people, nations, and languages should serve him; his dominion is an everlasting dominion, which shall not pass away." Again Isaiah:—" Behold, a virgin shall conceive, and bear a son. For unto us a child is born, unto us a son is given, and the government shall be upon his shoulder; and his name shall be called Wonderful, Counsellor, The Mighty God, The Everlasting Father, The Prince of Peace. Of the increase of his government and peace there shall be no end, upon the throne of David, and upon his kingdom to order it, and to establish it, with judgment and with justice, from henceforth even for ever."

Secondly, With respect to his character of rejection and suffering: " Who hath believed our report, and to whom is the arm of the Lord revealed? He is despised and rejected of men, a man of sorrows and acquainted with grief: and we hid as it were our faces from him; he was despised, and we esteemed him not. He was oppressed and he was afflicted; he is brought as a lamb to the slaughter, and as a sheep before her shearers is dumb, so opened he not his mouth. He was taken from prison and from judgment; and who shall declare his generation? for he was cut off out of the land of the living; for the transgression of my people was he stricken. And he made his grave with the wicked, and with the rich in his death."—Isaiah liii. David, too, says—"Dogs have compassed me, the assembly of the wicked have enclosed me; they pierced my hands and my feet. They part my garments among them, and cast lots for my vesture. But a bone of him shall not be broken. They shall look on him whom they pierced."

Thirdly. With respect to this being a willing offering for sin, Isaiah says in the same chapter, "Surely he hath borne our griefs, and carried our sorrows; yet we did esteem him stricken, smitten of God, and afflicted. But he was wounded for our transgressions, he was bruised for our iniquities; the chastisement of our peace was upon him, and with his stripes we are healed. All we like sheep have gone astray; we have turned every one to his own way, and the Lord hath laid on him the iniquity of us all." Jeremiah, too——

Here Mr. Fenton was interrupted. His man Frank entered booted, and all bespattered with dirt, and, having whispered something in his master's ear, Mr. Fenton turned aside his head to hide his concern from Harry, and stepping to his closet locked himself in.

CHAPTER V.

But it may now be thought full time to return to the head branch of this noble family.

Nearly nine years have now elapsed since the earl and his lady had seen or heard of their Harry, except by two or three anonymous notes in a year, giving a short account of his health and accomplishments; insomuch that time and long absence had, in a measure, worn him from the regrets of the family; excepting his brother Richard, on whom Harry's generosity, in taking his quarrel upon himself, had left an affecting and indelible impression.

Lord Clinton was indeed sweetly dispositioned by nature, and of an aspect and person extremely elegant; and, as he had tutors in all branches in which he chose to be instructed, he learned sufficient, by way of amusement, to render him one of the most accomplished youths in the nation. He was also naturally unassuming, and modestly disposed; but the unremitted adulation of domestics and dependants, with the complimentary artillery of all the neighbours and visitants, could not fail of some impression, at least so far as to make it evident that he was conscious of his condescension when he became familiar with you.

He was, however, easy to all who applied to him for any favour; exceeding charitable to the poor; and particularly fond of our Harry's foster-mother, and kind to her for Harry's sake.

He was turned of nineteen years of age when his parents,

for his amusement and the finishing of his education, resolved to accompany him on a tour to France.

They set out with a suitable equipage and a nominal tutor, whom they engaged, rather with a view of being a watch upon our young lord's motions, than the intendant of his principles or the former of his manners.

Nothing material happened till their arrival at Paris, where the earl took a sumptuous palace in the Rue de Vaugirard.

When he had settled his household, he went to inquire after his intimates of fifty years ago. Some three or four of them still survived. He renewed his acquaintance with them, and engaged them, their friends and families, to rich and frequent entertainments, whereby his palace speedily became the resort of one of the most elegant circles in Paris.

Young Clinton quickly entered into familiarity and confidence with such of the young nobility as frequented his father's; and they took him abroad on several parties of pleasure, and introduced him to the birds of their own distinguished feather.

Our young Englishman swam gracefully down the stream of pleasure; a warm imagination susceptible of the slightest impressions, a spirit apt to receive and impart the kindliest feelings, made him the idol of his home, and the desire of the brilliant society he moved in and adorned. But, alas for the stability of all earthly bliss! he was seized with the smallpox, which was then sweeping through Paris like a plague; and, though the eruption was but slight, yet on the seventh day Lord Clinton was suddenly taken with convulsions, and in less than an hour expired.

The old countess had never left his room since he had taken to his bed, and was now carried off in a deep swoon. She never after recovered her senses except by deplorable starts, to lament that she was the most wretched of all that ever was created, and on the second day she also expired.

The miserable earl, now an unit in creation, had their bodies embalmed and deposited in leaden coffins, ready for conveyance to his own vault in England, whither he now prepared to go.

At length he set out with his sighing and silent train; and after a voyage, lengthened by woe, arrived finally at Enfield.

Never was seen such a concourse at any funeral since the funeral of Jacob, on which all Egypt attended; they crowded from a distance of thirty miles round. But when they saw the old and reverend patron of the country all covered with sad and solemn weeds: when they beheld his countenance exceeding all pomp of sorrow, and conceived the weight and wringing that was then at his heart, envy was quite blunted and robbed of its sting. They now lamented the living more than they mourned the dead; and the poorest among the poor looked down with an eye of compassion upon the great man, now rendered, as they deemed, more pitiable and desolate even than themselves; without child or kindred; without any to continue his name or his honours; without any who could claim a share in his wealth or his woe; without any cause of further comfort, or further care upon earth.

During the following week the earl kept his chamber, and would admit of no visiter till Mr. Meekly arrived.

Mr. Meekly had long estranged himself to Enfield; he had gone elsewhere, seeking the houses of mourning, and breathing peace and consolation wherever he went; but, as soon as he heard of the affliction of his noble friend, he hastened to help him to bear up under the weight of his calamity. He entered and seated himself in silence beside the earl, he there wept near an hour without uttering a syllable.

My lord was the first who spoke—Mr. Meekly, said he,

my heart gratefully feels this melting proof of your love. You weep for me, my friend, because you see, and kindly feel, that there is no other comfort for me on this side the grave.

God forbid! God forbid! said Mr. Meekly; the best and greatest of all comforts is coming to you, my lord. Eternal truth has promised it, and he will make it good to you: "Blessed, blessed are they who mourn, for they shall be comforted."

Ah, Mr. Meekly! replied the earl, the comfort that you mention is promised only to the deeply contrite and broken of heart; to those who duly lament the baseness of their offences against so great and good a God. Neither do I despair, my friend, but that I also may finally share some portion of that same comfort; for, as I feelingly acknowledge myself the greatest of all sinners, so I wish for grace to make me the greatest of penitents.

God be praised, cried Meekly, for the grace already given! There was a time, my lord, when, as you told me, you had nothing of these divine dispositions; when the world, as you said, seemed to hold out happiness to you on either hand; when fortune, title, precedence, circling honours about you, and within you youth and health, and a revelling flow of blood and spirits, wholly disguised and concealed the state of your nature from you; when they hid from you your own body of frailty, distemper, sin, and death, and left you no occasion to call out for a Saviour, as you felt nothing from which you desired to be saved. But God has now been graciously pleased to send you his monitors, and to call upon you by affliction, that you, in your turn, may call upon him who alone can give you consolation.

It is not, my lord, to the mourners for sin alone to whom comfort is promised: the state of suffering and mourning is in its nature extremely salutary, and of happy tendency to man; and it is, therefore, that the suffering JESUS hath pronounced it blessed.

The God of all love takes no delight in the sufferings of his poor and pitiable creatures; neither would he have made this state of our mortality a vale of tears, and a state of misery, had it not been in order to conduct us through transitory evils to ever-enduring bliss, where "he himself will wipe all tears from our eyes."

When Adam, by his apostasy and falling off from his Maker, had converted all the goods of his temporary state into evil incitements to lust, covetousness, and sensuality, God determined, by a gracious reverse, to turn all the evils of corrupt and fallen nature into means of enduring good to his fallen and frail creatures: he therefore appointed pain, affliction, distress, and disease, to be his ministers, his monitors, and preachers within us, to convince us of all the evil of our depraved and mortal nature; to wean us from a world that is full of false promises, but empty of true enjoyment; to remind us that we are strangers and pilgrims upon earth; to turn our eye to the star that hath visited us from on high; and finally, through our sufferings, to accomplish the great work of his own salvation in us.

Thank you, thank you, Mr. Meekly! these are comforting things indeed. They pluck comfort from the very depth and abyss of affliction ; I love that my God should be lovely to my heart. You have now rent the dark veil that long hung before my eyes; and the Sun of righteousness breaks upon me through the clouds of my mortality.—But what of death, Mr. Meekly? what of death, my friend? I am interested in the question; my time is approaching. When this body shall fall to dust, and all these organs of sensation be utterly cut off, what remains—what then shall follow? by what means shall my spirit attain the powers of new perception? or am I to lie in the grave, in a state of total insensibility, till the last trumpet shall sound? My nature shrinks, I confess, from a total deprivation of the sense of existence.

It is no way evident to me, my lord, that body, or at least such gross bodies as we now have, are necessary to the perceptions and sensibilities of our spirit. God himself is a Spirit, an all-seeing, all-hearing, all-tasting, all-smelling, all-feeling, all-knowing, and all-governing Spirit. "He who made the eye, shall he not see? He who made the ear, shall he not hear?" Wherefore, as our spirits are the offsprings of his divine Spirit, we may justly presume them endowed with like capacities. But if body is necessary to the perception of spirit, as Zoroaster, the illuminated philosopher, seems to intimate, where, speaking of God, he says, "whose body is light, and whose soul is truth;" in this case, I say, we may reasonably suppose that, when our spirits shall be parted from these gross and frail bodies, they shall be instantly clothed upon with more pure and permanent bodies. Or, as I rather think that those pure and permanent bodies are already forming, and pregnant within our gross and corruptible bodies; and that when the midwife, death, shall deliver us from the dark womb of our woful travail and mortality, we shall immediately spring forth into incorruption and glory.

Of this, my lord, I am as confident as I am of my being, that he who by faith hath already put on Christ, shall break through death in the brightness of the body of his new birth, incorruptible, immortal, and blessed to all eternity.

Tell me, then, my dearest Meekly, what mean you by the body of this new birth? for, alas! I am but too apt to cry out with Nicodemus, "How can these things be?"

I mean, my lord, the forming of Christ within us: our being formed anew of a divine seed of our second Adam, even as our gross bodies were formed in the womb from a corruptible seed of the old Adam. I mean the clothing of our spirits with the heavenly substantiality of the spiritual body and blood of the heavenly Jesus himself; for, as the apostle says, "There is a spiritual body, as there is a carnal body." I mean a body the same as that in which the believing thief entered paradise with his Lord on the day of the crucifixion. "I am the resurrection and the life," saith Jesus: whoso believeth in me, though he were dead, yet shall he live; and he who liveth and believeth in me shall never die." Death shall become a new and divine birth unto him. And the great apostle says, "There are celestial bodies, and bodies terrestrial; but the glory of the celestial is one, and the glory of the terrestrial is another." And again he says, "For we know that if our earthly house of this tabernacle were dissolved, we have a building of God, an house not made with hands, eternal in the heavens."

These are great things indeed, Mr. Meekly, and full of hope, as well as incitements to divine ambition.

But why, my lord, should a new birth from Jesus Christ be thought wonderful? Is there any thing more wonderful in it than in the forming and unfolding of the whole stupendous mechanism of the body of our old man from a scarce visible speck of entity? Is there any thing more wonderful in it than in the growth and unfolding of any common vegetable from some latent principle or invisible speck in the seed, which not all the optics and glasses of a Galileo should be able to discover? Were not these the known facts of every day and hour, incredulity would have laughed the supposition to nought. But I think I have got about me something surprisingly analogous and apposite to the nature and manner of our new birth in Jesus.

Mr. Meekly then put his hand in his pocket and took out

a lump of matter, in form like a long and huge maggot, evidently without motion, apparently without life, and hard and incrusted all about to the feeling.

What have you got there, my friend? said the earl.—An old worm, my lord, that at this instant is pregnant with the birth of a new creature.—Impossible! cried the earl; the thing is absolutely dead!—The body of the old worm is dead, indeed, my lord; but there is certainly a principle of a new life within it, that will soon manifest itself in the birth of a very beautiful and wonderfully glorious creature. And this you will find if you leave it for a few days, where it may get the fostering warmth of the sun through one of your windows. Have you ever seen the fly they call the dragon-fly, my lord?—Yes; and have admired the elegance of its shape, the mechanism of its double wings, and the lustre of its irradiations.

This mass, my lord, of apparently insensible matter, is now actually pregnant with one of the same species. The parent, through whose death it is to attain life, was no other, as you see, than a vile and grovelling maggot; but the new creature that is to be born from it will be of a quite different nature and tendency. It will loathe the food and occupation of its foul progenitor; it will soar sublime over carnal and earthly things; it will drink the dews of heaven, and feed on the consummate nectar and fragrance of flowers.

This, indeed, Mr. Meekly, rejoined the earl, is to make the invisible things of God visible, even to the naked eye, by the things that are seen.

While my lord and his friend were thus deeply in discourse, Mr. John, the house-steward, came in and told his master that one waited in the hall with a letter for him.

A letter! cried the earl; what can I have to say, John, to any letter, or any of the writers thereof? But something is due to humanity, and it shall be paid; desire him to step in.

Hereupon a stranger entered, whose figure instantly caught the eyes and attention of the earl and his companion in an astonished captivity. The youth was dressed in a mourning frock; and his dark brown locks, tied behind with a black riband, flowed carelessly between his shoulders, while some of the front-straying curls, as in sport, alternately shaded and discovered a part of his lovely countenance. He bowed, he moved attraction; and, gracefully advancing towards my lord, he again bowed, laid a letter before him on the table, and then silently retired backwards a few steps.

They viewed him—they gazed on him—as it had been the sudden vision of an angel of light. Mr. Meekly was not able to utter a word; neither had my lord the power to lay a finger on the paper that was directed to him, till Mr. Meekly at last, giving a great stroke on the table, cried suddenly out—I would lay a thousand pounds of it!—it is he! —it is he!—my heart tells me he can be no other but your Harry Clinton!

Here Harry sprung forward, and, casting himself precipitately at the feet of the earl, he clasped his knees with an eager reverence, crying—My father, my honoured, my dear, my dear father! and broke into tears.

My lord, all in a tremor, attempted to raise him to his arms, and Harry, perceiving this, rose and threw himself into the bosom of his father. But the earl gently and fondly put him off a little, and gazing intently on a countenance that appeared to him lovely above all that was lovely in the circle of creation, he gathered new strength, and, catching Harry to his breast, he exclaimed in a transport— "Let me die!—let me die!—since I have seen thy face, my son."

Thus my lord, in the recent acquisition of such a son, forgot all his losses, and cast the whole weight of his late calamities behind him. His eye could not be tired with seeing him, neither his ear with hearing the sweetness of his voice; and he continued to hold, to gaze at him, to caress him, unmindful of aught else—unmindful even of his friend Meekly, who sat enraptured beside him.

Will you leave me again, my child? cried out the earl; do you intend to go from me again, my Harry? You must not—you shall not leave me—not for an hour—no, not for a minute, a second loss of my son would quickly bring my grey hairs with sorrow to the grave.—Never, never, my lord, will I leave you! tenderly cried Harry; never for a moment will I forsake you again, my father! I come purposely to watch over, to comfort, to tend you while I have life with all imaginable tenderness, affection and duty.

But where, hastily asked the earl—where is the murderer who stabbed my peace?—where is that old thief—that robber—who rent my child from me? Ah, my lord! cried Harry, he is very far from meriting such opprobrious epithets; he is a summary of all that is excellent—all that is amiable in nature. He respects and loves you too above the world, and all that is in it deserving of love. O, had you lately seen his grief for your losses—the floods of tears he shed—for—for—for—Here Harry could no more; but, on the recollection of his mother and brother, burst into tears.

But tell me, my dear, continued the earl—tell me who and what he is whom you commend so highly.

Even the son of your own mother, my lord; my much loved, my revered, my most honoured uncle.

Impossible, my child! That old despicable man, my brother! No, no, my Harry, he must have deceived you! My brother was all that was amiable upon earth—"the fairest among ten thousand"—the straightest cedar in the forest!

And such he is at this day, my lord. But, alas, alas! he has been broken by the batteries of many afflictions; a man wholly made up of sorrows, and acquainted with killing griefs! You wanted me not when he took me, my father; you had other and richer treasures—comforts that were infinitely more worthy your regard; but, little and despicable as I was, he had nothing but me. I became his only comfort—the only treasure in which he delighted. Yet, as soon as he heard that you wanted consolation, he chose rather to be without it himself, and so he restores me to you, if I may be any little matter of comfort to you, my father.

And where is this dear uncle—this precious brother—my Harry? Is he come with you? Shall I be so blessed to take him in with my eye—to take him in with my arms—to petition—to obtain his pardon—to press him to my bosom—to my heart—to my soul? Where is he—where is this precious brother—my Harry?

He is not come with me, my lord; he feared, as he said, that you would not forgive him the carrying off your Ganymede; but he is desirous of attending you on the first intimation.

Then you must write to him for that purpose to-morrow, my son; and despatch your invitation by some of our swiftest horses. The influence of his darling will, unquestionably, be greater than that of an offending and unnatural brother. Is this letter from him, Harry?—It is, my lord.—Then I will not peruse it till I get by myself. It probably contains reproaches but too well merited; or possibly matters of consolation too tender for me to bear. But, Mr. Meekly, my dearest Meekly, ten thousand pardons!—Harry, take to your arms the man in the world, next to your uncle, most deserving of your reverence—most deserving of your heart!

Here Mr. Meekly kissed and embraced our hero with

all the tenderness of a father, and the ardour of an old friend.

Mr. Meekly, cried Harry, looking earnestly and fondly at him, do I not remember something of that face, Mr. Meekly? Are you not the gentleman for whom I long since conceived such an attachment—to whom my heart cleaved, as I may say, from my infancy?

I am, my heavenly creature, answered Meekly; I am the man indeed whose soul was knit to yours, like the soul of Jonathan to David, the first moment I beheld you; and who saw in you then all those noble, generous, and divinely humane propensities that I see arrived to their maturity at this happy day.

While Mr. Meekly was thus rejoicing, Harry happened to turn his head aside, and, spying the lively portraits of my lady and Lord Richard, he started—he rose; and, gazing on them a minute, he went softly to the window, and, taking out his handkerchief, kept his back to the company, while he vented his emotions in a silent passion of tears. His father and Mr. Meekly perceived what he was about, but they did not disturb him. He brought fresh to their remembrance all the passages of late affliction, and they silently joined a flow of grief to his. But their tears were the tears of sympathizing humanity, or rather tears of delight on observing the sweet sensibilities of their darling.

In the mean time, Mr. Frank, who attended on Harry, had whisperingly given the mourning domestics an intimation concerning the person of the stranger who had arrived. Some of them well remembered him; and all of them had heard of him, and conceived a very kindly impression of our Harry. They first expressed their mutual joy by kisses, embraces, and silent shakes of the hand; but in a little space their congratulations became more loud and tumultuous, and the voice of exultation was heard through all the lower house.

Harry hereupon felt himself secretly hurt, and turning to his father his yet tearful countenance—My lord, says he, I beseech you to suppress this unseasonable sound of joy among your servants, in a house that ought so justly to be the house of morning. My love, mildly and kindly answered the earl, I cannot wholly refuse to my poor and afflicted people some share of that comfort which I myself feel on the return of my Harry. They are all my old and true servants, my child; this is no other than an expression of their love to you and to me; and I request you to receive them affectionately for my sake.

Here the earl rung a bell, and desired that all his domestics should come in.

They accordingly entered. Harry perfectly recollected Mr. John the steward, Mr. Samuel the butler, and old Mrs. Mary the cook. He called them by their names, and reminded them of old times, and took them in his arms with much affection. He then turned to the other servants. He took each of them by the hand in turns, and spoke to them with such a natural ease and lowliness, as though he himself desired, in his father's house, to become also "as one of his hired servants." Hereupon, gathering all about him, they catched and kissed his hand by force; and then, kneeling around, they promiscuously petitioned for blessings on his head; and rising, retired in a pleasing passion of sobs and tears; while the enraptured earl beheld all, with a mixture of such blissful sensations as he had never felt before.

It now began to grow late; and, after a short repast of some small matters, my lord proposed their retiring to bed. But, my friend, said he to Harry, you must content yourself with being my prisoner for the present; you must lie in my chamber; I will not trust my lamb from my side, for fear of its going once more astray.—Ah, my lord! cried Harry, there is no fear of that; my heart is wholly your property, and you have thereby a sure hold of all that I am.

The next morning Harry impatiently rose before the servants were stirring; and unlocking the great door, and closing it softly after him, he went out exulting on his premeditated expedition. He reconnoitered and recollected the quondam scenes of his childhood; and, flying like a bird over the hedges and other obstacles, he made the shortest way to his still precious mammy's.

When he approached the place of his infant endearments, he met his foster-father going forth to his field, with a solemn and melancholy air, on his usual occupations. Harry instantly remembered the features, once so delightful, and springing to him, and catching at him, he kissed and clasped him repeatedly, and cried aloud—My dear daddy Dobson! how glad am I to see you once again! How is my nurse, my dear nurse? how is little Tommy, and little Rachel, and all our dear family?

The old man then respectfully withdrawing a space—I don't know you, my sweet master, said he; I never saw you before.—Indeed, but you did; many and many a time and oft, cried Harry, you carried me in your arms, almost the livelong day, and pressed and hushed me to sleep at night in your bosom. Don't you remember your little Harry? don't you remember my two dogs? don't you remember my cock?

O! exclaimed the good old man, I now believe that you are my child, the dearest child that ever was born! But I never hoped to see him such a thing as you are; I never thought to see such a glorious creature upon earth!

Here old Dobson returned Harry's caresses with a twofold force, and, blubbering all aloud, had like to have smothered him with the intenseness of his embraces.

Bring me, bring me, cried Harry to the sight of my dearest nurse! I am all impatient to behold her.

Not so fast! said Gaffer Dobson—I love my old loving Kate; and should she find you out of a sudden, she would certainly die of joy. But I will bring you to her as a stranger, and so you may bring matters about. And indeed I fear that my own head is likely to be crazed by this business; for I do not find that I am the same man that I was a while agone. I shall grow too proud, I doubt, and look down upon all my better neighbours.

Goodman Dobson then conducted Harry to their ancient habitation. Nurse Dobson was just up, and preparing to comb the heads of her children, when they entered.

Kate, says he, I have brought to you a young stranger, who says he can give you some account of your little Harry; who says he is still alive, notwithstanding all your frights, and will shortly pay a visit to some parts of this country; and who knows then but that we, among others, may happen to set our eyes upon him, and that, I think, would be a great blessing, My Kate?

O no, no, no! exclaimed nurse, without deigning to cast her eyes on the stranger—he is dead, he is gone from me these many years! I once hoped to have his infant on my knee and in my bosom; but that hope is quite gone. Never, never shall I behold my darling again!

Harry had seated himself just opposite to nurse; when, looking up, she started, and stared eagerly in his face—Don't impose upon me, William, says she. Tell me, tell me at once; mayhap this is my child! Ah, against the world, the dimple in that smile is the dimple of my Harry!

Here Harry sprung up, and at one leap caught his rising nurse in his arms, crying—Nurse, my dearest nurse, do I live to be pressed once more to your dear bosom?

But the poor woman breathed short, and could not get out a word. Twenty times she put him from her, and catched him to her again, gazing at him by intervals with a frantic affection. At length she cast herself báck on the bench that was behind her, and, clapping her hands together, she gave a great shout, and burst into an hysterical passion of tears; while Harry seated himself beside her, and, gently drawing her head to him, placed it fondly on his bosom, and mixed his tears with hers.

This gush came very seasonably for our loving nurse's relief. She soon recovered her breath and her senses; and, seeing some drops on her Harry's cheeks, she drew them in with her lips, crying—Precious pearls be these! I would not exchange one of them for the brightest diamond in the mines.

Nurse, says Harry—I stole away to come and see you while my father was asleep, or else I should not have had leave to stir from him a foot. But you both must promise to come and dine with me; we will have a table by ourselves. And do you, my dear nurse, step to our house, and if my father should miss me, tell him I am gone into town, and will be back with him before breakfast.

Harry then stepped to the village, and, remembering Gaffer Truck's house, he went familiarly in, and inquired of the good woman how all the family was. Pray, how is my honest old Bartholomew? says he; and how is your pretty daughter, Molly? and, above all, what is become of my old friend Tom? The poor woman, all in amazement, cried—A pretty Tom he is, forsooth, to be friend to such a sweet young gentleman as you are. But the truth is, that our Tom is at prentice to a barber at next door.—Well, says Harry, when Gaffer Truck comes home, tell him that his old acquaintance, Harry Clinton, called to see him.

Tom had just finished an operation on a neighbour as our hero entered.—How are you, Tom? said he, carelessly. Tom gaped, and stared, and gaped; but answered not a word.— Will you give me a cast of your office, Tom?—Ah! that I will, master, as soon as you get a beard.—Why, Tom, you are grown a huge hulking fellow since I saw you last; will you step to yonder green, and wrestle one fall with me?— No, no, master, I would not hurt you; methinks I could throw a dozen of such fairweather gentlemen as you are, master.

Harry instantly seized Tom by the breast with one hand, and by the shoulder with the other; when Tom, feeling the hardness and hurt of his gripe, immediately exerted his powers, and grappled with his adversary. But Harry, giving him a slight foot, laid him on the broad of his back in the middle of his own floor; but kept him with both hands from being hurt against the ground.

I believe, said Tom, rising, you must certainly be the devil; and come, as they say, to fling poor sinners in the shape of an angel of light.—Ah, Tom, Tom! cried Harry, this is not the first struggle that you and I have had. Do you remember the bag of nuts, and poor blind Tommy? have you forgot your old friend, little Harry Clinton?

Blessed mercy! exclaimed Tom, can you be my young lord, my heart's dear young master?—I am, indeed, answered Harry, your old acquaintance, my dear Tom; your loving friend, Harry Clinton. And so saying, he took Tom about the neck, and kissed him very cordially.

Tom, says Harry, I want you to take a walk with me: Tom instantly assented, and out they went.

As they walked along, Harry began to grow sad.—Tom, said he, do you know where my dear brother Dicky was buried?—Yes, sir, said Tom, a great way off, in yonder churchyard below the town's-end.—Do you know where the sexton lives, Tom?—In a little white house, sir, just joining the yard.

As soon as they arrived, Tom called out the sexton, and Harry, putting a guinea into his hand, ordered him directly to unlock the family-vault.

The man looked astonished, but obeyed in silence; and Harry, as he entered, desired the sexton and Tom to wait at a distance, and promised to be with them by and by.

He put to the door after him, just leaving light enough to distinguish the recent deposits of the dead.

O! said he, as he advanced, thou truè house of mourning, thou silent end of all men, how sad art thou to sense! how sad to me above all, who bearest in thy dark bosom such precious and beloved relics!

Then casting himself on the coffins of my lady and Lord Richard, as they lay side by side, and clasping his arms about them as far as he could reach: O, he cried, my mother, my brother! my dearest brother, my dearest mother! you are gone, you are gone from me, and you never knew the love that your son and brother had for you! Ah, how did I flatter myself! what happiness did I not propose, in attending, serving, and pleasing you; in doing thousands of tender, kindly, and endearing offices about you! But you are snatched from me, my mother! you are snatched from me, my brother! all my prospects are defeated and cut away for ever. You will no more return to me, but I shall go to you; and O that I were laid with you this minute in this still and peaceful mansion, where hopes and fears cease, and all are humble together!

Meanwhile Mr. Meekly had gone abroad on his morning's walk. He met nurse on her way to the mansion-house, and accosting her in a kind of triumph—My good nurse, says he, we have blessed tidings for you; your Harry, your hero, is come to the country.—I know it, sir, I know it, answered nurse; it is but a little while ago that my babe left my bosom.

Mr. Meekly then proceeded in order to join his young friend, inquiring of all he met which way Lord Harry went, till at last he was directed to the churchyard. There he found Tom and the sexton, who, on further question, silently pointed to the door of the family vault that hung on the jar.

Mr. Meekly felt himself affected, and withdrew to a greater distance, but still keeping his tearful eye on the sad mansion that now held the living with the dead.

At length Harry came forth, drying his cheeks with his handkerchief. He assumed a constrained air of cheerfulness; and, joining Tom and the sexton, observed that a great crowd was gathering in the town.

Who are those, Tom? said he.—I suppose, answered Tom, your honour's tenants and old acquaintances, who are getting together to welcome you to the country.—If that is the case, Tom, we must go and salute them, and you shall introduce me, and tell me who is who; for, though my heart is heavy laden, it must not give a discharge in full to gratitude and humanity.

Mr. Meekly, perceiving that Harry was on his return, kept onward, aloof from him, but with an eye on his motions.

By this time the crowd had sorted themselves; the principals of the families into one group, the young men into another, and the fair maidens into another; and, as Harry approached, they all set up a joint shout of triumph.

Please your honour, says Tom, this is my father, and this is Gaffer Gubbins, and this Goodman Demster, and this Farmer Felster, and so on.

Harry, with the lowliness of a washer of feet, would have kissed and embraced them all in turns; but, pressing about him, they seized a hand on either side, and eagerly kissed them, as also the skirts of his clothes all round.

God bless your sweet face! cried Goodman Demster; who sees it in a morning can't fail, I think, of prospering the livelong day.

VOL. II.—11

When he came, in succession, to the companions of his infancy, as he kissed and shook hands with each in turn, some reminded him of his having beat them at boxing, others at wrestling, and all of his having played with them at prison-bars, leap-frog, shout the gate, and so forth.

Meanwhile the girls panted, gazed at him, and longed to get him to themselves.—Sir, says Tom, here is your old acquaintance, my sister, Molly; there is not a lad in the town whom she is not able to toss, except your honour. Molly looked full of health as Hebe, and rosy as the May, and Harry caught her about the neck, and kissed her very cordially.—Do you remember me, Molly?—O, answered Molly, I shall never forget, since your honour's lordship and I used to wrestle every day behind our house.

The rest of the girls now pressed for their share of Harry, and it was with difficulty that he divided himself with any satisfactory equality among them, as they all kissed him so close, and seemed so loth to part.

At length Harry's watch reminded him that it was time to attend his father, and as he parted they shouted after him— Long life, and health, and honours to our townsman, our own boy, our own dear, sweet child!

In the meantime Mr. Meekly had returned home, with his heart full of tidings to the earl. When Harry arrived, breakfast was on table, and he perceived that his father had been in tears; but no notice was taken of the affair at the charnel-house on either part.

When breakfast was over, Harry called in John.—Mr. John, says he, can you tell me how many families there are in this village of yours?—Twenty-five families exactly, my lord. Then Harry turned to his father and said—If your lordship will be pleased to lend me five hundred guineas for the present, I will pay you very honestly the hour that my uncle comes to the country.—Why, sirrah! cried the earl pleasantly, what right has your uncle to pay your debts, especially to such a great amount as you speak of?—O, my lord! answered Harry, I have already squandered away about fifty thousand pounds of his money; and this is but a trifle, which I am sure I may very safely add to the rest.

Here the earl looked truly astonished.—Fifty thousand pounds! he exclaimed. Impossible, Harry! Why, you had neither such ponds nor lakes as mine in London, wherein you might make ducks and drakes of them. How in the world could you contrive it? Where did you dispose of them?

In hospitals and in prisons, my father, answered Harry. In streets and highways, among the wretched and indigent, supplying eyes to the blind, and limbs to the lame, and cheerfulness to the sorrowful and broken of heart; and such were my uncle's orders.

Let me go, let me go from this place, my lord! cried Meekly; this boy will absolutely kill me if I stay any longer. He overpowers, he suffocates me with the weight of his sentiments.

Well, Harry, said the earl, go to my desk; here is the key of the drawer on the left hand, and I make you a present of the key and the contents; perhaps you may find there nearly as much as will answer your present exigencies.

Harry went, and, opening the drawer, was astonished to see it quite full of gold. However he took no more than just the sum proposed; and, returning to his father, said—What shall I do, my lord, with that vast heap of money?—Why, you extravagant rogue, replied the earl, there is not as much in it as will pay the debt you have contracted with one man! —O, cried Harry, I am quite easy upon that score! I will never affront my uncle by the offer of a penny. And don't you think, said the earl, that we have got poor among us in the country as well as you have in the city, Harry?—I believe you may have got some, my lord; but then I am much more difficult than you may think, in the objects on whom I would choose to confer charity. I look upon the money amassed by the wealthy, to have been already extracted from the earnings of the poor; the poor farmer, the poor craftsman, the hard-handed peasant, and the day-labourer, whose seven children perhaps subsist on the milk of a couple of cows. Wherefore, the objects on whom we bestow these gatherings ought at least to be something poorer, and more worthy of compassion than those from whom the money was exacted. So saying, he stepped out.

Amazing boy! cried Mr. Meekly; how new, and yet how just was that observation!—I am, cried the earl, as it were, in a kind of delicious dream, and can scarce yet believe myself so blessed as to be the father of such a child!

In the mean time Harry had called John aside.—Mr. John, says he, here are five hundred guineas. Be pleased to step and distribute them by twenty guineas to each of the families in the village. I would save you the trouble, and give them myself, but that for the present my heart turns with disgust from their thanks and their honours. Tell them, that this is a token in memory of my dear brother, to keep them in mind of him. Tell them further, that I will have no carousals, no rejoicing, on account of my arrival; and that it would please me infinitely better, if my return would bring their late losses to their remembrance, and set them all in tears and lamentations.

My lord now proposed a saunter in the park, in order to procure an appetite for dinner. Accordingly the gate was ordered to be unlocked, and they entered on a gravel walk, that was walled in on the left hand, and paled in on the right, along the verge of five canals, that fell successively in cascades, the one into the other.

As they talked and walked along, they met with a six-barred gate that directly thwarted their passage; and my lord reached his hand through the rails for the key, that the keeper had left in the lock on the inside, but he could not get at it. We are all at a full stop now, said he, unless Harry could make a shift to climb over the gate; but no, do not, my dear; your foot might happen to slip between the rails, and hurt you.—I will obey your lordship, answered Harry; I will not venture a foot upon one of them. So saying, he catched at the upmost bar with his left hand, and throwing himself slightly over, opened the gate for his companions. The earl and Mr. Meekly stood mute in utter astonishment. At length the earl cried—Child, you must surely be of more than mortal mould, or else you have a familiar spirit that conveys you through the air. Harry smiled, but was silent.

On their return, John called his master aside, and told him of his due distribution of Harry's bounty to the villagers.—But, my lord, says he, when I went down I found them all very busily employed in preparing bonfires and illuminations in honour of my young lord. This, however, I was obliged to countermand by his special order; and it has greatly mortified all your poor people.—Well, well, said the earl, it cannot be helped for the present; we must not dare to offend our Harry at any rate; and so those matters of rejoicing may rest in reserve till the arrival of my brother.

Soon afterwards our hero's fosterers came, decked out in their best attire; and Harry ordered a side-table to be covered for him and them, but my lord insisted on their dining all together.

Harry placed himself very lovingly between them at table, that he might help them, and prevail upon their bashfulness to eat.

When the repast was nearly over, nurse inquired after the little beggar-boy, whose absence she imagined had caused the elopement of her darling. He is come to great fortune, answered Harry; he has found his father and mother, and is heir to a large estate. Harry then told the manner in which Ned had been discovered, and they were all highly pleased and affected by the relation.

But, says Harry, what has become of my sister Nelly, on whose milk I was suckled? and what has become of my little brother Tommy, who was but two years younger than myself?—They are both dead, my precious; but God has been pleased to give me others in their room.—Well, nurse, I find we must all die, and, some time or other, that will be a great grief to one of us, whichever of us shall happen to outlive the other.—I am satisfied to die once, said nurse, but never let me hear again of your dying, my angel: I can't suffer the thought, she cried, and burst forth into tears—I could not bear, I could not bear to die a thousand deaths in the death of my Harry!

But, said Harry, in order to divert her passion, you have not yet inquired after the man with the beard.—O the old rogue! exclaimed nurse, I can't think of him with patience. —Ay, but you must know that that same old rogue is my own darling uncle, an own and only dear brother to my own dear father here.—If that is the case, said nurse, I don't wonder he should so greatly yearn after you; and indeed I would rather wonder if all the world did not yearn and long after you, my love!

And now, nurse, to show you how much you are obliged to this same darling uncle, he has ordered me to make you a present of five hundred pounds, in payment, as he says, of the grief he has cost you. And take no heed for your children, I will take that care upon myself; for this same dear uncle has made me a gift of the lands, and house, and plate, and furniture, that he has in this town, and so you see I am well able to provide for you all.

Here my lord cast an eye of tender jealousy upon Harry.

I perceive, my son, said he, that your uncle is your only trust, the only dependence that you choose to have upon earth.—Harry, with a glance of his eye, instantly caught the meaning of the eye of his father, and throwing himself at his feet—O pardon, my lord, he cried;. pray, pardon the overflowings of a grateful and simple heart! My uncle is my property; but I am yours, my father, to be disposed of in life and in death, at your pleasure. I do trust, I do depend upon you, my father; and you have already overpowered me with the weight of your affections.

My lord's eyes then glistened, and raising his son, and taking him fondly to his bosom—I believe I have been wrong, my love, said he, and hereafter I shall always think so, rather than think any thing amiss in my Harry. But tell me, my dear, and tell me sincerely; you speak of your uncle as one of the richest and greatest men upon earth—as a prince —as an emperor—enabled to give away fortunes and provinces at pleasure.

And he is, my lord, cried Harry—he is greater than any prince or emperor upon earth. To speak only of his temporal wealth or power—the most inconsiderable part of his value—he can do, as I may say, what he pleases in England. The ministry are at his beck—they profess themselves his servants; and even his majesty acknowledges himself deeply his debtor, and owes him, I daresay, half a million.

And yet this is the man, exclaimed the earl (turning an eye of penitence on Mr. Meekly)—this is the man, as I told you, my friend, on whom I looked down with such provoking contempt—whom I treated with such unpardonable insolence and ignominy!

My lord then inquired concerning the personal adventures of our hero in London, the account of which would have been more entertaining, had not Harry suppressed throughout his narration whatever he apprehended might tend to his own honour.

As soon as the fosterers had taken their leave, my lord proposed to his remaining guests a walk in the gardens, and after a few turns they sat down in a rural arbour, that was interwoven all about with jessamine and honeysuckle.

• Mr. Meekly, said the earl, I have often longed to hear the particulars of your life; and how you come to live by faith, and not by sight, and to hold your conversation in heaven, as you do at this day.

I can soon obey your lordship, answered Meekly; for my story is very short and very simple, and no way adorned with uncommon incidents.

My mother died a few hours after I was born. My father did not survive her two years; and I fell to the care of my only kinsman—an uncle by my father's side.

My uncle was an old bachelor, and though he was of a cold temper and had no tenderness for any one, he yet spared no cost in my education. He sent me to Eton school, and from thence to Cambridge, where I remained till I took my degrees. I then went to London, bought a sword and sword-knot, and commenced fine gentleman.

Though my head had been duly stored by my tutors in the rudiments of our religion, my heart had not yet felt any of its precepts, and I conceived that to go regularly to church, receive the sacrament, confess myself a miserable sinner, and avoid gross vices, was the sum of Christianity. I therefore entered without scruple into all the fashionable pleasures and vanities of the age; and I held that to pardon an affront would have been one of the deadly sins in a gentleman Christian.

One day, at St. James's coffee-house, Colonel Standard and another gentleman engaged at backgammon for five hundred guineas; and as the stake was so considerable, and both parties celebrated for their skill in the game, we all crowded about them to see the issue.

I happened to be next behind the colonel's chair, and others pressed behind me, eagerly bending and looking over my shoulders. At length he began to fret as the game was drawing to a close, and going against him. Pray, gentlemen, he would cry, don't bear upon me so; for heaven's sake keep off—you will make me lose the game! Hereupon, I did my utmost to bear back from him, but the company pressed me forward in spite of all I could do; till the colonel, giving an unhappily decisive cast, turned about in fury, and spat directly in my face.

Indignation gave me sudden and unusual strength, and casting all off who had borne upon me, I instantly drew my sword, and ran the colonel through the body. The company cried out that all was fair, and opening a window for me, they urged me to escape. Accordingly I got off, rode post to Dover, and there embarked for France.

The colonel, God be praised! did not die of his wound. He lay under the hands of the surgeons for above seven months, then recovered, and went to join his regiment in Flanders.

Of this my uncle sent me advice, telling me at the same time that I might return with safety. Yes, thought I, with safety to my life, but with death to my honour! I have taken revenge, indeed, but not satisfaction; the colonel must be compelled to make me personal reparation for the affront which he dared put upon me. His recovery has again dashed the spittle into my face; and I will pursue him through the world till it is wiped from the observation and remembrance of all men.

With this deadly determination I went post from Paris to Flanders, and traced the colonel from place to place, till I found him in a village on the road to Amsterdam.

I believe, sir, said I bluntly, you may not remember me, for our acquaintance was sudden, and of very short duration. I am the man in whose face you spit publicly at St. James's coffee-house.—Then, sir, said he, I am scarce yet recovered of the cause which you gave me to bear you always in mind; but, pray, what may your commands be with me for the present?—I am come to demand a remedy at your hands for the wound which you gave my honour, and which otherwise must remain for ever incurable.—Ah! he cried, no man ever exacted so severe a satisfaction as you have already taken; what, then, may be the nature of the further reparation that you are pleased to require?—Either to ask my pardon, or fight me within this hour.

That is very hard upon me, indeed, replied the colonel; the honour of my commission will not allow me to beg pardon of any man, at least in order to avoid a combat; so, sir, if you insist upon it, I must obey your summons, though very reluctantly, I confess.—Then, sir, said I, meet me in half an hour, with your pistols and sword, behind yonder little hill.

The colonel was punctual to the appointment. We both grasped a pistol at the distance of twenty paces, and advancing step by step, cried—Fire! Fire! Each seemed determined to make sure of his adversary, till, coming within arm's length, I fired directly in his face, but the ball passed through his hat, and only grazed the skin of his left temple.

The colonel then took his pistol into his left hand, and reaching out his right to me, with a smile of great complacence—I think, sir, said he, I may now ask your pardon with honour; and to convince you that I did not come to engage you in malice, be pleased to examine my arms, you will not find so much as a grain of powder in the one or the other.

Ah, colonel! I then exclaimed, I acknowledge you my conqueror both in honour and humanity. Had I been so unhappy as to kill you, and find your arms unloaded, I should certainly have done you justice by shooting myself through the head. But why did I pursue you from kingdom to kingdom? why was I unappeased by all the blood that I shed? Was it from any malignity of heart towards you? by no means. But while I lamented the misery I had already occasioned you, I was impelled to finish your destruction by a barbarian world, or rather, by the bloody prescribers of custom, whose censure I dreaded worse than death, or even futurity. Courage, colonel, incites soldiers to fight for their country; but it is cowardice alone that drives duellists together.

For three affectionate days I remained with my late enemy, but now warm friend. He then was obliged to return to quarters; and we parted with a regret much exceeding the hostility with which we had met.

On the departure of the colonel I went to Amsterdam, from whence I drew upon my uncle to the amount of £700. For I resolved, before my return, to take a tour through the seven provinces, though I had gone for a very different purpose.

During nine months I resided, or journeyed from place to place, among that people. Holland is, unquestionably, the wealthiest, the busiest, and most populous state upon earth. Not a hand is unemployed, not a foot of ground unoccupied; and, for a long time, I ascribed their extraordinary prosperity to an industry and ingenuity peculiar to them alone. But, on further observation, I discovered the true source as well of their industry as their opulence, and am persuaded that any nation bordering on the ocean might derive the like prosperity from the same spring.

Not, my lord, that I think opulence a real benefit to a

people, for "man's life consisteth not in the abundance of his possessions." But I look upon industry, the natural parent of opulence, to be as well a blessing as a duty to man, from the time that he was appointed to "earn his bread by the sweat of his brow." Many mental virtues, also, as well as temporal benefits, follow in the train of industry; it makes men healthful, brave, honest, social, and pacific. He who labours hard to acquire a property, will struggle hard to preserve it, and exercise will make him active, robust, and able for the purpose. As the man of industry hath, in himself, a living fund of competence for his own occasions, he will be the less tempted to plunder or prey upon others; and the poignant sense and apprehension of being deprived of a property so justly acquired, will give him the nicer and stronger sense of such an injury to others. Industry further incites to commerce and good neighbourhood, in order to dispose of mutual redundancies for the supply of mutual wants. And, lastly, it delighteth in peace, that its time and its labours may not be interrupted, nor the fruits thereof endangered, by rapine and invasion; and all this may be said of nations as well as of men.

Your observations, said the earl, are perfectly just; the works of industry are, unquestionably, the works of peace, and tend to open the avenues wherein the virtues may walk. But how to incite men or nations to industry, that is the question. The finer arts, we see, may be encouraged and promoted by national bounties, as now in France; but there is no inciting the bulk of the people to industry in like manner; that would be, as though the public should grant a bounty to itself. Nations certainly differ from nations as man differs from man; some are by nature industrious and ingenious, such as China and Holland—it is their propensity, their talent; while others, like Ireland, are naturally lazy and listless, and therefore remain in well-merited indigence.

You have greatly mistaken this point indeed, my lord. China and Holland are industrious and ingenious, because, whether it were through good hap or good policy, they hit upon the only method whereby industry and ingenuity could be duly promoted. Whereas Great Britain and Ireland are totally ignorant of the said method to this day, though both of them highly capable of having it put in execution.

You surprise me, Mr. Meekly, said the earl; a method to make men ingenious—a method to make them industrious! how can that be?

Experience has proved it to be even so, my lord; for where a method may be found for encouraging and promoting ingenuity and industry, that method will, infallibly, make people become both ingenious and industrious. No man will work, my lord, without some hire, or wages, or return for his labour; neither will any who are in want refuse to work, when assured of a due reward for so doing.

When the good householder walked out to the market-place, and found labourers loitering there when it was now toward evening, he asked them, "Why stand ye here all the day idle?" And when they answered, "Because no man hath hired or given us employment," he took this for a sufficient apology; he had compassion upon them, and he supplied them with the divinest of all kinds of charity, the means of earning their own bread.

Now, throughout China and Holland, no person is in want, because all are hired, all employed, the young and the old, the lame and the blind; and all find a ready sale, without anxiety or loss of time, without travel or delay, for products of their industry. Throughout Great Britain, on the contrary, nineteen in twenty are in real want; and in Ireland, as I am told, forty-nine in fifty are nearly in a state of beggary, merely for want of being employed—for want of encouragement to labour.

Permit me, then, to explain to your lordship, how some men and some nations came to be encouraged to industry, and others to be discouraged or in a manner prohibited from it.

Different men are endowed with different talents and powers, insufficient in many respects, though superfluous in others, to their own occasions. Different countries are also endowed with different productions, superfluous in many respects to the natives, though necessary or desirable for the well-being of foreigners.

Now, these alternate qualities of deficience and abundance, at once invite and impel all men, and all countries, to claim, and to impart that reciprocal assistance which is denominated commerce. Each gives what he can spare, each receives what he wants; the exchange is to the mutual advantage of all parties. And, could a method be found out for encouraging manufacturers to persevere in their industry, and improve in their arts, by a ready conveyance and sale of all their redundancies, neither want nor superfluity could find place upon earth.

All this is quite clear and self-evident, Mr. Meekly; but how to procure this ready sale is the question.

Your lordship must allow that the way to procure it would be to bring barterers and commuters, buyers and sellers, all who mutually want and mutually abound, together. For this is the end and purpose of every market upon earth.

Now, in Great Britain and Ireland, and in all continents or inland countries, the several deserts, mountains, marshes, and other obstacles, with the difficulty, danger, and toil of travel, and the great expense of land carriage, have utterly precluded all commerce and communication to any considerable extent. Insomuch that it would be easier and cheaper to convey a commodity of any burden to either of the Indies, than from many parts of Great Britain and Ireland to others, by land.

While God appears to separate the several nations of the earth from each other, by the intervention of seas, lakes, and rivers, he hath actually and intimately united them thereby.

Water serves to the art and navigation of man, as air serves to the wings of the feathered species. It is the easy and speedy medium, the ready conduit and conveyance, whereby all redundancies are carried, and all wants supplied. It makes man, as it were, a denizen of every country on the globe. It shortens every distance, and ties the remotest regions together. It carries and communicates the knowledge, the virtues, manufactures, and arts of each climate to all. It gives new springs and motives to industry, action, and invention. It gives a general importance to the meanest manufacturer. It gives to each man an interest in whatever is done upon earth, the productions of every region, and the tribute of every nation.

Now, China and Holland are the only countries upon earth who have considerably availed themselves of this capital benefit of water carriage, or water commerce; and therefore they are, incomparably, the most populous and most prosperous of all countries in the world.

China, as your lordship knows, extends from under the Tropic of Cancer to about thirteen hundred miles north, and thereby contains within itself all the variety of climate, and degrees of heat and cold, that are requisite for the sundry productions upon earth. Inspired by some forecast or sagacity, not imparted to the rest of mankind, they cut and quartered this vast continent by as many navigable canals as answer to the ducts and veins in the human body for the dispensation of life and nourishment. These canals serve as links or chords to the grand community of the Chinese; they bind region to region, house to house, and man to man, and hold the whole as one system or family together. This great kingdom is thereby become as one city, and the canals as so many streets, through which plenty is diffused by commerce to every part.. If any art or useful invention commences or receives improvement in any place, it is immediately conveyed to every place for imitation and promotion. No portion of this wide continent lies waste or uncultivated, because the canals are as so many markets brought to every man's door, and by the perpetual demand of whatever is saleable, incite the natives to exert themselves in providing all the redundancies they possibly can, that they may derive wealth to themselves by supplying the respective wants of others. Thus, throughout the expanded dominion of China, nothing is wasted, nothing lost, nothing superfluous, nothing wanting. All are employed, active, industrious, ingenious, and thriving. Their canals are intimately to them what seas are diffusely to the rest of the globe. They are thereby become as a world within themselves, sufficient to their own happiness and occasions. They never change their manners or policy. They never enterprise war against others. And China is affirmed at this day to contain one hundred and twenty millions of prospering inhabitants.

The Dutch also, about a hundred and forty years ago, followed the example of the Chinese. Their country is now become as one great and extended metropolis to the universe; and through their canals, as through paved and spacious high-ways, the world resorts with all its wealth. So encouraged and so incited, neither the lame, nor the blind nor the maimed, sit unemployed. Every child is taught its trade from the moment it can apply its little hands to a regular motion, and they bring to the parents vast sums, in lieu of an infinite variety of toys and trifles that are dispersed among the idle of the other children of men. For, barterers and commuters, buyers and sellers, manufacturers and merchants, like Pyramus and Thisbe, want nothing but the removal of envious obstacles to meet and to multiply a similar progeny.

From what has been premised, my lord, it is most evident that industry is the parent of the wealth of this world. That no man's industry is sufficient to his own occasions. That the mutual assistance denominated commerce is, therefore, necessary to the well-being of all people. That the reciprocal advantage of this commerce consists in supplying mutual wants with mutual redundancies. That this commerce, however, cannot be carried on without a medium for the conveyance of such supplies. That such a medium by land, even where it is practicable, is tedious, toilsome, expensive, extremely discouraging, and cannot be pushed to any considerable extent or effect. That God, however, hath opened for the purpose an easy, speedy, and universal medium of seas, lakes, and rivers, part of which he hath left unnavigable, that man might finish by art what nature had prepared, and contribute in some degree to his own advantages. That, accordingly, China and Holland (and France of late) have pursued the path so divinely appointed, and that power, wealth, and prosperity have flowed in upon them, in proportion as they have opened the medium of water-carriage for their reception. And that causes which have produced their concomitant effects, without variation, from the earliest ages to the present period, must be presumed to produce the like effects through all countries and ages to the end of time.

I protest, Mr. Meekly, exclaimed the earl, you have pushed this matter into mathematical demonstration. What a happy —what a glorious prospect now opens to my view! How easily, how speedily, how profitably, might this method be put in execution throughout the earth! There is no deficiency of rivers or collateral streams for the purpose. The sinking into the earth would give vent to new springs, and extract plenty of water in all places for an inland navigation; and half the number of hands that perish through war and want, might be peacefully and plentifully employed in accomplishing this weal of mankind. Famine and depredation would then cease. Nation would no longer rise up against nation, nor man against man. The earth, by culture, would soon become capable of sustaining tenfold the number of its present inhabitants. We should no more be tempted to push each other from existence. We should find ourselves mutually interested in preserving and multiplying the lives of all from whose labours we were to derive such advantages. All would be plenty, all peace and benevolence throughout the globe. The number of inhabitants, instead of being a burden, would then become the riches of every climate. All hands would be set to work, when thus assured of a purchaser for every effect of labour. The buzz of wheels, reels, and looms; the sound of hammers, files, and forges; with the shouts of vintage and the songs of harvest, would be heard in all lands! I am quite astonished that a work, so full of benefit and blessing to the universe of man, is not already commenced, advanced, and completed.

How comes this to pass, Mr. Meekly? have you yet mentioned this matter to any of our great ones?

I have, my lord, to several. They confessed themselves convinced of the utility of the scheme; and, could each of them be assured of engrossing to himself the most considerable part of the profits that would thereby accrue to the public, the work would instantly be begun, and would shortly be perfected. For, such is the nature of unregenerate man, that he grudges to others any portion of those goods which he so eagerly craves and grapples after for himself. He would hedge in the air, and make a property of the light. In proportion as he sees his neighbours in comparative want, he exults in the accumulation of imaginary wealth. But should he deem them, in a measure, more prosperous than himself, he sighs at his inmost soul, and grows wretched and repining.

I protest, cried the earl, were I young, I would to-morrow morning, at my own cost, set about this great work of national, or rather of universal, beneficence. But my Harry here has youth enough, with an abundance of benevolence also for the purpose; and I recommend it to him as the greatest of charities, a charity to Great Britain, a charity to mankind.—What would you think, my lord, said Harry, of my expending your whole drawer of gold upon this business? Great as it is, it would be but a small matter towards the value of purchasing peace upon earth, and the sons of peace upon earth will be likeliest to be the sons of love in heaven. So that we cannot lay out our money to better advantage in any purchase for the benefit of the brothers of our own frailty.

Alas, my love! rejoined Mr. Meekly, though you were master of half the wealth of the people of England, and were willing to employ the whole for their emolument in this way, the people themselves would oppose you in every step you should take. Some would be too proud to accept a benefit from you. Others would tell you that no man should dare to violate their property with either spade or pickaxe; and others would indict you even for treading on their grounds. Nothing less than the act of the whole legislature, to whom the people have committed their confluent powers, can avail for an undertaking of such national import.

Then, my dear Mr. Meekly, be pleased to let me have in writing what you have already set forth on this head; and if I live to come to the lower house of parliament, I will bend all my powers to this capital charity. And, if no other oratory will avail for the purpose, I will bribe the members with a hundred thousand pounds, and corrupt them, if possible, into one act of patriotism.* But, Mr. Meekly, I interrupt you. Pray, proceed in your narrative.

On my return to Amsterdam, I grew affected one evening in a manner I had never before experienced. I did not feel myself any way sick or in pain, and yet I wished to exchange my sensations for any other species of malady. I was wholly pervaded by a gloomy despondence. I looked abroad for comfort, but it was nowhere to be found; every object gave disgust to my discontented imagination. I secretly inquired of my soul, if riches, honours, dignities, if the empire of the world would restore her to joy? but she turned from them, and said—All these things are strangers and aliens to my peace. Alas! said I, tell me then where your peace may be found?—I know not, she replied; but I feel that I am wretched.

For three days I continued under this oppression of spirit; and on the third night an increasing horror of deep and heavy darkness fell upon me. All hope died within me, and misery seemed to open a gulf of ever deepening destruction in my soul. I lay all night bathed in drops of unutterable anguish. I wished and struggled to arise and change my situation; but I felt that my mind was its own place, and its own hell, from whence there was no removal, no possible escape.

* It is observable that, within ten years subsequent to the period of the above promise, the inland navigation of England commenced. Since which time, the river Isis has been made navigable from Oxford to Cricklade in Wiltshire, and to Abington in Berkshire. The river Avon in Warwickshire, from Stratford to the Severn. The Avon from Bath to Bristol. The Medway, from Maidstone in Kent to Tunbridge. The Lug in Herefordshire, to the Wey. The Lea, from Ware to the Thames. The river Kennet in Berkshire, to the Thames at Reading, containing twenty locks in seventeen miles. The river Are in Yorkshire, containing sixteen locks, whose tolls are now valued at about £10,000 yearly. Beside the Stroud, the Nen, and the Wey, with many others now in hand.

I now concluded that, somehow, I must have sinned beyond the measure of all sinners, since my damnation was deeper than that of any other. I therefore turned towards God and wished to repent; but, as I did not feel conviction for the sins of which I accused myself, no place for repentance was found in my soul.

Tremendous author! I cried, I find that thou canst sink and slay at pleasure; but canst thou not also raise up and make alive? If all things have their existence in thee, O God, is it not near and easy unto thee to impart to us some sensation of thine own existence also? some sensation of thine own peace, the sense that it is thou alone who canst be our sustainer? Save me, Jesus, save me from the hell of mine own nature! Save me, thou Son of David! O save me from myself!

While I thus prayed in an agony, my whole frame was suddenly overpowered, and sunk, as I suppose, into a state of insensibility, till the following day was far advanced. At length I perceived that I still existed.

I dreamed that I found myself in a deep and noisome dungeon, without a single ray that might even suffice to shew me the horrors of my situation. I attempted to rise and grope about, but perceived that I was tied and fastened down to earth by a number and variety of bands and fetters.

At length a sudden light appeared, and diffused itself throughout the darkness of my mansion; when, looking up, I observed that the keeper of my prison had entered, the doors being yet locked. His head, as I thought, was bound about with a tiara, from whence the glory arose that shone around me. In the coronet, instead of gems, were inserted a number of thorns, whose points streamed with incessant and insufferable brightness; and on the golden circlet was engraved in all languages, Jesus of Nazareth, King of the Jews.

Immediately my shackles loosened and fell away of themselves, and I wished to cast my whole existence under the feet of my Lord, but was so overcome with ecstasy that I could not rise; when, looking upon me with a smile of ineffable graciousness, he approached and took me by the hand, and at the contact I sprung up a great height in my bed, and awoke to sensations of indescribable blessedness.

You are come, then, my Lord, my salvation! you are come, my Master! I cried; and I will cling inseparably to you. Never, O never more will I suffer you to depart! Ah; I have felt, severely felt, what it is to be without you! for in your absence, though but for a moment, lies the essence of hell and misery; but in your presence, my beloved, in your presence is peace unspeakable, and joy for evermore!

From that day my nature became, as it were, wholly inverted. All the honours and worldly respects for which I formerly risked my life, were now my aversion; and I turned from carnal indulgence and sensuality with loathing.

Nothing could now affront, nothing could now offend me. As I totally despised myself, so I wished, after the process of my divine Master, to be despised and rejected of men. This made all others, the very meanest of human creatures, respectable unto me. Even in reprobates methought I discerned some unerased traces of the image and superscription of my God, and I bowed down before it.

If any attempted to injure or defraud me of my property, I yielded it without variance, and thereby I found myself cordially enriched.

I grew weary of my own will and of my own liberty, and I earnestly prayed my Lord that he would rid me of them, and be instead thereof a controlling principle within me, ever influencing and directing me according to his own pleasure.—Turn me, Jesus, Master! O turn me! I cried, from all the evil propensities of my own evil nature; though thou shouldst turn me, as thou didst Sennacherib, with thy ruling rein on my neck, thy bridle in my mouth, and thy hook in my nose! Take my heart and affections captive, and into thine own divine guidance! Compel me into all the ways and all the works of thy commandments, till thy yoke shall become easy, and thy burden light and delightsome; till I shall move, as down a descent, wherever thy goodness would guide me; till I shall feelingly find and know that all thy ways are ways of pleasantness, and all thy paths the paths of peace!

This, my lord, may look somewhat like boasting; but it boasteth of nought excepting Christ crucified, or rather arisen in me, whereby all worldly matters are crucified unto me.

Within about a fortnight after my conversion, I received a letter from a friend in London, informing me that my old uncle had secretly married a young creature who was lately delivered of a son; that he now openly acknowledged her for his wife; and that this, as he feared, did not bode me any good.

At another time these tidings would have greatly alarmed me; but I was now equally resigned and indifferent to all events.

In a few days after, as I was stepping out of my lodgings, I was arrested, in the name and at the suit of my uncle, for £700, the precise sum for which I had drawn upon him about nine months before. All the consequences of this caption immediately occurred to me. I perceived that my uncle intended to deprive me of my patrimony in favour of his new family; and, as I had no means for opposing his machinations save what lay in his own hands, I concluded that a jail was to be my portion for life. Wherefore I lifted up my heart, and said within myself—To prison and to death give me cheerfully to follow thee, O thou who in death art the life and resurrection!

My spirit had no sooner uttered this short ejaculation, than I felt such a weight of peace descending upon me, that my heart leaped within me at the prospect of suffering, and I would not have exchanged my prison for a throne.

While I quietly walked with the officers towards the place of my durance, they came to a great tavern, where they entered, and proposed to regale themselves at my expense.

Meantime a Dutch merchant, of great eminence, happened to be with his lady in the principal room, and, hearing a bustle in the house, he inquired the cause, and sent for the chief bailiff.

Soon after, I was conducted into their presence. They both rose as I entered, and the gentleman approaching took me familiarly by the hand, and said in Dutch—Mr. Meekly, I hear you are in distress, and that is sufficient to recommend you to my services; but your appearance exacts something more from my inclinations. Pray, let me know wherein and how far it may be requisite for you to command me?

I muttered somewhat, as I suppose, inarticulately towards an answer; for I protest, my lord, I was so struck, so awed, so confounded by his presence, that I was lost for the time to the consideration of my own affairs. Meanwhile he placed me at table, just opposite to the heavenly vision of his bride, and then went and resumed his seat beside her; while I, gazing in silence and utmost wonder, recollected those lines of Milton, where, speaking of Adam and Eve, he calls them

> "The loveliest pair
> That ever since in love's embraces met:
> Adam, the goodliest man of men since born
> His sons; the fairest of her daughters, Eve."

The gentleman perceived my astonishment, and, graciously smiling, again asked me what sum was requisite to extricate me from my present difficulty?—Ah, sir! said I, it is a sum that far exceeds all human bounty; and, indeed, I would not accept the obligation from any man unless I were assured of being shortly in a capacity to reimburse him, of which I see no likelihood, I think no possibility.

Here I told him, in a few words, how my father had left me an infant at the disposal of my uncle, who had now put me under arrest for £700, which, some time since, he had freely remitted to me, as in my own right.

I see, said the gentleman, your uncle is a villain, and means, by casting you into prison in a strange and distant place, to deprive you of the power of bringing him to account. But he must be detected; it is a justice which you owe to the public as well as yourself. And as the amount of the pretended debt is not sufficient for that purpose, here is an order on the bank in town for double the sum. For this you must give me your note of hand. Be pleased to reimburse me when it is your convenience. If that should never happen, be under no concern; for I hold myself already repaid with usury, in the opportunity of serving an injured and a worthy man._

O sir! I cried; I cannot, indeed I cannot—I will not accept it on any account. I am patient, nay, I am pleased with the lot that is appointed me. Shall I, in an instant, break the yoke, and cast the burden which my gracious Master but this instant has laid upon me? No, sir! I submit myself to it with thankfulness; I take this cross to my bosom, and press it to my heart.

O Meekly! said he, you are a very misdeeming Christian, if you think yourself entitled either to assume or retain your proper crosses at will. There is too much of self-righteousness in such a zeal, Meekly. Humility would rather bid the will of our Master to be done; and he offers you enfranchisement by my hand. Do, my dear sir, cried the angel beside him—do let me petition, let me persuade you to accept this little instance of our good-will to so good a creature. Though my lord here has not been able to prevail, a lady has superior claims, and I must not be refused.

Quite sunk, quite overwhelmed, I dropped involuntarily on my knees before them. Blessed pair! I exclaimed, blessed and beauteous beyond expression; if angels are like you, what happiness must be in heaven! I could no more, my words were choked by my rising emotions.

My benefactor then rose, and, coming tenderly towards me, he took me warmly in his arms. Mr. Meekly, says he, do not oppress me, I pray you, by this excess of acknowledgment. I am but a worthless instrument in the hands of your beloved; for from him, and him alone, is every good gift, and even the will of the giver.—O Mr. Meekly! added the lady, her eyes glittering through water, we thank you, we cordially thank you, Mr. Meekly; you have occasioned us much pleasure this day, I assure you; and the means of our happiness should be delightful in our eyes.

My patron then rung a bell, and ordered his principal gentleman into his presence; when, putting the order into his hand—Here, says he, take this, with the bailiff, directly to the bank; there pay him his demand of £700 and fees; and bring me a hundred pounds in cash, and the remainder in bills on London. Then, calling for pen and ink, he drew the following short note—"I owe you fourteen hundred pounds;" to which I signed "Charles Meekly."

On the return of the messenger, I was put in possession of the cash and bills, and a dinner of little elegances was served up.

After a short repast, the decanters and glasses being placed, and the attendants dismissed, my two patrons gave a loose to social joy, and invited me to be a partaker in their festivity. Never was I, nor ever shall I again, be witness to such flights of fancy, such a spontaneous fluency of heart-springing glee. With what pleasure did erudition cast off its formal garb; how delightfully did wisdom assume the semblance, and at times the very phrase, of childhood! They laughed, they rallied me, themselves, and the world. Their merriment was as the breaking forth and exuberance of overflowing innocence and virtue. Conceive to yourself, my lord, a large room surrounded with benches, whereon are seated the principal philosophers, literati, lawyers, statesmen, chief captains, and chief conquerors in all ages; then think you behold two sportively observant children in the midst, looking and laughing at the insignificance of the several sages; taking off and holding up the solemnity and self-importance of each profession in caricature, and setting the whole world, with all its wisdom, its toils and boasted acquirements, its solicitudes, applications, and achievements, at nought.

The gentleman indeed pretended—and only pretended—to defend the sophists, the valiant, and the renowned of his sex, but he evidently exulted in his own defeat; while the lady, with a drollery amazingly voluble, ran through the schools of philosophy, the systems of human policy, and histories of heroism, unpluming the crested, bringing the lofty low, and depreciating and reducing all magnitude to miniature. And all this she did with an archness of such pleasant meaning—with such looks, eyes, and attitudes of bewitching transition, as would have infused fascination into old age and ugliness; what then must it have done when accompanied by a beauty that scarce ever was equalled, that could not be exceeded? Did the Sarah of the patriarch Abraham resemble her, I wonder not that nations should have been enamoured of her at the age of fourscore.

At length the enraptured husband, no longer able to contain, bent towards her with looks of soul-darting delight, and restraining his arms that would have crushed her to his bosom—O my Louisa! he cried, you are too much, too pearly, too precious a treasure for me! But, giving him a sweetly petulant pat on the cheek.—Away you rogue! she cried, I'll none of your mockeries!

What can expression add further to this divinely pre-eminent of human creatures? Whatever was her present glance, aspect or posture, you would have wished to fix her in it, that you might gaze and admire for ever; but when she varied the enchantment of her action and attitude, you forgot the former attractions, and she became, as it were, a newness of ever-rising delight!

Alas, how transient, how momentary, was the bliss I then enjoyed! A chariot and six pied horses drove up to the door, attended by a retinue of ten or twelve men, all armed, gallantly mounted, and in rich apparel.

My dear Meekly, mournfully said my benefactor, I am sorry that we are destined to different departments. I lodge to-night at a villa belonging to one of my correspondents, and to-morrow we set out to visit some of the German courts. Fare, fare-you-well, Meekly, for a short season at least!

I would have cast myself at his feet. It was an emotion, a propensity, which I could not resist; but he prevented me, by kissing and casting his arms affectionately about me. The lady then turned to me, and with a smile of heart-captivating graciousness—God be with you! God be with you, my good Mr. Meekly! she cried; perhaps we may meet ere long in your own England. I answered not; but, bending on one knee, I caught her hand, pressed it fervently to my lips, and permittted her to depart.

Alas, they did depart! I saw them for the last time.

They mounted their carriage, and, being seated, they bent forward, and bowing to me with a fixed regard, off they drove, and tore away with them, as I thought, the best part of my soul.

I followed them with straining eyes. When out of sight methought I held them still in view, and I blessed and kissed, in imagination, the very ground over which they went. At length I awoke from my delirium, and with slow and heavy steps turned back into the house.

I had not yet, through shame, so much as inquired the name of my benefactor. I therefore called to my host, in order to inform myself of all that I could learn concerning him; as also to make out a bill—for it had not been called for—and I pleased myself with the thought of discharging a reckoning that my friends had forgotten. When I questioned my host on this head, he put his hands to his sides, and broke into a violent fit of laughter—No, no! master, said he, there's nothing for any one to pay in this house, I assure you. Mynheer never troubles himself about those matters; his major-domo pays all; ay, and for many a guest too that happens to be in the same inn with his master.

Why, pray, said I, is he a lord?—A lord? quotha; not so little as that comes to neither. No, sir; he is a prince—the very prince of our merchants; and our merchants are princes above all lords.—And, pray, how do they style or call him?—He has many names and titles. When our traders speak of him, they call him Mynheer Van Glunthnog; but others style him my lord of merchants, and others my lord the brother-man, and my lord the friend of the poor.

The remainder of my story is very short, and still more insignificant. I soon set out for England, in order to file a bill against my uncle, and compel him to discover what patrimony my father had left me. But God was pleased, in the mean space, to cut off all debate; his wife and child had died of an epidemic distemper, and he did not survive them above a fortnight. He left me a penitential letter, with a small will enclosed, whereby I became entitled to three hundred a year in right of my father, and an additional four hundred in right of my uncle, with a sum of near three thousand pounds in ready money.

If I know my own heart, the only cause of rejoicing that I felt on that occasion was, that it put it in my power to discharge my pecuniary obligations to my late generous preserver. I immediately wrote, and transmitted bills to Holland for the purpose; but the bills were returned, and I could hear no tidings concerning the residence of my patron. I then put out his £1400 on the best securities that I could procure. It is now close upon five-and-thirty years since I saw him; and in that time the principal, with interest upon interest, yearly turned into capital, has amounted to nearly £5000, one penny of which I never touch, but hold the whole as sacred.

Meantime, it has cost me hundreds upon hundreds in correspondences, advertisements, and even in special messengers to several parts of Europe, to discover where this greatest, this most eminent of men could have concealed himself; but, alas! my search proved as fruitless as that of the miser in hunting after the pearl of mighty price.

During those five-and-thirty years, the image of the persons of those my two gracious patrons never left my memory—were ever at my heart. Ah! I would say to myself, they are dead—they are dead; or rapt, perhaps, like Elijah, alive into heaven; flesh and blood refined as theirs might easily pass from its little impurities, through the fire of the love of God to the place of its bliss. And again, it was my daily and ardent petition that, if their mortal was not swallowed up of immortality, I might once set my eyes upon them before I died.

Here Mr. Meekly ended.—I thank you, my dear friend, said the earl, for your history; it has entertained me most pleasingly, and I have also been highly edified by some passages in it. But, with respect to the glimpse that you had of your two wonderful friends, I think it must have been a vision, or merely a matter of imagination; for I never saw in nature, nor read in fiction, of any thing comparable to the excellences that you have described in that exalted pair.—If it was a vision, my lord, it must have been one of blessed angels indeed; but I hope you will allow that the benefits which they conferred were no way visionary.—O Mr. Meekly! said Harry, with a sigh, the picture that you have drawn of this dear lady has almost given me a distaste to all the rest of her sex. Ah! might I meet hereafter some daughter—some descendant—some distant likeness of her—how happy should I think myself!—May heaven succeed your ominous wish, my dearest child! cried Meekly. It is just, perhaps prophetic, that it should be so. For never did I see so perfect a resemblance between any two creatures, as between the consort of that bewitching woman and yourself—it struck me the other night the moment you entered the room; and I thought that I beheld my very benefactor newly arisen, like a young phœnix, from the ashes of old age.

Near a fortnight now elapsed without any news or notice from Mr. Clinton, or from the messenger who was sent despatch for him. Harry daily advanced in the favour and familiarity of his father; and Mr. Meekly continued with them in a most pleasing society.

On a fine morning, as they were walking together towards the village—This is the first time, my Harry, said the earl with a sigh, that I have ventured to turn my face this way since the death of my wife, and the interment of your dear brother.—O my lord! cried Harry, I would gladly exchange my lot in life with the meanest of yonder cottagers, who earns his daily bread by the labour of his hands, provided I might thereby restore them both to your bosom.—Not so, not so, my son! fervently replied the earl; I would not lose my Harry, though I were thereby to resuscitate all that are dead in England. I have no cause, no manner of right to complain; I am still happy—wonderfully happy—too happy in the possession of such a child!.

Just then a great shouting and uproar was heard in the village. The huge mastiff belonging to Peregrine Pelt, the tanner, had run mad, and came foaming up the road, pursued by thirty of the townsmen, armed with staves, spits, and pitchforks. The dog rushed on at such a rate that there was no possibility for our company to escape him; and Harry, observing that he made directly towards his father, threw himself full in his way. Instantly the envenomed monster sprung up and cast himself open mouth upon our hero; but Harry, with a wonderful presence of mind, having wrapped his left arm in the skirt of his coat, dashed it into the frothing jaws of the terrible animal; when, giving a trip at the same time to his hinder legs, he threw him flat on the ground, and springing up into the air, he descended upon him with all the force of his heels, and dashed his bowels to pieces; whereupon the creature uttered a faint howl, sprawled a while, and expired.

The earl and Mr. Meekly stood yet a while, pale, astonished, and unassured; and my lord, looking about in a panic, cried—Where is the dog?—what's become of the mad dog? In the mean time the villagers came on in full pursuit, crying out—The mad dog!—the mad dog!—take care of the mad dog! But when they all arrived, and beheld their huge enemy looking formidable even in death, never was amazement equal to theirs. They stared at the earl, Meekly, and Harry, in turns, and seeing no weapon in any of their hands

—God! cried Goodman Demster, God has been wonderfully gracious in your deliverance, my lord; for nothing less than a thunderbolt could so suddenly have stricken this monster dead.—I protest, said the earl, I was so much alarmed that I know not how it happened; I remember nothing further than that my dear child here thrust himself between his father and danger.—But I beheld, said Meekly, when with one stroke of his arm he dashed the creature to the ground, and then instantly crushed him to death with his feet.—Not I, Mr. Meekly, modestly replied Harry; God gave me strength for the season in defence of my father.—But are you not bit—are you not hurt, my child? cried the earl, coming up tremblingly to his son.—Not touched indeed, my lord.—Glory for that in the highest! exultingly cried the earl.

I knew, exclaimed Tom Truck, with a shout and look of triumph, I knew it could be no other but my brave and noble young master who did the feat.—On my life, cried Farmer Felster, he is able with his naked arm, like another young David, to save his lambs from the jaws of the lion and the paws of the bear.

Though these praises served only to put our hero to confusion, they went trickling, like balm of Gilead, to the heart of his father.—Pelt, said the earl, let it be your task to flay and tan me the hide of your own dog. I will have his skin stuffed with incense, and his nails of solid gold; and he shall hang up in my hall from generation to generation, to commemorate the piety and prowess of my son! Mean while, my good friends, I invite you all, with your families, kinsfolk, and neighbours, to come and feast with me this day. Sorrow hath endured her night; but joy cometh with my child, and ariseth on us as a new morning!

In the afternoon all the townsfolk and neighbours, with

their wives and children, convened to the great house, having their cattle and themselves heavy laden with fagots for a magnificent illumination. The whole court was spread with tables, and the tables with victuals and liquors; besides two hogsheads of October that stood apart.

The earl, in the joy of his own escape, and the recent prowess of his young hero, went forth with a cheerful countenance, and graciously welcomed all his guests; whereat they wished health and long life to his lordship and their young lord, and giving a joint huzza, sat down to their banquet. From whence, after a night far spent in carousal, their great fire being out, and their great hogsheads exhausted, they peacefully helped each other to their respective homes; regretting, however, that they had not been honoured with the presence of their young master among them; for Harry had besought his father to dispense with him yet a while from partaking in any part or scene of festivity, especially when appointed in his own honour; and Mr. Meekly highly approved and applauded his motion.

On the eve of the following day, Mr. Meekly rode abroad on a charitable visit to a dying man in the neighbourhood; and my lord was fondly toying and patting the cheek of his darling, as they stood at the hall door, when Harry spied a mourning coach turning up the lower end of the great avenue, and instantly cried out—There's my uncle! my lord; my uncle! my dearest uncle! and off he shot like lightning. The coach drove but slowly; Harry was up with it in a twinkling, and, vaulting in at the window, was in an instant in the bosom of his best friend and patron.

In the mean time the earl had retired into the house in great agitation. He feared and was jealous of the manner in which his brother would meet him; and this gave him equal doubt and hesitation respecting the manner in which he ought to receive his brother. Mr. Clinton, on the other hand, was not wholly without some similar emotions; so that, when Harry introduced his uncle into the parlour, no two noble personages could salute each other with a more distant respect.

The earl, however, on casting a glance upon the face of his brother, felt a tide of returning affection, and lifting up his hands and eyes, exclaimed—It is he! it is he! my Harry! my Harry Clinton! my dear, my long lost, my long sought brother! then hastened forward in a gush of passion, and caught him in his eager arms; when Mr. Clinton, alternately folding the earl to his bosom, cried—I am content, O my God! give me now to depart in peace, since at last I find and feel that I have indeed a brother!

Our hero, observing the violence of their emotion, interposed with a gentle care, and supporting them to seats placed them tenderly by each other.

For a while they both sat silent, with a handkerchief at their eyes, till the earl turned, and plaintively said—You do not forgive me, Harry Clinton! you never will, you never can forgive me, my brother! Whereupon Mr. Clinton caught up the earl's hand to his lips, and, pressing it with a fervent respect, cried—my brother and my lord! my brother and my lord!

O then, said the earl, you do forgive me, I find; but never can I, never will I forgive myself! My faults towards you, my noblest brother, for these many long years, have been ever before me; my neglects, my pride and insolence, my contemptuous treatment of one so highly my superior—of my Harry, the only boast and glory of our house!

Mean while our hero stood aloof, with his head averted, weeping and sobbing with evident agitation, till Mr. Clinton cried—No more, my brother! no more, I beseech you! It is already too much; I cannot bear my present excess of grateful affection for you; it struggles to rush forth, but utterance is not given. Beside, we shall break the heart of our dear child there; his nature is too tender to support such a scene as this.

Harry then smilingly turned his face towards his parents, all shining through tears, as the sun in a shower; and advancing, and kneeling before them as they sat, he took the hands of each alternately, and pressed them in silence to his lips.

In about an hour after, while their affections were still at the highest, but their spirits somewhat composed, Mr. Meekly returned. The earl immediately rose, and, advancing, took him by the hand with a cordial familiarity.—Mr. Meekly, says he, I shall now have the pleasure of introducing you to that inestimable brother, of whom you have heard me speak so often. Brother, this is Mr. Meekly, my best and worthiest friend!

Mr. Clinton rose and advanced; and Meekly approached with an abased reverence, not venturing to look up, but saluted him as he would have saluted an angel of light.

Meekly! Meekly! cried Mr. Clinton; I have surely heard that name before! Pray, Mr. Meekly, were you ever abroad? have you travelled, sir? Were you ever in Holland, Mr. Meekly?

Here Meekly started, as awaked by the sound of a voice whose recollected tunings went thrilling to his heart; and lifting up his eyes, and beholding the traces of features once so lovely, and ever deeply endeared to his memory, he started, and, staggering back some steps, he sunk down on a chair behind him almost in a fainting fit.

The earl, greatly alarmed, went up, and taking him by the hand—What is the matter, my friend? says he. Are you taken suddenly ill? are you not well, my Meekly?

O, my lord! he pantingly cried, there he is—as sure as I live—my patron—my benefactor—the wondrous man that I told you of; there he stands in his own precious person before us!

Mr. Clinton then approached, and, taking a seat beside him, leaned towards him with a melting complacence.—Mr. Meekly, said he, I expected ere this to have embraced you in heaven; but I rejoice to meet you even on earth, for I have ever retained a very affectionate impression of you; and I more especially rejoice to meet you in the present society.

But then—but then you come alone—you come alone, my lord and master! Alas! you wipe your eye. O, then, it must be so! and here he broke into a passionate gush of tears.

My lord and our hero, hereupon recollecting the engaging circumstances of a character of whose description they had been so lately enamoured, could not refuse their tribute to the memory of that admirable lady, to whose person they now found themselves endearingly attached by affinity.

At length Mr. Clinton, distressed to the last degree for the distress in which he saw the forlorn Meekly, sweetly turned from his own affliction to the consoling of that friend whom he found so deeply afflicted for him.

Mr. Meekly, said he, let us not weep for the dead, but rather for the living; for those who are yet in the vale of mortality. Shall we mourn the condition of angels? shall we lament that a weight of glory is fallen on those whom we loved! No; let us rather rejoice in the prospect of being speedily partakers!

When supper was over, Harry laid hold of the first interval of converse to inquire after his friends in town, more especially Mr. Clement, his Arabella, and their little Dicky.— They are come, said Mr. Clinton, to sudden and great affluence. Old Clement is thoroughly reconciled to his son, and is doatingly fond of Arabella and her child.—I am glad of it with all my heart, cried Harry, clapping his hands; but pray, how did the matter come about, sir?—By an event, my dear, in which this arm of Providence was signally visible. Old Clement's supposed wife was detected, and is dead, as is also her paramour, the villain who betrayed, and lately also attempted to murder, your Hammel. His history is wonderful; but it is long, and too horrid to relate.

What an astonishing distance there is, exclaimed the earl, between the characters and dispositions of man and man! And how does my brother, my revered Harry Clinton, rise supreme above all his species, in every excellence, in every virtue, scarce less than divine?

Oh, my lord! I am persuaded, said Mr. Clinton, that could it please God at this instant to withdraw from me the influence of his holy and happy Spirit, I should become altogether as evil as the worst, as evil as the vilest.

I cannot think so, my brother, replied the earl; you would still continue a rational and free creature. There is certainly a distinction in the nature of things! There is the beautiful and deformed, the amiable and detestable; your judgment would approve the one and reject the other; and your freedom of agency would act conformable to your election.

Ah, my lord! cried Mr. Clinton, what things, what beauty, what amiableness, what freedom is this that you speak of? Have you found out another universe or another deity beside HIM in whom our life subsists? Are there any things in nature save the things of our God? Or what beauty or amiableness can they possibly exhibit, save what they derive from him; save some quality or impregnation, some manifestation or impression, of his own beauty or amiableness?

To make this matter clear, let us go somewhat deeper; quite back, if you please, my lord, to the very birth of things.

Throughout nature, we find that God can impart to his creatures a being, an identity, a fire of life, an intelligence or sagacity, a consciousness, a force or action, a will, and a freedom, distinct from himself, and distinct from each other: and this is the utmost extent of creaturely nature,· whether respecting the powers that are in hell or in heaven; whether respecting the highest seraphim that are in bliss, or the lowest fallen spirits in perdition.

Now all these powers or high prerogatives, although distinct from God, are infinitely far from being independent of him; for he will not, he cannot, depart from his supremacy, nor that universality of essence, by and in which alone all essences subsist. He can, indeed, impart the fore-mentioned powers to any limited degree that he pleases; but then, in their highest degree of fire, life, or sagacity, force, action, or freedom, you will perceive, on the slightest reflection, that there is nothing of the beautiful or amiable that you spoke of; but that they are equally applicable, and may be equally exercised to evil or good purposes, according to the nature or disposition of the agent.

I have already specified the many great and wonderful powers that God can impart to his creatures distinctly, though not independently, from himself. But there is one power, one quality which God cannot make creaturely; which with all his omnipotence he cannot possibly impart, in any kind of distinction or separability, from himself, and this quality is called Goodness.

And now, my dear lord, in order to convince you of this most capital and most important of all truths, a truth upon which time, eternity, and the universe all turn, as on their axis, it may be necessary to inquire what Goodness is.

There is no species of allowed or conceivable virtue that is not reducible under the standard of their great leader, and all-generating parent, called Love. Good-will is the eternal blesser of all to whom it is beneficent, and also generates its own blessing in the very act of its love.

Here lies the great and impassable gulf between God and his productions, between the creature and the Creator. The will of God is an eternal fire of love towards his creatures, and goes forth in blessings upon them as wide and universal as his own existence. But the will of the creature is confined and limited, like its essence. While it is distinct from, or uninformed by the will of God, it cannot possibly act beyond or out of itself; it cannot possibly feel for any thing except itself; it cannot wish any welfare except its own welfare, and this it endeavours to compass by the exertion of all its powers.

From this distinct, selfish, and craving will of the creature, springs every possible evil, whether natural or moral. From the preference of its own identity to that of others, ariseth pride; from the eagerness of its grasping at all advantages to itself, ariseth the envy of any imaginary advantage to another. Pride, covetousness, and envy, beget hatred, wrath, and contention, with every species and degree of malevolence and malignity; and the disappointment of these passions produce rancours and misery; and all together they constitute the whole nature and kingdom of hell itself in the soul.

But when God is pleased to inform the will of the creature with any measure of his own benign and benevolent will, he steals it sweetly forth in affection to others; he speaks peace to the storm of rending passions; and a new and delightful dawning arises on the spirit. And thus, on the grand and final consummation, when every will shall be subdued to the will of good to all, our Jesus will take in hand the resigned cordage of our hearts; he will tune them, with so many instruments, to the song of his own sentiments, and will touch them with the finger of his own divine feelings. Then shall the wisdom, the might, and the goodness of our God, become the wisdom, might, and goodness of all his intelligent creatures; the happiness of each shall multiply and overflow in the wishes and participation of the happiness of all; the universe shall begin to sound with the song of congratulation; and all voices shall break forth in an eternal hallelujah of praise, transcending praise and glory, transcending glory to God and the Lamb.

Purblind reason here will say, even the goodness of God himself in the human heart will say—If our God is all love, if he is a will to all rectitude and happiness in his creatures, why did he suffer any evil to begin in nature and creature? Could evil have arisen contrary to the will of Omnipotence, if Omnipotence had willed that it should not arise?

Ah, my friends! no evil ever did, nor ever can approach the will of God; neither can he will or effect any species of evil in nature or creature; but he can allow a temporary evil in the creature, as a travail toward its birth into the more eminent degree of that goodness and happiness which God effects. God cannot effect or take delight in the sufferings of the most abandoned reprobate that ever blasphemed his name; but he can will that the sinner should be reclaimed to happiness, even by suffering, when there are no other means in nature whereby he may be reclaimed.

Could creatures, without the experience of any lapse or evil, have been made duly sensible of the darkness and dependence of their creaturely nature, and of the distance and distinction between themselves and their God; could they have known the nature and extent of his attributes, with infinity of his love; could they have known the dreadful consequences of falling off from him, without seeing any example, or experiencing any consequences of such a fall; could they have otherwise felt and found that every act of creaturely will, and every attempt at creaturely power, was a forsaking of that eternal wisdom and strength in which they stood; could all intelligent creatures have been continued in that lowliness, that resignation, that gratitude of burning affection which the slain will of the mortified sinner feels when called up into the grace and enjoyment of his God; could those endearing relations have subsisted in creation, which have since newly risen between God and his lapsed creatures wholly subsequent thereto—those relations, I say, of redemption, of regeneration, of a power of conversion, that extracts good out of evil, of a love that no apostasy can quench, that no offences can conquer—if these eternal benefits could have been introduced, without their ground or foundation in the admission of evil, no lapse or falling off would ever have been.

Here Mr. Clinton paused, and his auditors continued in a kind of respectful musing, as attentive to what he might further offer. At length the earl exclaimed—Never, never more, my brother, will I debate or question with you, further than asking your advice or opinion, to which I shall instantly and implicitly submit, as I would to that of the highest seraph in heaven. Our dear Meekly here, and I, had some former converse on a few of these deep subjects, and I received much satisfaction and instruction from him; but he was not quite so explicit and convincing as you have been.

Ah, my lord! cried Meekly, were I as intimate with the fountain of all knowledge as your precious brother is, you would not then have opposed me in the conversation we last held on those heads.

On the following day, at breakfast, Mr. Meekly took out his pocket-book, and produced bank and stock-bills to the amount of something upward of five thousand pounds. He then presented them to Mr. Clinton, and said—Here, sir, is a little matter towards repayment of the loan I had from you in Holland. I bless—I bless my God that he has enabled me thus far to approve myself an honest man; but, above all, I bless him for giving me once more a sight of the gracious countenance of my patron.

But for you I had miserably perished in a dungeon; to you, sir, I owe my liberty, to you I owe my life, to you I owe the recovery of the inheritance of my fathers. With respect to such obligations, I am indeed a beggared insolvent. But my heart is pleased with the thought, that the connection between us, of creditor on your part and debtor on mine, should remain on record to all eternity.

Here the worthy Meekly became oppressed under sensations of grateful recollection; and, putting his handkerchief to his eyes he sobbed out his passion.

In the meantime, Mr. Clinton held the bills in his hand, and, carelessly casting his eye over them, perceived the amount. As soon as he saw that his friend's emotion had partly subsided, You have, Mr. Meekly, says he—you have been quite a gospel steward, and have returned me my own with most unlooked-for usury; and I heartily pray God, in recompense of your integrity, to give you the principality of many cities in the coming kingdom of his Son. But what shall I do with this money, my dear Meekly? My wealth already overflows; it is my only trouble, my only encumbrance. It claims my attention, indeed, as it is a trust for which I know I am strictly accountable; but I heartily wish that Providence would reclaim the whole to himself, and leave me as one of his mendicants, who daily wait on the hand that supplieth all who seek his kingdom, with necessary things; for my Harry has enough, and more than enough now, in the abundance of his noble father. You must therefore keep these bills to yourself, my worthy friend; retain, or give, or dispose of them, even as it shall please you; whether as your property or as my property, it matters not sixpence; but take them back, you must take them back indeed, my Meekly. And so saying, he shoved them over from him, on the table.

Ah, my most honoured sir! exclaimed the repining Meekly; surely you would not serve me so. My soul is but just eased of a load that lay heavy on it for many, many years. Be not then so severe as to replace the burden upon me. It would break my very heart should you persist in refusing this little instance of acknowledgment from one of your warmest lovers.

Here Harry found himself affected and distressed for the parties; and, in order to relieve them, took the decision of the matter upon himself.

Gentlemen, says he, I will, with your good pleasure, put a very quick end to this dispute; and I offer myself to you, as your joint trustee, to be your almoner and disposer of these bills.

As I was lately on my rambles through some villages near London, the jingle of a number of infant-voices struck my ear; and turning, and looking in at the ground floor of a long cottage, I perceived about thirty little girls neatly dressed in an uniform, and all very busily and variously employed in hackling, carding, knitting, or spinning, or in sewing at their sampler, or in learning their letters, and so forth.

The adjoining house contained about an equal number of boys, most of whom were occupied in learning the rudiments of the several handicrafts; while the rest were busied in cultivating a back-field, intended as a garden for these two young seminaries.

I was so pleased with what I saw, that I gave the masters and mistresses some small matter; and I resolved within myself, if ever I should be able, to gather together a little family of my own for the like purposes.

Now, gentlemen, here comes Mr. Meekly's money, quite in season for saving just so much of my own. But hang it, since I am grown suddenly rich, I think I will be generous for once in my life, and add as much more out of my proper stock. I shall also make so free as to draw on my uncle there for the like sum; and these, totted together, will make a pretty beginning of my little project.

As to my poor father here, he has nothing to spare, for he has already lavished all his wealth on his naughty boy.

My lord and the company laughed heartily at Harry's little pleasantry. But harkee, honest friend, added the earl, you must not think to expose me by leaving me out of your scheme; can't you lend me as much, Harry, as will answer my quota?—Yes, my lord, said Harry, upon proper securities I think I may venture.—You are a rogue, and a darling, and my treasure, and my honour, and my ornament, cried the earl, turning and bending fondly towards him. While Harry's eyes began to swim with pleasure, and, casting himself into his father's bosom, he there hid the tears of his swelling delight; while Mr. Clinton and Mr. Meekly sat silently wrapped in the enjoyment of the touching scene.

After dinner the earl said—Tell me, my ever amiable Harry Clinton, where in the world could you hide yourself from my inquiries these twenty years past? I have got some scattered sketches of your history from Mr. Meekly, and my son here, and have been burning to learn the whole, but dreaded to ask you that favour, lest the recollection of some passages should give you distress.—I refuse no pain to do you a pleasure, my brother.

Here the Honourable Mr. Clinton began his story as formerly recited, and that night sent his auditors weeping to bed.

On the following morning, when he came to that part of his narrative where Lady Maitland broke away, he proceeded as followeth:—

Having travelled through several parts of France and Italy, I took Germany in my tour. I stayed some time at Spa, where I drank the waters, and within the year arrived in perfect health at Rotterdam.

On a visit to Mr. De Wit, at his villa near the city, he told me, over our bottle, that he had at that time in his house and in his guardianship, one of the most extraordinary women in the universe. Though she is now, says he, advancing towards the decline of life, she is by far the most finished female I ever beheld, while all she says and all she does give a grace to her person that is quite indescribable. She hath a youth, too, her son, with her, who is nearly as great a rarity as herself; and were it not that his complexion is sallow, and that he is something short of a leg and blind of one eye, he would positively be the most lovely of all the human species.

You put me in mind, said I laughing, of the Baratarian wench who was commended to governor Sancho as the most accomplished beauty within a league; with this exception only, that one eye was blind, and that the other ran with brimstone and vermilion. But pray, who are these wonders?

That, said he, I either cannot or must not declare. They are evidently people of the first fashion; and must have some uncommon reasons for their present conduct, as they live quite retired, and admit of no company.

I protest, said I, you have raised my curiosity in earnest; is there no managing so as to procure me a short *tête-à-tête* with them?—I wish there was, says he, for I long to know how far your sentiments agree with mine in this matter. Yesterday the lady told me that she intended to go and reside some time in England, and that I would oblige her by getting a person duly qualified to initiate her and her son in the language of the country. And now, if such a fine gentleman could condescend to undress himself, you might come to-morrow as a person who wanted hire, and I might introduce you to an interview by way of treating, provided you are upon honour not to reveal any thing concerning them or their place of abode.

The next morning I waited on Mr. De Wit, under the appearance of a reduced gentleman, a character that excites a mixture of contempt and compassion.

The lady received and spoke to me with that dignified complacence which awes while it engages, and while it attracts, forbids an irreverent familiarity. She was indeed every thing that my friend had boasted of her; for though her person was all majesty, her manner was all grace.—Will you answer for the discretion of this young man, Mr. De Wit?—I will, madam, said he. I bowed to them both.

On turning, I perceived that her son eyed me with much attention, and I, on my part, surveyed him with the utmost astonishment. He laboured, indeed, apparently under all the disadvantages that my friend described; but enchantment lurked in his accents and in the dimpling of his lips; and when he smiled, heaven itself was infused through the fine roundings of his olive-coloured countenance.

In short, I felt such a sudden attachment to these extraordinary personages, that I resolved to keep on the deception, at least for a few days, and accordingly engaged with them at a stated salary.

I entered on my province. My young pupil especially began to improve apace; and, as I was particularly cautious in observing the distant respect that suited my station, I grew into great favour with both mother and son.

How long, Mr. De Wit would say, do you propose to carry on this farce?—Till I can prevail upon them, I answered, to accompany me to England; for I feel my affection so tied to them, that I cannot think of parting

On a day as I sat with my pupil in his apartment, he

happened to let his book fall; and as I stooped to take it up, the picture of my Matilda, that was richly enamelled, and set with brilliants to a great value, suddenly loosed from its riband, and dropped through the bosom of my shirt upon the floor.

I stood concerned and greatly abashed by this accident; but my pupil, still more alarmed, started up, and, catching at it, gazed upon it intensely.—Ha, my friend! said he, I doubt you are an impostor. The proprietor of this jewel would never set himself out to hire without some sinister design. Who, sir, and what are you?

I own, said I, my sweet fellow, that I am not what I seem. I am of noble descent, and of riches sufficient to purchase a principality.—And what then could induce you to impose upon us as you have done?—Curiosity at first, and then the strong inclination which I took both to you and your mother at our first interview; neither did I propose to reveal myself till we should reach my native country, where all sorts of honours and affluence attend you.—Tell me then, said he, whose picture is this, a very lovely one, indeed? Is this the face, sir, of your mistress or your wife? (looking very inquisitively at me).—Ah! said I, she was once mistress of thousands of hearts; nobles waited before her drawing-room, and dukes near her toilet. She was once also my wife; but the dear saint is now eternally blessed in a more suitable Bridegroom.

Will you indulge me, sir, said he, with the story of your loves; it may atone in a great measure for your late deception, which, however, well meant, was very alarming.

Here I related to him the short pathetic history that I told you of my Matilda, with which he was so affected, and in such agitation, that I was quite affrighted for him, and stopped several times; but he insisted on my proceeding.

Ah! said he, when I concluded, should I ever be comforted in the manner that you and your Matty were, how blessed I shall think myself!—I have, said I, a little cousin in England, and perhaps the loveliest child in the world, and if you will marry her, when you both come to proper years, I will settle ten million of French money upon you. Meantime, I beseech you to say nothing to your mamma of what has passed.—I will not, said he, unless I see a discretionary necessity for it.

That night I went to the city to settle the affairs of my household. On my return next morning, I met Mr. De Wit at the gate of his court.

Ah, my friend! said he, our amiable guests are departed. —Gone! I cried. Gone! which way? where to, I pray you? —That also is a secret, said he, which I am not permitted to tell you. Late in the evening there arrived a retinue of about twenty servants, strongly armed and mounted, with a flying chaise and six horses, and a packet of letters. The lady did not go to bed, but ordered all things to be in readiness for their departure against the rising of the moon. When they were near setting out, and going to bid me adieu—Have you no commands, madam, said I, for the good young man, your tutor?—Not a penny, says she; I cannot afford to pay wages equivalent to servants of his quality.— How, madam, said I, is my friend then detected? But it was a very innocent and friendly fraud, I assure you; I should not have imposed upon your ladyship, did I not know you to be safer in his honourable hands than those of any other.

I then gave them an account of your family, your vast fortune, nor was I quite silent as to your merits, my dear Harry; and I added, that I was sensible you would be deeply afflicted at the departure of persons to whom you were so strongly attached.—There is no help for it, replied the lady; we have reasons of the utmost import for not disclosing ourselves to him. Tell him, however, that we esteem him highly, affect him tenderly, shall think of him, shall pray for him, and, lastly, that you saw us drop a grateful tear to his remembrance.

As I could extort no further intelligence from my friend Mr. De Wit, I parted in a half kind of chagrin, and prepared to pursue my fugitives, though I knew not what road to take, nor where to turn me for the purpose. At all adventures, however, I set out on the way to France; as they appeared to be of that country, as well by the elegance of their manners as by their fluency in the language.

I was attended by eleven of as brave and faithful fellows as ever thrust themselves between their master and danger.

On the fifth or sixth day, as we got on the borders of French Flanders, in an open and desolate way, with a forest far on the left, a man rode towards us on the spur, and, approaching, cried out—Help, gentlemen, for heaven's sake! Help to rescue my dear ladies, who are plundered and carried away by the banditti! They have already killed twenty of my companions, and I alone am left to cry out for relief.—I bid him lead, and we followed.

In a few minutes we came where we saw a great number of the dead and dying covering the sand and thin herbage; but our leader cried out—Stop not here, my noble friends! Yonder they are! yonder they are! They have but just taken away all our horses, luggage, and coach, and are now at the plunder. I am weak through loss of blood, but will help you the best I may.

Here he spurred again towards the enemy, but his horse would not answer his courage. I then looked about to observe if any advantage could be taken—for I perceived that the ruffians were still very numerous—about thirty—who had survived the late combat; but seeing that the country was quite open, and that we had nothing but resolution and our God to help us, I commended myself to Him in so good a cause, and, putting my horse to speed, I rode full at the foe, confident of being well and gallantly seconded.

When the banditti perceived us, they instantly quitted the plunder, and, gathering into a group, they prepared their carabines, and discharged them full at us as we drew near.

As I happened to be foremost, I received the greatest damage. One of their balls gave me this mark in my neck; another passed through the flesh of my left shoulder; and another through my hat, and left this scar in my head.

But when we came in upon them, as the Romans say, *cominus ense*, hand to hand, had they doubled their numbers they would have been as nothing to us. My faithful Irishman levelled half a score of them with his own hand, and in less than three minutes we had no opponent in the field. I then rode up to the coach, and perceived two ladies in it, pale as death, and sunk senseless to the bottom.

Immediately I ordered James, my surgeon's mate, to take a little blood from them, and, on their recovery, to follow me, with all my people, and all the horses, baggage, etc., to the nearest inn. Then, feeling my wounds begin to smart, I took my surgeon with me, and galloped away.

In about a league we came to a large house of entertainment, and finding myself sick and qualmish, through the great effusion of blood, I had my wounds directly dressed, and, taking a draught of wine whey, got into a warm bed.

After a night of uneasy slumbers, the curtain of my bed was gently drawn aside, and awaking, I heard a voice say, in soft music—Ah, my dear mamma, it is he! it is he himself!

On lifting my feeble eyes, I perceived a vision at my side of a female appearance, but more wonderful and more lovely than any thing I had ever conceived of the inhabitants in bliss. Her eyes swam in glory, and her whole form seemed a condensing, or substantiation, of harmony and light.

While I gazed in silent astonishment, I heard another voice say—Don't you know us, my son, my dear Mr. Clinton? Don't you remember your pupils? Don't you remember your blind, lame, and tawny Lewis? He is now turned into that passable girl there, whose honour and whose life you yesterday preserved, at the great peril of your own.

Here, seizing her hand, I pressed it to my lips and cried— Am I then so blessed, my honoured madam, as to have done some service to the two dearest objects of my heart's fixed affections?—Soft, says she; none of these transports: your surgeon tells us that repose is necessary for you. Meantime, we will go and prepare the best regimen that the place can afford for your nourishment, and after that I will send a despatch to my lord, and let him know how far, how very deeply, he and we, and all his house, are indebted to you.

For that day, and the following week, as my fever grew something high, I saw no more of the daughter; and the mother stayed no longer than to administer something to me, or barely to inquire how I was. At length I got a cool, and began to recover, when the former vision descended upon my ravished senses; the vision of that Louisa, the sight of whom never failed to bring cheer to the eyes, and delight to the hearts, of all beholders.

They sat down by my side, and my lady, taking my hand and looking tenderly at me—what would you think, said she, smiling, of my Louy for a wife?—Ah, madam! I exclaimed, she would be too much of bliss, too precious, too glorious, too overpowering for the heart and senses of any mortal!— Don't tell me, cries my lady; in my eyes, my Harry, you are full as amiable for a husband as she can be for a wife. Beside, you have earned her, my son; she is your own dear purchase by a service of infinite value, and at the price of your precious blood. She has told me the story of your first love, and the recollection of it never fails to bring tears from my eyes. But I must, hereafter, hear the whole from your own mouth, with all your other adventures; the smallest incident will be very interesting to me, I assure you. O my dear, my sweet fellow! you are to a hair the very man I wish for my Louisa—the brave, the tender, gentle, and generous heart; just the thing I would have wished for myself when I was at the age of my Louy.

But, my dearest, my honoured madam, loved and honoured next to heaven, you have not yet told me how your Louisa is inclined. Whereupon the bewitching creature, archly smiling and blushing, and reaching forth a polished hand of living alabaster—Here, she cried, I present you with this trifle in token that I do not hate you—very much.

Mr. Clinton, said my lady, I have sent off my favourite servant Gerard with my despatches to my lord. He is the only one that remains of all my retinue. Your surgeon has dressed his wound, and pronounced it so slight as not to incommode him in his journey. I chose him more particularly for the carrier of my purposes as he was the witness of your valour—as he can testify to my lord with what intrepidity you rushed foremost into the thick of the assassins, and with what unexampled bravery you defeated, in a short time, a body of four or five times your number. These things, I trust, will have their due weight; for, though my my lord is of a lofty and inflexible nature, he is yet alive to the feelings of honour and justice, so that our affairs have a hopeful and auspicious aspect. But you are a little flushed, my child; we will not encroach further upon you till to-morrow.

During the three following weeks, though confined to my bed, I was permitted to sit up, and my wounds, though not skinned, were healing apace. What happiness did I enjoy during that ecstatic interval! The maternal and filial angels scarce ever left my side. One morning, when I just awoke from a terrifying dream, they both entered with peace, and comfort, and healing in their countenances.

What is the matter, my Harry? said my lady; your face does not seem composed to that fortitude and complacence which is seated in your heart.—Ah, madam! I cried, I have been all night tormented with the most alarming and horrible visions I ever had in my life. Three times I dreamed successively that my Louisa and I were walking hand in hand through the fields of Elysium, or on the banks of Meander, or in the gardens of Alcinous, gazing and drinking in large draughts of love from each other; when at one time a huge and tremendous dragon, at another a sudden earthquake, and at another an impetuous hurricane came, and caught and severed us far asunder.

But my visions, my honest friend, said the heavenly smiling Louisa, have been of a very different nature. I dreamed that, while we were standing on the bank of a frightful precipice together, your Matilda descended, all celestial, and a thousand times more lovely than she appears in the lovely portrait that you carry about you. At first I feared that she came to reclaim you to herself; but instead of that she smiled upon me, and began to caress me, and, taking my right hand she put it into yours. Then, ascending in her brightness, she hovered a while on high, and casting down upon me a look of fixed love, she gave me a beck with her hand, as it were to follow, and was immediately lost in glory.

O, my dear children! cried the marchioness (for such she was), might I but once see you united, how I should lift my head! or, rather, how satisfied I should be to lay it down in peace, having nothing further to care for on this side of eternity!

That night I slept sounder than usual, and did not awake till the day was something advanced. On opening the curtain I saw James seated in a moody posture by the side of my bed.—How are the ladies, James? said I.—Gone, sir.—Gone, gone! I cried out.—Yes, sir, gone indeed; but with very heavy hearts, and both of them drowned in tears. Here has been a large body of the gens d'armes sent for them, so that there was no resisting. Poor Gerard went on his knees to his lady to beg permission to throw himself at your honoured feet, as he said, and to bid you adieu, but she would not allow him. Meantime she charged me with this watch and ring, and this letter for your honour.

I catched at the letter, and tearing it open, read over and over, a thousand times, what will for ever be engraven in my memory and on my heart.

"We leave you—we leave you, most beloved of men, and we are miserable in so doing; but, alas! we are not our own mistresses. My lord, for this time, has proved unjust and ungrateful; and refuses your Louisa, as well to my prayers as to your infinite merits. He has affianced her, as it seems, to a prince of the blood, and his ambition has blinded him to all other considerations. Be not yet in despair, we shall exert our very utmost to get this injurious sentence reversed; and, if your Louisa inherits my blood or spirit, not all the engines in France will ever compel her to give her hand to another. In the meantime, follow us not; come not near us, we beseech you. Should you be discovered, you will inevitably be assassinated, and we also should perish in your loss, my son. We are distracted by our fears for you, and it is this fear that has prevented us from disclosing ourselves fully to you. Keep up your correspondence, however, with our friend De Wit, and through him you shall learn the first favourable turn that happens in our affairs. I leave you my ring, in token of your being the wedded of our heart; and Louisa leaves you her watch, to remind you of time past, and to look upon when at leisure, and think of

"Your ELOISA DE——
"Your LOUISA DE——"

Yes I cried, ye precious relics, ye delicious memorandums, to my lips, to my heart! Be ye the companions of my solitude, the consolers of my affliction! Sooner shall this arm be torn off, and time itself pass away, than one or the other shall be divided from my custody.

Ah, how useless are admonitions to the impatience of a lover! Fervent love can know no fears. I was no sooner able to sit my horse than I set off directly for Paris, with this precaution only, that my people were to call me by my mother's maiden name of Goodall.

As we knew not the names or titles of those after whom we were in search, our eyes became our only inquisitors; and we daily ranged the town, peering into every carriage of distinction for a sight of the mother or daughter; and even prying among the lackeys and liveries for the face of our friend Gerard.

On a day, as my valiant Tirlah and I rode abroad, reconnoitring the suburbs, we heard a noise and shout of distress that issued from a distant farm-house; and as we hastened up the tumult grew louder, and the cry of Help! and Murder! was several times repeated.

We instantly knocked at the door, but were refused admittance, when Tirlah alighted, ran against it, and breaking through bars and all with his foot, threw the door off its hinges.

On entering, we saw a man with four others about him, who were going to slit his nose, and to use him very barbarously.—Stay your hands, I cried; I will shoot the first man through the head who shall dare to proceed in this business.

Why, sir, said a young fellow, this man wanted to be gracious with my pretty young wife; I caught him in the very attempt; and so I think it but fair and honest to spoil his beauty for such sport for time to come.—Ay, but, said I, you might murder him, and I cannot suffer that. Come, my friend, no harm, appears to be done as yet; and if he pays a handsome penance for the wickedness of his intention, I would advise you to pass matters over for the present. Say, how much do you demand?—Five hundred louis-d'ors, said the fellow; if he pays that he shall be quit for this turn.

Five hundred louis-d'ors! I exclaimed; why, all the clothes on his back are not worth the hundredth part of the sum.—True, master, said the peasant, winking, but his pockets may happen to be richer than his clothes.—Well, said I, if he secures you in half the sum I think you may be satisfied.—Why, master, since you have said it, I will not go back. Whereupon the astonished prisoner was permitted to rise.

What do you say, you very bad man? Are you willing to pay this fellow the sum I agreed for, in compensation of the injury you attempted to do him?—I am, sir, said he; with many thanks for your mediation. Then, hastily putting his hand to his pocket, he took out a note on the customs, which, with some small matter of cash, made up the money, and we departed the house together.

As I was just going to mount, he came up and accosted me with elegance and dignity. Sir, said he, you have made me your debtor beyond expression, beyond the power of princes to pay. Be pleased, however, to accept the little I have about me; here are five thousand louis in this little note-book.—Not a penny, sir, indeed; I am by no means in want.—You must not refuse, said he, some token of my acknowledgment; here is a stone, valued at double the sum I offered you. Then, taking from a pocket the diamond button of his hat, he presented it to me.—You must excuse me, sir, said I; I can accept of no consideration for doing an act of humanity; and I rejoice to have preserved a person of your distinction and generosity. I then turned my horse, and, though he called after me, I rode away, being neither desirous of knowing or being known.

My researches hitherto being altogether fruitless, I imagined I might with better likelihood meet my beloved in the public walks, public theatres, or rooms of distinguished resort.

One night, as I sat alone in a side-box at the opera, intently gazing and hungering around for some similitude of my Louisa, there entered one of the loveliest young fellows I ever beheld. He carelessly threw himself beside me, looked around, withdrew his eyes, and then looked at me with such a long and piercing inquisition as alarmed me, and gave me cause to think I was discovered.

Though the French seldom hesitate, he seemed at once backward and desirous of accosting me. At length he entered upon converse touching the drama and the music, and spoke with judgment and elegance superior to the matter; while I answered him with due complacence, but in a manner that partook of that regardlessness for trifles which then sat at my heart.

Between the acts he turned, and cast his eye suddenly on me.—Sir, says he, do you believe that there is such a thing as sympathy?—Occasionally, sir, I think it may have its effects; though I cannot credit all the wonders that are reported of it.—I am sorry for that, said he, as I ardently wish that your feelings were the same as mine at this instant. I never saw you before, sir; I have no knowledge of you; and yet I declare that, were I to choose an advocate in love, a second in combat, or a friend in extremity, you—you are the very man upon whom I would pitch.

I answered not, but seized his hand, and pressed it to my bosom.—I conceive, sir, continued he, notwithstanding your fluency in the language, that you are not a native. My name is D'Aubigny; I live at such a place; and if you will do me the pleasure of a single visit, all the honours, respects, and services that our house can confer, shall be yours without reserve.—Sir, said I, I am of England; my name is Goodall; and, as soon as a certain affair allows me to admit of any acquaintance in Paris, you shall be the first elected of my arms and my heart.

In a few nights after, as Tirlah and I were turning a corner of the Rue de St. Jacques, we saw three men with their backs to the wall, attacked by nearly three times their number. We did not hesitate a moment what part to take. At the first pass I ran one of the assassins through the body; Tirlah levelled two more with his oaken staff, and the rest took to flight.

Gentlemen, said one of the three, I thank you for this brave and seasonable assistance. Roche, run for a surgeon; I am wounded, I doubt dangerously. Pierre, lend me your arm. Come, gentlemen, we have but a little way to my house.

Though the night was too dark for examining features, I thought that the voice was not quite unknown to me. Within a few minutes we arrived at a palace that retired inward from the houses that were ranged on either hand. On pulling the hanger of a bell, the great door opened upon a sumptuous hall, which led to a parlour enlightened by a silver sconce that hung from the vaulting.

As we entered, the master turned short upon me, and looking full in my face, and starting and lifting his hands in surprise—Great ruler of events! he cried; the very man I wished my brother and companion through life! and this is the very man you have sent to my rescue.

Just then the surgeon arrived, and I heard him hastily asking where the marquis was. On entering, he said—I am sorry for your misfortune, my lord; but matters may be better than we apprehend; and immediately he took out his case of instruments.—One of the ruffians, said the marquis, before I was aware, came behind, and run me through the back.

The surgeon then ripped open his lordship's waistcoat, and changed colour on seeing his shirt drenched in blood. But getting him quickly undressed, and having probed his wound, he struck his hands together, and cried—Courage, my friends! it is only a flesh business; the weapon has passed clear of the ribs and vitals.

As soon as the marquis's wound was dressed, and that we had got him to bed—I fancy, sir, said I to the surgeon, I may have some small occasion for a cast of your office; I feel a little smart in my sword-arm.

On stripping he found that a chance thrust had entered about half an inch into the muscle above my elbow, and had ripped up some of the skin. But he quickly applied the proper dressing, and I was preparing to take my leave, when the marquis cried out—You must not think of parting, my dear friend; you are the master of the master here, and lord of this house, and of all that is in it.

The surgeon then ordered his lordship to compose himself as soon as possible; and, having wished him a good-night, I sent Tirlah to my lodgings to let my people know that I was well, and in friendly hands. I was then conducted by the domestics to a superb apartment, where a bed was prepared, and where a small supper of elegancies lay fuming on the sideboard.

Having swallowed a few bits, with a glass or two of wine,

I rose and sauntered through the room, musing on my Louisa, heavily sighing, and nearly despairing of being ever able to find her.

Some time after, I sat down to undress and get to bed, when a number of the officers of justice silently entered my chamber, seized my sword that I had put off, and, coming whisperingly to me, commanded me to accompany them, without making any noise.

I saw that it was madness to resist; and, as I went with them, I observed that two of the family-liveries had joined themselves to the officers. It then instantly occurred that I was in the house of my rival; that the marquis was the very person to whom my Louisa had been destined; that I was somehow discovered; and they were conducting me to the Bastile, of which I had heard as many affrighting stories as are usually told of the Inquisition.

Ah, traitor! said I to myself, is it thus you serve the man who but now saved your life at the expense of his own blood? Let no one hereafter trust to the bleating of the lamb, or the courting of the turtle; the roaring of the lion, and the pounces of the vulture, may thus deceitfully lurk under the one or the other.

After passing some streets, they took me to a large house, where dwelt one of their chief magistrates, being also a member of their parliament. Having knocked respectfully at the gate, and waited some time, at length we were admitted, and they took me to a kind of lobby, where we stayed, while one of the posse went to advise the justiciary of my attendance. At length he returned, and, accosting me in a tone of surly and discouraging authority—Friend, says he, my lord is engaged, and not at leisure to-night; to-morrow, perhaps, he may hear what you have to plead in your own defence. So saying, he and his fellows thrust me into a waste room, and locked and chained the door upon me; and, laughing, bid me to warm or cool my heels at pleasure.

Fool, fool that I was! said I, to quit the side of my brave and faithful companions; how quickly should we have discomfited this magistrate and all his host! But I must be a knight-adventurer forsooth, and draw my sword in defence of every scoundrel who goes the street.

I then went and felt the windows, to try if I could force a passage for making my escape; but finding that all were grated with strong and impassable bars of iron—Oh! I cried, that this marquis, this ungrateful D'Aubigny, were now in his fullest strength, and opposed to me point to point, that I might reclaim from him in an instant the life I have given!

I then traversed the room with an inconsistent pace, now rashly resolving on furious events, and again more sedately deliberating on what I had to do, till, having ruminated thus for the remainder of the night, I at last became more at ease, and resigned myself to the dispensations of all-disposing Providence, though, I confess, with a gloomy and reluctant kind of content.

When the day appeared, and was something advanced, I heard my door unlocking, and the chain taken away, and I concluded that they came to summon me to my trial. But, instead of the officers of justice, I saw near twenty men in the marquis's livery, who silently bowed down before me, and respectfully showed me with their hands the way out of my prison. I followed them also in silence, and, getting into the street, I wished to know if I was really free, and turned from them down the way that led to my lodgings; whereupon they cast themselves before me, and in a supplicating posture besought me to go with them.

Finding then that I was still their prisoner, I gave a longing look-out for my valiant fellows; but, as they did not appear, I suffered myself to be reconducted to the marquis's palace, and followed my obsequious commanders into the proud apartment to which they had led me the preceding night, and where, bowing to the ground, they all left me and retired.

As I had been much fatigued in body and mind, I threw myself on the bed, leaving events to their issues, and fell into a kind of starting and intermitting slumber, when I heard a voice at my side shout out in once-loved accents— Oh, my dearest mamma, it is he! indeed it is he! it is he himself!

On this, I awoke and roused myself, and lifting my languid eyes, and fixing them on the object that stood before me— And are you then, I cried, are you also, Louisa, in the confederacy against me? Say nothing, you are not the Louisa I once knew. I will arise, I will go forth; not all your gates and bars and bolts shall hold me; I will tear my body, and my soul too, if possible, from you for ever! Go to your betrothed, to your beloved! and leave me to perish; it is a matter of no import. I am yet pleased that I saved your chosen, as it may one day serve to reproach you with the merits of the man whom he has so unworthily treated!

I could no more. A long silence on all sides ensued, save the language that was uttered by heavings and sobbings, when the marchioness, coming and casting herself on her knees by my bed—You have reason, sir! she exclaimed— you have reason to reproach and to detest every branch of our ungrateful family for ever! You saved myself, you saved my daughter; and yet the father and the husband proved averse to your deservings, and turned your benefits into poison.. You have now saved our son, the only one who can convey our name to posterity; and yet, from the beginning, you have received nothing in return save wounds, pains, and sickness, losses, damages, and disappointments, and at this very day the most ignominious usage, where you merited endless thanks and everlasting renown. Blame my Louisa, then, and me; but blame not my son, sir, for these unworthy events. He is shocked and distracted by them; he is quite innocent of them; he respects and loves you more than ever Jonathan loved the son of Jesse; but he will not, he dare not see you, till we have in some measure made his peace.

How, madam! I cried—but no more of that posture; it pains me past bearing. Is it a fact, can it be possible, that the Marquis d'Aubigny should be your son? Is he not of the blood-royal, the very rival whom your letter rendered so formidable to me? and was it not by his order that I was disgracefully confined in a dungeon all night?

No, no! said my lady; he would have suffered the rack first! He is in despair, quite inconsolable on that account. Let us go, my dearest Harry; let us go and carry comfort to him of whom you are the beloved.

Ah, no, my mamma! cried out Louisa; let us put no constraint on Mr. Clinton, I pray you! There has been enough of confinement; we leave him now to his liberty; let him go, even where and to whom he likes best. Once, indeed, we could have tied this all-conquering champion with the spinning of a silkworm; but now he tells us that neither gates, bars, nor bolts shall hold him to us.

Here I threw myself precipitately at her feet—Pardon, pardon, my Louisa! I cried; O pardon the misdeeming transports of your lover, and pardon the faults that love alone could commit! My enemies are foreign to me; they and their injuries affect me not; but you are regent within, my Louisa! you sit throned in my heart, and the presumption of an offence from you makes strange uproar in my soul!—Well, says she, reaching her hand, and smiling through tears, since it is so, poor soul, here is the golden sceptre for you; I think I must take you to mercy.

I caught her hand, and impressed my very spirit on the wax; and my lady, casting her arms about us, and kissing us both in turns, requested that we should go and carry some consolation to her dear, repining Lewis.

As we entered his chamber, the marchioness cried out—Here he comes, my son! we have brought your beloved to you; yet not your Mr. Goodall, as you thought, but one who is at once both your good angel and our good angel, even our own Harry Clinton, the betrothed of our souls!

I took my seat on the side of the marquis's bed, and, looking fondly upon him, would have inquired of his health, but my speech for the time was overpowered by my affections. Then taking my hand in his—The power of this hand, says he, I have found to be great; but has your heart the power to pardon the insults and outrage you have received in the house of him who is so deeply your debtor?—My lord, said I, I have already drank largely of Lethe on that head; nothing but my diffidence of your regard can offend me.

You know not, said my lady—you know not yet, my dear Harry, how this provoking business came about. I will explain it in a few words:—

On our return to Paris, and on our remonstrances to my late lord, of the inestimable services you had rendered to his family, he inquired your character among the English; and, notwithstanding the report of the nobility of your birth, and your yet nobler qualities, hearing also that you had acquired part of your fortune in trade, he conceived an utter contempt for you, and took an utter aversion to you.

Some time after, as he took notice that Louisa and I wanted our watch and our ring, I dreaded his displeasure, and gave him room to think that the robbers had taken them from us in Flanders, and this report became current among our domestics.

In the mean time, my lord became importunate with our Louisa respecting her marriage with the Prince of C——, who was then with the army; and her prayers and tears hitherto had been the only artillery which she had used in her defence.

But when the couriers brought word that the prince was on his return, my lord sent for Louisa, and gave her instant and absolute orders to prepare for her nuptials; but she full as positively and peremptorily replied, that her soul was already wedded; that she would never prostitute her body where her heart was an alien; and that all the tortures of the Inquisition should not change her resolution. Her father thereupon rose to such ungovernable fury, that with one blow of his hand he struck her senseless to his feet; but when he saw my lamb, my darling, all pale, and as dead before him, the tide of nature returned, and the conflict of his passions became so violent that an imposthume broke in his stomach, and falling, he was suffocated, and expired on the spot.

Soon after the prince arrived. He had never seen my daughter; but his ambition to possess a beauty, of whom the grand monarch himself was said to have been enamoured, had caused him to demand her in marriage: for that purpose he also did us the honour of a visit. Louisa refused to appear; and I told his highness, with the best grace I could, that she happened to be pre-engaged. In a few days after he met my son on the Tuileries, and accosted him to the same intent; but my son had been previously prejudiced in your favour, my Harry, and answered the prince with so cold or so haughty an air, that further words ensued, they both drew, and his highness was slightly wounded; but, as company interposed, the affair was hushed up, and, shortly after, the prince was killed in a night broil upon the Pont-Neuf. We then wrote to our friend, De Wit, to advertise you of these matters, and to hasten you hither; but you arrived, my child—you arrived before there could be any expectation of an answer.

Two days ago, as I observed that my lamb's spirits were something dejected, I prevailed upon her to take an airing to our country villa. On our return this morning, we were struck half dead with the news that our Lewis was wounded, and dangerously ill in his bed. We flew into his room, and were still more alarmed to find him in a fury that is not to be imagined; while Jacome, his old steward, was on his knees, all pale and quaking, at a distance before him.—Villain! he cried, what have you done with my friend? What have you done with my champion; the preserver of my life? —Please your lordship, said he trembling, I took him for a highwayman; I saw my lady's ring and my young mistress's watch in his custody; I will swear to the property before the parliament of Paris, and so I lodged him in prison—till —till——

Go, wretch! cried my son, recall your information; take all your fellows with you, and instantly bring me back my friend, or your ears shall be the forfeit; but conduct him to his own chamber; I cannot yet bear to see him, I cannot bear the reproach that his eye must cast upon me.

All afflicted, and yet more astonished, my Louisa and I sat down by the side of my son, casting looks of surprise and inquiring doubt on each other. At length I said—What is this that I hear of our ring and our watch? Alas! he is no highwayman who took them from us; they were our own free gift, a mite in return for a million of services. But do you know any thing of the possessor?—I know, answered Lewis, that he is the loveliest of mankind, the preserver of my life, and that his name is Goodall.—Ah! screamed out

Louisa, there we are lost again. This Goodall must certainly have murdered our precious Clinton, and possessed himself of our gifts; he would never have parted with them while he had life.—Oh, my sister! said my son, when you see my friend Goodall, you will think nothing of your Harry Clinton! Why, why were you so hasty, so precipitate in your choice? A robber, a murderer! No; had I a thousand lives, I would pawn them all for the probity that heaven has made apparent in the face of my preserver.

It is with shame and great reluctance, my dearest brother, that at times I recite passages tending so much to my own praise; and yet, did I omit them, I should do great injustice to the kind and amiable partiality of those who were so fondly my lovers and my beloved.

But, Madam, said I to the marchioness, did you not hint something of his majesty's being enamoured of my Louisa? Ah, such a rival would be a terrible business indeed, especially in a country of unlimited power!

There is no fear of that now, said my lady. The king has changed his fancy, from young mistresses and old counsellors, to young counsellors and old mistresses. But what I mentioned was once very serious and alarming.

My Louisa was scarce turned of fourteen, when the Duchess de Choisseul requested her company to Marlay, where the court then was. The king fixed his eye on her, and inquired who she was; but took no further notice at that time. Missing her, however, at the next, and again at the following drawing-room, he asked the marquis what became of his fair daughter; said he had a place in his eye for her; and desired, in an accent of authority, that he would send her to court.

The marquis instantly took the alarm. He was ever jealous of his honour, and singularly nice in matters of female reputation. He gave his majesty a sort of equivocal consent; and, hurrying home, ordered me directly to prepare for carrying my daughter out of the French dominions. The night was employed in hastening and packing. We disguised our Louisa in the manner as you saw her metamorphosed at Rotterdam, and set off for Holland before day. The rest you know, my Clinton, as you were the principal mover in all our concerns.—But tell me, my Lewis, can you conjecture on what account those assassins set upon you?— I declare, madam, said the marquis, I cannot; perhaps they mistook me for another; or, now I recollect, it might be owing to some familiar chat which I had the other night with a pretty opera-girl, who is said to be in the keeping of a very great man. But, madam, you forgot to tell my brother how my father was banished, on account of Louisa, to his paternal seat in Languedoc, on the borders of the Mediterranean.—Very true, said the marchioness, and was not recalled till Madam Maintenon was taken into supreme favour.

But I wonder what has become of our faithful Gerard; I thought that he would have been the first to come, and to throw himself at the feet of his hero. Indeed, my Harry, he would have tired any, who loved you less, with his praises, and perpetual talking of you and your exploits. O, here he comes! Step in Gerard. Is there any one in this company that you remember beside the family?

Gerard then advanced with a half-frantic aspect, and, kneeling and grappling at my hand, seemed desirous of devouring it. God be praised! he cried; God be praised, my noble, my glorious master, that I see you once again! and above all, that I have the blessing of seeing you in a place where a throne of beaten gold should be raised to your honour. O, had I been here, all sorts of respects and worships, instead of indignities, should have been paid to your deservings! But I have provided for the hang-dog Jacome; I have tied him neck and heels, and tumbled him into a dark vault.

Ay, said I; but my good friend, Gerard, I have not yet got my share of satisfaction upon him; pray, shew me where he is. I then followed Gerard to the place where the deplorable wretch was cast; and, cutting all his cords, I led him back to the company, and warmly joined his petition for pardon and restoration.

As soon as Jacome and Gerard were withdrawn—Ah, my brother! cried the marquis, what new name shall we find for a man of your new character? Moreover, what shall we do for you? You have quite overpowered us; we sink, we drown under the sense of our obligations! We have nothing worth your acceptance save this simple wench; and what is she in comparison of what we owe you?—Ah! I cried, she is that without whom all things are nothing; she is the living treasure, the Rachel of Rachels; seventy times seven years were too short a service for her! I would not exchange this little pearly joint of this very little finger for all the gems that grow in the mines of India; and so saying, I pressed the precious finger with my lips, while Louisa turned upon me an eye of such ineffable satisfaction and melting acknowledgment, as sunk upon my soul, and wrapped it in elysium.

Ay but, my Harry, said the marquis, you ought not to prize your Louy as much as me; she did not fall in love with you at first sight, as I did.—How did you know that, honest friend? cried Louisa. Is there a necessity that our tongues as well as our blushes should be tell-tales? Are maidens to trumpet forth their thoughts, like you broad-fronted men, whose ornament is your bold-facedness?

Thus happy, above all styled happy upon earth, we joyed and lived in each other, continuing a mutual commerce of delightful sensibilities and love for love.

Alas! our blissful junto was soon to be broken in upon. In a few days, one of the royal pages came and intimated to the marchioness that his majesty required her immediate presence at court; and we remained in a kind of fearful and fluctuating suspense till her return.

As she entered, the consternation in her countenance instantly struck an alarm to all our hearts. O, my children! my dear, my dear children! we must part, she cried; and that, too, speedily. Our hour of bliss is past; our sunshine is over, and the clouds gather thick upon us, heavy laden with wretchedness. Alas! my heart misgave me ever since that inauspicious encounter the other morning. As we came from our villa a great funeral met us (a bad omen as I have heard); our carriage stopped to let them pass, and the carriage of the Duke of Ne——rs drove up beside us. As we remained within a few paces of each other, he gazed at Louisa with such enamoured intenseness as caused her to colour and turn aside. However, he accosted us not, nor inquired concerning us; it seems our arms and livery were too sure an indication of our name and quality. In short, on my approaching the presence, the king affected to smile very graciously upon me, and said—I have provided, madam, a noble and princely husband for your daughter; it is the Duke of Ne——rs.—Ah! I cried, bending my knee in a supplicating posture, my daughter is already engaged, by bands of the most endearing and indissoluble obligations, to a man who has preserved the lives and honours of all our family; to a man who, I trust, by his eminent courage and qualities, will become the brightest jewel in your majesty's crown.— Madam, said he, severely, you must withdraw your election. I find I have ordered matters superior to your merits; but my will is the law here, and shall be obeyed.—I rose dejectedly, curtsied, and withdrew without reply.

Ah! I exclaimed, on what summit does this rival hold his

abode? I will instantly go and scale it, and at once put an end to his life and his pretensions! My lady then, throwing her arms about my neck, and pressing her lips to my cheek—What romance, says she, is this? my Harry; would you at once fight the duke and the king, and the whole army of France? No, my child, prudence reduces us to more salutary, however deplorable, measures. We must part, my Harry—we must part this very night, and my Louisa must depart with you. My chaplain shall, this minute, unite you by ties that death alone can sunder. Alas! my precious babes, I little expected that your nuptials should be celebrated by tears and wailings! But better these than no nuptials. When you are once joined, I shall care little for myself. And, if we meet no more here, we may yet meet hereafter, as happily as the barbarians who tear us asunder.

The chaplain was then summoned, and, having performed his office, no congratulations nor salutations ensued, save a kiss and a sigh of mine on the hand of my angel. The marquis then called me, and drawing me down to him, he pressed me ardently to his bosom, cried—O my Harry! O my Harry! burst into tears, and dismissed me.

Meanwhile, all was in bustle and hurry throughout the palace. No festival was prepared, no bridal bed laid. Horses, arms, and carriages, were all the cry; and the marchioness, with an anguishing heart, but amazing resolution, issued her orders with a presence of mind that seemed serene in the midst of tempest.

I then sent for my brave fellows, with orders to double their arms, and to double their ammunition. They came accordingly. It was now within three hours of day. All was despatched—all in readiness; the carriages were at the gate. Silence sat on every tongue, and a tear on every cheek. I threw myself at my mother's feet, I clasped, I clung to them; she wept aloud over me, but neither of us utterred a word. When, rending myself away, I took my sobbing Louisa under my arm, seated her gently in her chariot, placed myself to support her, and away we drove.

When we got clear of the town, and were speeding on the way, my Louisa started and cried out—O how fast—how very fast they take me from you, my mamma! Whither, whither do they carry me, perhaps never to return, never to meet again? I answered not, but kissed her head, and drew her gently to me, and she seemed more at ease. But, after a while, I felt her agitation at my bosom, and she exclaimed —From my birth to this hour of woe, my blessed mamma, never was I from those dear arms of yours! shall I ever, shall I ever again behold those eyes that used to look with such fondness upon me?

Here I could no longer contain, but taking her hands between mine, and weeping upon them, I said—Will you then, my angel—are you resolved upon breaking the heart of your Harry?—O no! says she; no! not for worlds upon worlds would I break that dear and feeling heart, the heart of my heart, the heart of which I became enamoured. She then leaned her head fondly over, and in a while fell fast asleep; while my arms gently encircled and my soul hovered over her, as the wings of a turtle over her new-begotten.

When she awoke, and found herself so endearingly situated, she gave me a look that overvalued the ransom of a monarch; she kissed my hands in turns, she kissed the skirts of my garments. O, she cried, I will endeavour, I will do my best to be more composed! I know I ought not to repine. I am too rich—too happy. I ought to wish for nothing more, I ought to wish for no one more; since my Harry is so near me, since I have him to myself. But—but —and here her lovely lips began again to work, and the drops that trembled in her living brilliants could hardly be restrained from breaking prison. Soon after the grief of her heart overweighed her spirits, and she fell asleep into my arms, that opened of themselves to receive her.

On setting up for the night, I rejoiced to find that my Louisa was something more easy; and that her repose on the way had greatly deducted from the fatigue that I apprehended.

At length we reached Calais, and immediately sent to the beach to engage a ship for wafting us over to the land of freedom and rights, but the wind was contrary.

Meanwhile the day advanced towards evening, and my Louisa and I sat together in the arbour of a little pleasure garden that lay behind the house, when James came hastening to us and cried—Hide yourself, madam, for heaven's sake hide yourself! Here is the Duke de Ne——rs, with a large party of the king's light horse.

Poor Louisa started up and attempted to fly; but she trembled and grew faint, and sunk down again on her seat.

James, said I, stay and take care of your mistress, then, turning with hasty steps to the house, I recommended my spirit in a short ejaculation, and entered, determined that the duke should accompany me in death. His highness was in the parlour. I advanced fiercely towards him. So, sir, says he, you have cost us a warm chase—Heavens, what do I see! and so crying out, he threw himself back into an arm-chair, all panting, and his aspect working with distraction and disappointment.—Cursed chance! he again exclaimed; are you the man, Clinton? Ah! I must not hurt you, I ought not to injure you; but what is then to be done? Where have you put my Louisa? But no matter; let her not appear, let me not see her. I could not answer the consequence. I would be just if I could, Clinton. O love, O honour, how you do distract me! You refused my treasures and jewels, Clinton; but then you have rent from me a gem more estimable than my dukedom. Help saints, help angels, help me to wrestle with myself! Honour, virtue, gratitude! O, compel me to be just! Tear, tear me away, while there's strength to depart! Adieu, Clinton! you are recompensed; should we happen to meet again, I may assail you without reproach. And so saying, he rose suddenly, and rushed out of the house.

I then hastened to seek my love, but had scarce entered the garden when I saw James on his knees before her, endeavouring to oppose her way to the house. But she cried—away, villain, let me pass! They are murdering my lord, they are murdering my husband! I will go and perish with him. Then, breaking away from him, she shot along like a lapwing, till, seeing me advancing, she sprung upon my bosom, crying—O my Harry! O my Harry! are you safe, are you safe? and fainted away in my arms.

The rest of my story, my lord, is no way material or entertaining. The serene of heartfelt happiness has little of adventure in it, and is only interesting to the possessors.

Having settled my affairs in London, and carrying my Eden along with me, I passed into Holland to settle, and be quit of matters there also; for the world that I wished was in my holding, and all things else appeared either nugatory or encumbering.

It was there that I met our Meekly; and, taking a pleasant tour through the skirts of Germany, we entered France, and, leaving Paris on the right hand, we reached the marquis's country seat, situate near twenty leagues beyond the metropolis.

What a meeting! what an interview! My Louisa sunk into tears for half an hour on the bosom of her mother; and the marquis would put me from him and pull me to him again, all panting with transport, and insatiate of his caresses. It was too much of joy; it was pleasure too paining. The domestics would no longer be restrained from their share of the felicity; they rushed in, and, as though we had been new descended divinities, they dropped on their knees; they fell prostrate, and clung about us; kissed our feet, our hands, our garments, and broke forth into cries as though it had been the house of mourning and lamentation.

On retiring, they got my Louisa's Gerard to themselves. He now became a man of mighty importance among them. They crowded about him, and in a joint voice, but a distraction of questions, inquired after our travels, our adventures, our good and evil occurrences, and all that concerned us.

The marchioness then coming, and casting her honoured arms around me, and weeping upon me, cried aloud—O Harry, my son, my son! I delivered my daughter to you, even as Edna committed her Sarah, of special trust, to Tobias, and I see that you have entreated her very kindly, my son, my son!

As my Louisa now began to be apparently pregnant, I earnestly pressed my precious mother and brother to accompany us to England; the place where law was regent; where there was no apprehension of inquisitions or bastiles; and where the peasant was guarded, as with a bulwark of adamant, against every encroachment of arbitrary power. They assented with joy; and the marquis, going to his escritoir, brought forth bills to the amount of ten millions of livres, the produce of some concerns which he had disposed of for the purpose. Here, my brother, says he, if I am not able to be grateful, if I am not able to be generous, I will at least be just; here is the patrimony to which my lovely sister is entitled.—But I said to the marquis, my Louisa can admit of no accession of value. Keep your goods to yourself. Remember how Esau said to Jacob, I have enough, enough, my brother; these things can add nothing to the abundance of my blessings.—But then, he cried, you must accept them as a token of our loves; and so he constrained and impelled them upon me.

Soon after we passed to London, where we continued some months, and where my Louisa was delivered of my little Eloisa, who was said to be the beautiful likeness of her father.

We then retired to my seat near Stratford, on the fatal Avon, the chief of the landed possessions that Mr. Golding had bequeathed me, where we remained something upwards of five years, happy, I think, above all that ever were happy upon earth; for my Louisa was perpetual festivity to our sight and to our hearts; her eyes beamed with living and sentimental glory; her attitudes were grace; her movements were music; and her smiles were fascination. Still varying, yet exhibiting the same delight; like the northern aurora, she shone in all directions; and she sported as though she had gone to heaven from time to time, and borrowed all her plays from the kingdom of little children.

But she needed not to go to heaven, since heaven was ever in her and round about her, and that she could no more move from it than she could move from herself. She had been, from her earliest years, the beloved disciple of the celebrated Madam Guion; and the world, with all its concerns, its riches and respects, had fallen off from her, as the cloak fell away from the burning chariot of Elijah. She looked at nothing but her Lord in all things; she loved nothing but him in any thing; and he was, in her heart, a pleasure passing sense, as well as a peace that passed understanding.

Our friends now prevailed upon us to accompany them, in our turn, to France; together with our prattling Eloisa, who was become the darling and inseparable companion of her grandmother and her uncle. We again took London in our way. I there renewed, for a while, my old acquaintance with my fellows in trade, and they persuaded me to join them in a petition to his majesty for the restoration of some of the lapsed rights of their corporation, as your lordship may remember.

From Calais we turned, and by long but pleasant journeys at length arrived at the marquis's paternal seat at Languedoc, that opened a delightful prospect on the Mediterranean. And here we continued upwards of five years more, even as Adam continued in paradise, compassed in by bliss from the rest of the world.

During this happy period, I often pressed my dear marquis to marry; but he would take me to his arms and say —O my Harry! shew me but the most distant resemblance of our Louisa, and I will marry, and be blessed without delay.

In the meanwhile my angel made me the joyful father of a little son, who was also said to be the happier resemblance of his happy father. Then, though I had long disregarded the world and all its concerns, as I saw a family increasing upon me, and also considered the poor as my appointed and special creditors, I resolved once more to return and settle my long-suspended accounts.

As for the marchioness, she protested that she could not think of parting with her little Eloisa, and that she should not be able to survive her absence ten days. So my Louisa and I, and my little Richard, who was named after you, my lord, set out by sea, and after a favourable voyage arrived in England; comforted, however, with the promise that our friends would join us as soon as possible in Britain.

Within the ten subsequent months we received the joyful tidings that our brother was married to the third daughter of the Duke of Alençon—that they were all in the highest triumph, and would speedily be with us in a joint jubilate on the banks of the Avon.

Soon after, as my Louisa and I rode along the river, pleasing ourselves with the prospect of a speedy union with persons so dear to us, and talking and laughing away at the cares of the covetous, and the ambition of the high-minded, a fowler inadvertently fired a shot behind us, and my horse, bounding aloft, plunged with me into the current, from whence however I was taken, and unwillingly reserved to years of inexpressible misery—of a misery that admitted not of a drop of consolation.

Meanwhile my love had fallen, with a shriek, from her horse, and lay senseless on the sod. Some of my people flew back, and bringing a carriage, conveyed us gently home, where my Louisa was undressed and put into a bed, from whence she never rose. Her fright had given such a shock to her blood and spirits as threw her into a violent fever.

On the second day, while I sat with the physicians by her side, James put in his head and beckoned me forth.—Ah, my dearest master! says he, I pray God to give you the strength and patience of Job; you have great need of them, for your calamities, like his, come all in a heap upon you. Here is a messenger despatched from France with very heavy tidings —that my sweet young lady, your darling Eloisa, was cast away in a sloop, upon a party of pleasure, and that the good old marchioness did not outlive her five days. Then lifting my eyes to heaven—Strip, strip me, my God! I cried—to the skin—to the bone: leave but my Louisa, and I will bless thy dispensations!

On the next day, my little Dickey was taken ill of a severe cold that he caught, through want of due attention during the sickness of his mother. As he was of a florid complexion, his disorder fell suddenly in an inflammation on his lungs, and in less than twenty-four hours he went to join his little brothers and sisters in their eternity. Did I not feel these losses? Yes, yes, my friends, they wrung—they rent my vitals; yet I still lifted my heart in an eager prayer, and repeatedly cried—Take, take all—even the last mite; leave, leave me but my Louisa, and I will bless thee, O my Creator!

Alas! what could this avail? Can an insect arrest the motion whereby the round universe continues its course? On the fifth day I perceived that the eyes of my Louisa— the lamps of my life—began to lose their lustre. The breath that was the balm of all my cares and concerns, grew difficult and short. The rose of my summer died away on her cheek. All agonizing, I felt and participated her changes; and she expired while I dropped and lay senseless beside her.

I knew not what our people did with her or me afterwards. For three weeks I lay in a kind of dosing but uneasy stupor; neither do I recollect during that period when or whether I received any kind of sustenance.

At length I awoke to the poignancy and bitterness of my situation. I did not awake to life, but rather to the blackest gloom of the regions of death; and yet it was from this depth and enfolding of death alone that my soul could find or would accept an alleviation of its anguish.

O earth! I cried, where is thy centre? How deeply am I sunk beneath it! how are the worms exalted over me! how much higher are the noxious reptiles that crawl upon earth! I will not accuse thee, thou great Disposer. I have had my day—the sweetest that ever was allotted to man; but O, thy past blessings serve only to enhance my present miseries, and to render me the most accursed of all thy creatures!

I then rose, and threw myself along the floor, and my faithful and valiant companions immediately gathered to me; but finding that I would not be removed, they cast themselves around me.

All light was shut out save the glimmering of a taper; and for seven nights and seven days we dwelt in silence, except the solemn interruptions of smothered sobs and wailings.

At length my spirit reproved me. What property, said I to myself, have these people in my sufferings, or why should I burden those who love me with my afflictions? I then constrained myself, and went and took out a drawer. Here, my friends, I said, here is something that may help hereafter to dry up your tears. Divide these thousands among you; neither these counters nor your services are now of further use. Fare ye well!—fare ye well!—my worthy and beloved brothers! God will give you a more gracious master; but —but—such another mistress you never—never will find! I then took each of them to my arms, and kissed them in turns, and the house was instantly filled with heart-tearing lamentations.

I now expected and wished to be left wholly alone; but James and two domestics remained against my will. I then endeavoured to seem easy—I even struggled to appear cheerful, that I might communicate the less of grief to the voluntary sharers in my misery. O world, world! I said to myself; thou once pleasant world, we have now bid a long and eternal adieu to each other! From thee I am cut asunder—thou art annihilated to me—and we mutually reject every kind of future commerce.

Ah! how much deeper was my death than that of those in the tomb—"where the wicked cease from troubling, and where the weary are at rest!" While I was dead to every relish of light and of life, I was wholly alive to all the gloom and horrors of the grave. The rays of the sun became an offence to my soul—the verdure of the fields, the whole bloom of nature, was blasted and blasting to my sight; and I wished to sink yet deeper, and to dig a lower bottom to myself of darkness and distress.

I no longer regarded what the world thought of me, or what it did to me; and I left my hairs and my nails, even as those of Nebuchadnezzar, to grow like eagles' feathers and birds' claws.

My friend James, in the mean time, took a place for me in this town, in order to remove me from scenes that could only serve to perpetuate or aggravate my misery, by reminding me of the blessedness that I had once enjoyed. He was now become my controller. I was patient and passive to any thing—to every thing; and so he conducted me hither— I neither knew nor cared how.

In all this time, though I panted after a state of insensibility, even as a traveller in the burning desert thirsts after a cool and slaking stream, I never attempted to lay a violating hand on the work of my Creator. I did not even wish an alleviation of my misery, since my God had appointed that I should be so very miserable.

At length my spirit rose from its blackness to a kind of calm twilight. I called for a Bible, and, since this world was incapable of a drop of consolation, I wished to know if the next had any in store.

As I read, the whole of the letter and of the facts contained therein, appeared as so many seals and veils that removed from before my eyes, and discovered depths under depths, and heavens above heavens, to my amazed apprehension. I had no vision, no revelation of these matters; but the conviction was impressed as strongly on my soul as though an angel of God himself had revealed them to me.

How this came to pass I know not. Homer gives to his heroes a sight into futurity, at the time that their spirits are breaking away from the shackles of flesh and blood: and it is not unlikely that the eye of the soul, when wholly turned from all carnal and earthly objects, can penetrate with the greater scope and clarity into concerns that are merely celestial and divine.

I have now told you the whole of my dreary history, my friends, till I met with our Harry; and the rest our Harry can tell.

But Harry was in no manner of vein at present for entertaining, or receiving entertainment, from any one. His eyes were swelled with weeping, his spirits totally depressed, and getting up, as with the burden of fourscore years on his shoulders, he retired slowly and silently to his apartment.

On an evening, after coffee, as the earl stood fondly fooling with his Harry, as one child with another, he turned to Mr. Clinton, and said—How came it to pass, my brother, that Jesus suffered near four thousand years to elapse before he became incarnate for the salvation of the world, although it was by him alone that the world could be saved?

We may as well demand of God, said Mr. Clinton, why he suffered near four days of creation to elapse before he compacted yon glorious body of far-beaming light; for this matter was barely a type, and the sun himself but a shadow of the Christ that was to come.—But did the world want light before light became incorporated in its illustrious circumscription?—No, my lord. Jesus, who was from eternity the illumination of the dark immensity of nature; Jesus, who alone is the living light of spirit, soul, and sentiment, the perpetual fountain of the streams of beauty and truth, he said—Let there be light; and instantly, through the darkness of a ruined world, the internity of his ever-living light kindled up an externity of corporal irradiation, that has its effluence from him, and cannot be but by him.

Now as a day is as a thousand years, and a thousand years as a day, in the sight of God, you see that the fourth day of creation, wherein the light of this outward world was compacted into the glorious body of the sun, precisely answers to the four thousandth year wherein Jesus, the light of eternity, was to become embodied and incarnate in Christ the son of righteousness.

But as the world wanted not light before the sun opened his first morning in the east; neither did it want the means of salvation before the blessed doctrine of Messiah was promulged upon earth!

All sorts of sectarians, all persons of selfish and little minds, would make a monopoly of the Saviour; they would shut him up into a conventicle, and say to their God—"Thus far shalt thou go, and no farther." But he is not so to be confined. The spirit of our Jesus bloweth wide and where he listeth; and he is at once both the purifier and redeemer, as well of all nations, as also of all nature.

Accordingly we see that the Turks, who are wholly unblessed by true religion or liberty, who live the slaves of slaves, without a form of civil government, temporally subjected to the will of a tyrant, and spiritually to the worship of a sensual impostor, yet want not the feelings of our Jesus in their heart.

Even the wild Indians, who never listened to the toll of a bell, nor ever were called into any court of civil judicature, these want not their attachments, their friendships, their family feelings, nor the sweet compunctions and emotions of the human heart, by Jesus forming it to divine.

The truth is, that people live incomparably more by impulse and inclination than by reason and precept. Reason and precept are not always within our beck; to have their due influence, they require frequent inculcation and frequent recollection; but impulse and inclination are more than at hand; they are within us, and from the citadel rule the outworks of man at pleasure.

When the apostle, speaking of Christ, affirms that "there is no other name under heaven whereby a man may be saved;" and again, when he affirms that "those who have not received the law, are a law unto themselves;" he intends one and the same thing. He intends that Christ, from the fall of man, is a principle of redemption in the bosoms of all living; that he is not an outward but an inward redeemer, working out our salvation by "the change of our depraved nature;" that in and from him alone arise all the sentiments and sensibilities that warm the heart with love, that expand it with honour, that wring it with compunction, or that heave it with the story of distant distress; and that he alone can be qualified to be judge at the last day, who from the first day to the last was internally a co-operator and witness of all that ever passed within the bosoms of all men.

Hence it is, that although the Christian countries have received the two tables of the laws of Christ, his external as well as internal revelation, each witnessing to the other that the God of our gospel is the God of our nature; the nations, however, who are strangers to his name, yet acknowledge his influence, they do not indeed hear, but they feel the precepts of "that light which lighteth every man who cometh into the world."

My dearest brother, said the earl, my conceptions are quite clear with respect to the omnipresence of Christ's divinity; but as his body is circumscribed by external features and lineaments, I can form no notion of its being in several places at once: how then will it be, I pray you, at and after the last day? Will he be present to, and approachable only by, a select number of the saints; or will he go certain journeys and circuits through the heavens, blessing all in rotation with his beatific presence?

Is not the body of yonder sun circumscribed, my lord?— Most certainly.—It is now, said Mr. Clinton, at a distance of many millions of leagues from you; and yet you see it as evidently, and feel its influence as powerfully, as if it were within your reach. Nay, it is more than within your reach, it is within your existence: it supplies comfort and life to your animal body and life; and you could not survive an hour without its influence and operations.

Now this is no other than the apt type and prefiguring promise of what Christ will be to his new-begotten in the resurrection, "when corruption shall be swallowed up of glory, and mortal of immortality." The same blessed body which, for the redemption of commiserated sinners, went through the shameful and bloody process of scourges, thorns, spittings, and buffetings; which hung six agonizing hours on the cross; which descended into the grave, and thence opened the way through death into life, and through time into eternity; even this body shall then shine forth in ineffable beauty and beatitude, in essentially communicative grace and glory, through the height and through the depth, through the length and through the breadth, beaming wide beyond the universe, from infinity to infinity!

Father, Son, and Holy Spirit will then become coembodied in this divine body; they will be the repletion of it; they will operate all things by it. To bring the Creator nearer to his creatures, the invisible godhead will then become visible, the infinite circumscribed, the unapproachable accessible, and the incomprehensible comprehended, within the humanity of our Christ.

Then will his cross be exalted, for an ensign to the circling, bending, and worshipping universe; his wreath of thorns will kindle all nature with the dartings and castings forth of its coruscations; and the reed of mockery will become the sceptre of unlimited domination!

From his five wounds shall be poured forth incessant floods of glory and wide-diffusing blessedness upon all his redeemed: adoring worlds, in self-abjection, shall strive to sink beneath the abjection that became their salvation: these ever-apparent ensigns of so dearly purchased benefits, shall inevitably attract the wills of all creatures; they shall cause all hearts and affections to rush and cleave to him, as steel-dust rushes to adamant, and as spokes stick in the nave whereon they are centred. There shall be no lapse thenceforward, no falling away, for ever; but God in his Christ, and Christ in his redeemed, shall be a will and a wisdom, and an action and a mightiness, and a goodness and a graciousness, and a glory rising on glory, and a blessing rising on blessedness, through an ever-beginning to a never-ending eternity.

O brother, brother, brother! exclaimed the earl—I am enraptured, I am entranced! I see it all, I feel it all. I am already, with all my corruptions, with all my transgressions, desirous of being crushed to nothing under the foot of my Redeemer. But he comforts instead of crushing me. O that I were this night, this very moment, to be dissolved, and to be with my Christ!

That night the earl was quite happy, and pleasant and affectionate, even beyond his custom. He said and did every thing that could be endearing to his Harry, and to his friends. He caressed them at parting for bed. He smilingly shook hands with all the domestics that approached him; and in the morning was found dead, without any notice or warning to the servants who attended and lay in the room.

A sudden and grievous alarm was instantly given through the family, and quickly reached the town, and spread through the adjacent country.

Harry fell upon his father's face, and wept upon him, and kissed him, and wept aloud, and kissed him again, crying— My father! O, my father!

And they laid his remains in a plated coffin, under escutcheons and a sable canopy of velvet; and the house and the court were circled with mourners from all parts; and they mourned for him fifty and nine days; and on the sixtieth day he was deposited in the family tomb; but Mr. Clinton would not permit Harry to attend the funeral of his father.

Our hero was now the master of millions, approaching to the prime of youth, glowing with health, action, and vigour —of beauty incomparable, beloved of all who knew him, and the attraction and admiration of every eye where he passed. Yet all these advantages, with all his higher accomplishments, became as matters of no value; they sunk and sickened to his sense, while he felt a void in his bosom, eager after he knew not what, sighing he knew not why; keen and craving in his desires, yet pining and languid in the want of possession.

What is the matter, my love? said Mr. Clinton. My dear brother died in a good old age. Such things should be expected; we know that they must be; and we ought not to grieve as persons who are without hope.

True, sir, said Harry; and yet it is a very melancholy thing for a poor man to reflect how very rich he was a very little while ago. I lately had a dear brother, a dear mother, and the dearest of fathers; but where are they all now? I look around the world and see nothing but yourself therein; and—should you, too—should you, too—here Harry could no more. His uncle also broke into tears at the thoughts of parting with his beloved Harry, though it were to join his Louisa.

My Harry, says he at last, we have yet too precious treasures left upon earth, if we did but know where to find them: it is your cousin, the Countess of Maitland; and the brother of my Louisa, the Marquis d'Aubigny. Let us go in search of them, my son! Next to my Louisa, they are the loveliest of all living. They abound in all human and divine affections, and will caress us with kindred and corresponding hearts.

Soon after they set out for France, and, by a roundabout tour of short but pleasant journeys, arrived at Paris, where Mr. Clinton ordered his large retinue to his ancient inn; and, taking only two footmen, he and Harry went in their postchaise to the marquis's palace.

On the ringing of the bell, and the opening of the gate, a single domestic came forth. Mr. Clinton perceived that all was dark in the hall, and this instantly gave an alarm to his ever-ready feelings.

He alighted, however, and stepping, with his Harry, up the flight of marble—Where is your master? says he; where is my brother, the marquis?—Heaven bless us! cried the fellow, are you my master's brother? I have heard a deal of and about your lordship, though I never was so happy as to see your face before. Ho! he continued, and rung another bell, come all of you! Attend the brother of your lord! attend the present master and lord of your household!

Immediately the palace was in commotion, the parlour and hall were lighted up, and all seemed to have acquired a set of wings to their motions.

Mr. Clinton looked with eagerness at each of the domestics, endeavouring to recollect the features of some old acquaintance; but all the faces were strange to him.—Pray tell me, my friends, says he, where is your master? where and how are he and his lady? are they still in good health? has he had any children by her?

Please your honour, said an elderly man, my master's first lady died of childbirth, and her infant perished with her; but he is since married to one of the loveliest women in the world. He is gone, a year since, on an embassy into Africa; his lady would not be left behind. We lately heard from them; they are both in health, and we expect that less than a month will bring them safe to us. Indeed, the sum of our prayers is for their happy and speedy return.

What! said Mr. Clinton, are there none of my old friends, not one of our ancient domestics, to be found?—Please your lordship, Jacome, the whiteheaded steward, is still left; but, though in good health, he is very little more than half alive. —Pray, go and tell him that an old friend of his is here, and would be very glad to see him; but don't do things suddenly, and be very tender and careful in bringing him to me.

Old Jacome was wheeled in, wrinkled, pale, and paralytic; and, all enfeebled as he sat reclining in an easy-chair, he seemed to recover life and new spirits as they brought him forward.—Bring me to him! bring me to him! my eyes are wondrous dim. Bring me closer, that I may know if it is my very master indeed! Bring me but once to know that it is his sweet pardoning face, and then let me die with all my sins upon me! I care not.

Mr. Clinton then took him very lovingly by the hand—My good friend Jacome, says he, we are both growing old, I find; I rejoice, however, to see you once more upon earth.— O! cried the old man, a well-known and a sweet-tuned voice is that voice. It is you, then—it is you yourself, my master! Alas! for all your losses since last we parted. I have got a salt rheum in my eyes of late, and I never thought of you but it began to come down.

Here Jacome, sobbing aloud, provoked the joint tears of his attending fellow-servants, though they had never been partakers in the foregoing calamities further than by the ear, whence they were now recollected and carried home to their hearts.

My lord, says Jacome at last, I am not the only one that remains of your old servants. Your Gerard, too, who (blessings on his hands) once tied me neck and heels—Gerard, too, is forthcoming, and near at hand. Your honour's wonderful bounty made a gentleman of him at once, and he is now in a high way, with a wife and three children. A hundred and a hundred times have we washed your remembrance with our tears; and indeed I think your honour ought not to send for him, lest he should suddenly die, or run distracted at your sight.

In the mean time one of the lackeys had officiously gone and informed Gerard of the arrival of his patron. He came panting, and rushed forward, as it were, to cast himself at the feet of his lord; but stopping suddenly, and drawing back some steps, he nailed his eyes, as it were, on the face of Mr. Clinton, and, spreading his hands, cried—You live, then, my lord! you still live, my dearest master! You survive all your deaths and sufferings, and the weight of ten mountains has not been able to crush you! O the times— the times, my master, never more to return! Will there be such times in heaven, think you? Will there be such angels there as we once lived with upon earth?

Here he clapped his hands together, and set up such a shout of bitter lamentation as was enough to split the heart of every hearer, and in a manner to split the graves of the persons whom he deplored.

As soon as Mr. Clinton and his two old friends had parted for the night—Tell me, my dear sir, said Harry, are there different kinds of grief; or is it merely that grief affects us in different manners?

When I wept for my dear father, my mother, and brother, my affliction was anguishing and altogether bitter, without any species of alleviating sensation to compensate my misery. But it was far otherwise with me to-night. When I grieved in the grief of your old and faithful domestics, I felt my heart breaking, but I was pleased that it should break; I felt that it was my happiness so to grieve, and I could wish a return of the same sweet sensations.

The reason is this, my love: When you lamented your parents, you lamented yourself in your private and personal losses; your affliction was just, it was natural, it was laudable; but still it was confined; it participated but little of the emotion that is excited by the affliction of others; and the anguish was the keener by being nearly limited to your own bosom, and your own concerns.

But in the griefs of my old and loving servants this night, you became wholly expanded; you went beyond, you went out of yourself; you felt, without reflection, how delightful it is to go forth with your God, in his social, generous, noble, and divine sensibilities; and you delightfully felt, my Harry, that such a house of mourning is more joyous to your soul, than all the festivals that flesh and sense can open before you.

And now, my child, I will finally and at once for all lay open the very horrible and detestable nature of Self in your soul.

Self appears to us as the whole of our existence; as the sum-total of all in which we are interested or concerned. It is as a Narcissus, self-delighted, self-enamoured. It desires, it craves, and claims as its right, the loves, attachments, and respects of all mankind. But does it acquire them, my Harry? O never, never! Self never was beloved, never will be beloved, never was honourable or respectable in the eye of any creature. And the characters of the patriot, the hero, the friend, and the lover, are only so far amiable or so far reverable, as they are supposed to have gone forth from the confines of self.

As Mr. Clinton proposed to wait the return of the marquis, he employed the mean season in endeavours to amuse his darling, and to dispel the cloud of melancholy that continued to hang over him.

For this purpose he went with him to Versailles, and to

the many other elegant environs of Paris. He also shewed him the Tuileries and other public walks, where our hero became oppressed by his involuntary attraction of all eyes upon him.

One night, happening to go to the play without the company of his guardian, as he came forth with the crowd a carriage was opened for him, which he took to be his own, and in he stepped, and away he was taken.

In the mean time Mr. Clinton waited supper for him, and began to grow uneasy when the clock struck twelve. At last his carriage and servants returned, with tidings that they stayed for him above an hour at the theatre after the play was over; and had ever since been in search of him, to no purpose.

Though Mr. Clinton was by nature of an intrepid spirit, and was still more assured by his reliance on Providence, he yet found himself agitated in a very alarming manner. He therefore retired to his closet, and there, on his knees, fervently commended his Harry to the protection of his God.

At length the clock struck three. Soon after the bell was heard from the hall; and Harry entering, with a page in a rich livery, flew like lightning up-stairs, and cast himself into the bosom of his patron.

My father, my-father! he cried, I have been in sad panics for you. I knew the love that you bore to your good-for-nothing Harry. But indeed I could not help it. I could not get to you till this instant. I have been a prisoner, sir, and here is my dear deliverer.

As soon as they were something composed, and all seated, Harry proceeded to satisfy the impatience of his uncle.

As I came out of the theatre, ruminating on a passage in one of Racine's tragedies, I found a chariot in the spot where I had left my own, and stepping heedlessly into it, I was soon set down, and, hastening through the great hall, flew up-stairs to salute you. But think how I was surprised, when I suddenly found myself in the most sumptuous chamber, perhaps, in the universe. It was wainscoted with mirrors of the most perfect polish, whose plates were artfully buttoned and buckled together by diamonds and other gems of a most dazzling lustre.

All astonished, I recoiled, and was going to withdraw, when I was met by a lady who gracely accosted me.—Have you commands, sir, says she, for any one in this house?—A thousand pardons, madam; I perceive my error. I really thought I was set down at my own lodgings.—No great offence, sir; but now that I look at you again, I think you ought to pay the forfeit of your intrusion, by giving me one hour of your company at least.—You must excuse me, madam, my guardian would be under the most terrifying alarms for me.—A fig for guardians! she cried. You are now my prisoner; and nothing less than my friend Lewis, with his army at his back, shall be able to take you out of my hands.

So saying, she rung a bell, and immediately a folding-door of panelled looking-glass flew open, and shewed us to another apartment, where a supper, composed of all the elegances of the season, was served up as by magic, and lay fuming on the table.

She then took me by the hand, and, having graciously seated me, placed herself opposite. A number of servants then vanished on the instant, leaving a dumb waiter of silver behind them.

Sir, said she, we are not to have any further company. You alone were expected, you alone are desired; all others are forbidden.

In short, I have seen you often at the public walks and theatres. You did more than strike my fancy; you laid hold on my heart. I inquired every thing about you. I know your rank, title, and fortune. I made use of this night's stratagem to decoy you to me; and, though there are few women in Europe of equal opulence or dignity, I think I cannot much demean myself by an alliance with a sweet fellow whom I so ardently love. But come, our supper cools.

I gazed at her with admiration. She was indeed the most finished beauty I ever beheld; and I was inwardly flattered, and in a manner attached to her, by her partiality in my favour.

After supper, and some futile and insignificant chat, she drew her chair nearer to me. What say you, my lord, says she fondly; am I to live, or to perish?

Ah, madam! I cried, love is as a little bird; if you cage it, it will beat itself to pieces against its prison. Not that I regard your late threats of confinement; my own arm is at all times sufficient to deliver me from your thraldom: but, in truth, I am partly become a willing prisoner to you, and time may, possibly, reconcile me to your different customs.

What customs, I pray you?—Why, madam, the ladies in my country use no paint except the rouge of nature's blush, and the paleness of chastity. Love also, in England, is a kind of warfare between the sexes, just such as once happened between the Parthians and old Rome; our ladies conquer by flying, and our men are vanquished while they pursue.

Persons, sir, of a certain rank, said she, are dispensed with from conforming to little matters of decorum. However, if you will endeavour to adopt the manners of my country, I will do my best, on my part, to conform to those of yours.

So saying, she drew her chair quite close; when, by an involuntary motion, I put mine further back.—Don't be alarmed, my lord, says she; women of my condition know always where to stop.—Right, madam, said I; but possibly you might not be quite so successful in teaching me where to be stopped.

Cold-constitutioned boy! she cried (indignantly rising and

colouring), your bed lies yonder; you may go to it, if you like, and ruminate till morning on the danger of slighting and insulting a princess. So saying, she swept haughtily out of the room, and locked me in.

During an hour after she had withdrawn, while I walked about, considering what I had to apprehend from the threats of this extraordinary woman, I heard a great bustling in and about the palace; but within another hour all was quiet and still again.

I then conceived thoughts of attempting my escape. But again I held it beneath me to be caught in the manner; and so I resolved to wait till morning, and then to force my passage through her guards in open day.

In the mean time, I imagined that a panel in the wainscot stirred; and soon after it was removed, and my young friend here entered my chamber on tiptoe. He beckoned me to silence, and, taking me by the hand, he led me through the way by which he came.

We then descended a narrow pair of back-stairs, and groping along a dark entry, he cautiously unbolted a door that opened into a garden; and, hurrying with me across, he unlocked another door that opened to the street, and out we got rejoicing!

Soon after we met a party of the guards who were patrolling the streets; and putting a few pieces into their hand, I requested their safe convoy, and they conducted us home.

My lords, said Pierre (for that was the page's name), it would be extremely dangerous for you to remain another day, or even till morning, in Paris. The princess is the most intimate friend of Madam Maintenon, and through her can do what she pleases with the king. During my residence with her, she grew tired of two handsome lovers in succession; but they told no tales, and no one can yet tell what became of them.

Mr. Clinton was quite of Pierre's opinion. He instantly sent for his people. All was hurry, pack, and despatch, and towards dawning they set out on a road that led to the Cantons. But, changing their course again for several successive mornings, they arrived at Calais by a long tour of near five weeks' travel.

Mr. Clinton set up at his old inn, and after dinner the host entered to pay his compliments. Have you any news, landlord?—Nothing at present, my lord; all is quiet again. But here has been a fearful bustle about three weeks ago. The king's army came down in pursuit of a young Englishman, who ran away with a lady of quality from Paris. For my share, continued he, looking earnestly at Harry, I fear that you pretty young English lads will hardly leave us a lovely wench in the nation. Harry looked quite secure, being wholly innocent of any present design on the sex; but poor little Pierre turned as pale as the table-cloth.

I remember, continued our talkative host, that just such another affair happened when I was a boy and servant in this house. Here came a young Englishman, just such another sweet fellow as this before me; and he brought with him an angel of a creature, the like of whom my eyes never did, nor never shall open upon till they close in death. After him came one of our great dukes, with a party of the king's army, and terrible things were expected. But they made it up in a manner I know not how, and my Lord Anglois carried off his prize in triumph. Mr. Clinton stooped his head, and dropped a silent tear, but held no further converse with our landlord on the subject.

That evening a gale sprung up, and, going on board, they were safe anchored before morning in the bay of Dover.

They then mutually embraced; and Harry, catching his beloved deliverer to his bosom—We are now upon English ground, says he; welcome to my arms, my dear Pierre, no longer my page or servant, but my friend and my brother! You cannot conceive what pain your officiousness has hitherto cost me; but there must be no more of this. You shall hereafter be served and attended as I am; nay, I myself will gladly serve you to the utmost of my power, and the extent of my fortune.

Ah, my lord! cried the lovely Pierre, if you deprive me of the pleasure of serving you, you deprive me of all the pleasure that the world can afford me. If you knew the delight I find in being always about you, in watching your thoughts and motions, in looking into your fine eyes, and there reading your desires before they rise to expression, you could not find in your heart to deprive me of such a blessing.—Well then, said Harry, raising him fondly in his arms, our future contest shall be, which of us shall serve the other with most affection and sedulity.

After dinner, the evening being calm and shiny, Harry took his Pierre with him along the shore that stretches under the stupendous cliffs of Dover. They had not walked far, when, getting out of the sight of people within the winding of a creek, a man advanced towards them, and, taking out a pistol, called to Harry, and ordered him to throw down his purse. Our hero did not regard his money; but, thinking it an indignity to be robbed by one man, he put his hand to his sword. Hereupon the villain cocked and levelled his pistol; and the faithful Pierre, observing that he was going to fire, instantly jumped in between his master and danger, and received the ball into his own bosom.

Harry saw his darling drop, and flying all enraged at the robber, he ran him thrice through the body, and pinned him to the ground. Then, flying as swiftly back, he threw himself by the side of his dying Pierre, and, gently raising his languishing head, placed it fondly on his bosom.

You are wounded, my friend—dangerously wounded, I

fear, says Harry.—Yes, my lord, I am wounded just as I could wish; and I would not exchange my present blessed death for the longest and happiest life that the world could bestow. But it is time to undeceive you, and reveal a secret which nothing but death should ever have extorted from me. I am not what I seem, my most beloved master! I am a foolish and fond girl, who at the first glance conceived a passion for you. My name is Maria de Lausanne. I am niece to that bad woman whom you justly rejected. But what did I propose by this disguise? First, your deliverance, my lord, and that I effected. But did I further aspire to the honour of your hand? Far from it—far from it. I felt my own unworthiness; I did not think you could be mated by any thing less than an angel. But then to see you —to hear you—to serve—to touch—to be near you—to fix my eyes on you unheeded—and, if possible, to win your attention by the little offices of my fondness—this was my happiness—the whole of the heaven that I proposed upon earth. I have had it—I have enjoyed it, and I ought to die content. But, alas! to part from you—there is the pang of pangs! O, if this day merits any thing by the offer of my own life for the preservation of my beloved, then cause my chaste clay to be kindly deposited in the tomb of your ancestors—that—when time shall come—my dust may be neighboured——to your precious dust——and there sleep in peace—beside you—till we spring——together——from corruption——to glory and——immortality!

During these short sentences and difficult respirations, Harry could answer nothing. He was suffocated by his grief; but, putting his speechless lips to the fading lips of his Maria, he drew her latest breath into his own affectionate bosom, and angels instantly caught her spirit into the regions of purity, of love, and of faith unfailing!

Harry then, plucking up strength from oppression, and

courage from despair, pressed his lips to the pale and unfeeling lips of his lover, and cried—Yes, my Maria, our dust shall be joined, and I feel that our spirits too shall shortly be wedded! Then raising her in his arms, and pressing her to his bosom, he bore her to the town, while he poured upon her all the way the two fountains of his affection.

When he got to the inn, and came to his uncle—Here, sir, said he, I present you with a very precious little burthen—a burthen that lies much heavier on my heart than it did in my arms. He then related to Mr. Clinton the whole of what had passed; when, heavily sighing, and shedding a tear, Mr. Clinton cried—Ah, my Harry, I would to heaven that your Maria had lived! her beauty—her services—but above all the excess of her love, made her truly deserving of you.

Harry ordered a carriage on purpose for himself and his beloved. She was deposited in a coffin hurried up for the occasion; and, notwithstanding all the remonstrances and entreaties of his parent, Harry proved a rebel for the first time, and would not be divided from his Maria till they reached London.

There our Harry ordered a coffin of unalloyed and beaten silver to be prepared for her reception; and, though near five days had passed since the departure of her spirit, her chaste flesh remained as pure and untainted as that of a lamb newly slain.

While they were putting her into her solemn repository—Ah, sir! said Harry, I pretend not to compare with you; your losses, I own, have been greater than mine. You are a man, like your divine Master, wholly made up of sorrows, and acquainted with killing griefs. But still you must allow that, for my little time, I have had a competent share. It matters not. I am reconciled to them. I begin to be pleased with them. And, indeed, joy is become my utter aversion while I think on this loved creature, who willingly bled and died for my sake.

As Harry thought it his duty, so he thought it to be his delight, to weep and lament his Maria. But passions seldom are permanent; and time, though it may not wholly efface, daily wears away an insensible portion of the deepest impressions.

Harry caused the coffin of his deliverer to be exalted on a cabinet in his bed-chamber, that it might be always in his sight. But the familiarity of affecting objects daily lessens their force; and Harry, week after week, began to contemplate the repository of the loved remains of his Maria with abating affliction.

In the mean time, Mr. Clinton received a letter by the French mail, in answer to one which he had left for his brother-in-law at Paris. And this letter informed him, under the marquis's hand, that he had returned from his embassy to the court of Morocco, and that he and his lady would be shortly in England. And at the bottom he found written in a different character, "Will it be any satisfaction to see them accompanied by your once loved—FANNY GOODALL?"

We have found them, my Harry! he cried; we have found them, our long and far-sought friends! the two treasures which our God had graciously laid in store for the comfort of us poor people who have lost all beside! But don't let us do them the disgrace, my son, of meeting and receiving them with tears and dirges. Let me then prevail upon you to permit your faithful Pierre to be conducted by some of our people, with an honourable train of undertakers, to Enfield, and there to be treasured up in your family vault, where I shall speedily join her, and whereunto even my Harry must finally adjourn. Harry wiped his eye, and said —Be it as you please, my father!

Within the following fortnight, Harry, attended by his page, put on a footmanlike frock, and gripping his quarterstaff of polished yew, took a walk towards the custom-house to inquire if any French vessels had lately arrived, in hope of tidings respecting the Marquis and the Countess of Maitland.

As he approached the wharf, he observed a crowd all in motion, and shouting as in the midst of some affray. Immediately he hastened up, and, making way through the savage populace, perceived that they were insulting, beating, and dragging a number of unhappy foreigners, without any apparent provocation, save that their garb, complexion, and language were different from their own, the very reason that should have induced them to have treated these abused strangers with courtesy and kindness.

On the instant his humanity was at once melted by compassion and fired into rage; while a lady, who stood with her woman on the stairs, cried out in accents of the bitterest distress—One hundred, two hundred, five hundred pounds, to any one who will save my poor people!

In little more than twenty seconds, Harry laid near as many of the assailing mob maimed or sprawling on the area; and advancing on the crowded spectators with a threatful and agile whirl of his staff, they fell back in a hurry upon each other, and, dispersing, left our hero peaceable master of the field of battle.

Then turning to the bruised and bleeding strangers, he raised some, and supporting others, conducted them all to the feet of their lady.

While he approached, she eyed him over and over in mute and wondering astonishment.—I think myself happy, madam, says he, in having done some small service to a lady of your fair and noble appearance; of what country, may I presume?—Of England, sir, says she; and I am ready to present you with five hundred pounds, in recompense of the gallant, the miraculous rescue, you so seasonably brought to me and my people.

No, madam! said Harry smiling, my circumstances do not lay me under the smallest temptation of setting any instance of humanity to sale. But I shall not be easy till I see you and your attendants safe out of the reach of these London barbarians.

He then called to some porters, and throwing them a parcel of silver, ordered them to bring all the coaches they could muster.—And go you, says he to his page, go to the shipping, inquire after the friends that I told you of, and then follow me to the Whitecross tavern in Cheapside.

The coaches came, and Harry assisted his porters in carrying, helping, and gently stowing the maimed and the wounded into some of them. He then handed in the lady; and next, coming to a blackamoor boy, who had a coronet of diamonds inserted in his cap, he offered to lift him in. But the youth, bending one knee to the dust, and seizing on Harry's hand, eagerly and repeatedly kissed it, crying out, in French—Heavenly, heavenly creature! and then, breaking into tears, he sprung into the coach, and sat down by the lady.

Our hero then bestowed the four female attendants, with such luggage as was brought on shore, into the remaining coaches. Then grasping his quarterstaff, and ordering the porters to attend, he guarded and escorted all safe to the Whitecross.

The first thing he then did was to order private apartments for the lady and her attendants. He next despatched the waiters for all the surgeons in the neighbourhood. He then locked the room where he saw the luggage safe lodged; ordered a sumptuous dinner to be prepared as soon as possible; and, lastly, discharged the coaches and porters who poured their parting blessings upon his head; and all this he did with wonderful despatch, for Harry was now in the wide element of his beneficence, as a whale in the ocean.

Three surgeons then came, and our hero, putting five guineas apiece into their hands, desired them to examine and dress their patients; and stay till he heard the delightful tidings that none of them were incurable. He then sent up to the lady to desire permission to attend her. She rose and met him as he entered.—Child of heaven! said she, from which of the orders of angels have you descended? I have heard as well as seen what you have wonderfully done for us. Madam, said Harry, endeavouring to turn the discourse, I would not advise you to remove your people for some time: I have ordered beds and apartments for them in this house, where those that are tolerably well may assist the doctors to attend their sick fellows till all shall be restored. In the mean time, I have sent to my father's for his coach and chariot, to convey you and this young gentleman and your woman to our house, where you can want no servants, since my father and I, and all, will be truly and tenderly your servants.—We are your property, sir, said the lady, dispose of us as you please.

In a little time after, dinner was served up, and Harry, happening to turn his head, perceived the black youth by stealth kissing the hat and pressing the gloves to his bosom that he had laid on the table.

Whatever the darkness or deformity of any aspect or person may happen to be, if the sentimental beauty of soul shall burst through the cloud upon us, the dark becomes light, the deformed quite comely, and we begin to affect what was lately our aversion. Thus it was that Harry found himself suddenly and inevitably attached by the two recent proofs that this outlandish youth had given of his affection.

Being all seated, Harry looked earnestly at the young Moor, and turning to the lady, said—I now perceive, madam, how ridiculous all sorts of prejudices are, and find that time and observation may change our opinions to the reverse of what they were. I once had an aversion to all sorts of blacks; but I avow that there is something so amiable in the face of this youth, and his eyes cast such a lustre over the darkness of his countenance, as is enough, as Shakspeare has it, to make us in love with night, and pay no more worship to the gaudy sun.

The Moor hereat smiled celestial sweetness, and joy beamed from his eyes, and throughout his dimpling aspect.

But who can you be, my sweet fellow? said the lady; who are the picture, the image, almost the thing itself, that I was so sadly in love with five-and-thirty years ago?—Why, madam, said our hero, you could not have been born at that early day.—Ah, you flatterer! says she, I am turned of forty. —But pray, madam, who was he that was so happy as to attract your infant affections?—His name was Harry Clinton. —Why, madam, Harry Clinton is my name.—Harry Clinton, Harry Clinton! screamed out the lady, and started up from her chair.—Yes, madam, I am son to the late Earl of Moreland; and I almost dare to hope that you were once the enchanting Fanny Goodall.—Yes, my lovely kinsman, I am indeed your Fanny Goodall!

Harry then sprung forward, and, seizing her hand, kept it dwelling on his lips. But, disengaging it, she opened her arms and clasped him to her bosom, and wept over him as a mother would over a long-lost son; while the young Moor ran and danced about the room like a mad thing, clapping hands, and springing like an antelope, almost to the ceiling.

When they were something composed, the Moor caught the lady about the neck, and kissing her, cried—Joy, joy, my dearest madam, the greatest of all joys! Then, turning to our hero, he took each of his hands in turns, and pressed them to his lips; while Harry, kissing his forehead, cried—My brother, my brother!

When they were again set to dinner, the page entered. My lord, said he, I have been all along the quays and the shipping, but can learn no tidings of the Marquis D'Aubigny, nor of any French family save that of the Duchess Bouillon, who this morning came up the river with a numerous train.

Well, says Harry, our happiness has been already quite sufficient to the day. To-morrow may crown our wishes with full success.

No, my love! said the lady, you cannot see the marquis for some time. The truth is, that you find in me, your Fanny Goodall, the Marchioness D'Aubigny and the Duchess de Bouillon. But these matters shall be explained more clearly when I am blessed with the sight of your precious uncle.

News was now brought that the carriages were at the door; when, taking a hasty bit or two, they visited and left orders for the care of the sick and wounded, and then set out in a hurry for Pall-Mall.

When they arrived, the duchess hastened in, inquiring for Mr. Clinton; and when she came where he was, she cried out as she advanced, and as he rose to receive her—Your Fanny, your Fanny Goodall, my cousin! and, throwing herself into his arms, dwelt there for a minute. Then recoiling a while, she looked fondly at him and cried—Your sister also, my brother; your sister D'Aubigny! the wife of the brother of your heavenly Louisa! Then, clasping him to her arms, she broke into tears; and, again quitting him, sat down to quiet her emotions.

Mr. Clinton, having seated himself affectionately beside her, said—These are wondrous things that you tell me, my precious sister! By what miracle have these blessings been brought about?

I am too much agitated at present, says she; let me have a little coffee, and the matter shall be unravelled.

As they were settling to the tea-table—Give me leave, sir, said the duchess, to introduce my little black companion to your notice. He is a sweet fellow, I assure you, notwithstanding his complexion. He is child to our royal friend the Emperor of Morocco, who has intrusted him to our guardianship for his travel and education. However, he might have come by his sable outside, his father, the great Abenamin, is the least of the tawny of any man I saw in Africa, and his mother is one of the fairest and finest women that ever opened a pair of living diamonds to the light. But, my brother, I shall more particularly recommend him to your regard, by telling you that he is an exceedingly pious Christian.

She then turned, and, taking the little Abenamin by the hand, led him up and placed him before her brother; when the youth, suddenly dropping on his knees, looked up to Mr. Clinton with eyes that spoke love and reverential awe, and besought his blessing.

The old gentleman found himself surprisingly affected, and, lifting up his hands, cried—God be gracious to you, my child, and make your soul as bright as your countenance is sable! and may the Sun of righteousness shine with power upon you, and soon disperse or illumine every shade that is about you! The prince embraced his legs, kissed his knees, and arose.

Soon as the coffee was removed—You may remember, my dearest cousin, said the duchess, in what a hurry I last parted from you. Mr. Fairface, with whom the bulk of my fortune was deposited, went off with above a hundred thousand pounds of my substance, beside four times that value intrusted to him by others.

I traced him to Paris, and there he had the impudence to give me an interview; but, at the same time, had the impudence also to bid me defiance.

Immediately I commenced suit, and sent despatch to London for my papers and witnesses.

On the opening of my cause in court, I was summoned by the title of Countess of Maitland, otherwise Frances Goodall. On hearing the name, a gentleman who was near me started, and turning and coming up—Pray, madam, says he, are you any way related to the Honourable Harry Clinton, who once went by that name in this city?—I am, sir, said I, almost the nearest relation that he has upon earth.—He is, madam, my dearest friend and brother. Pray speak to your advocates to postpone your suit for a few days, till I am informed of the nature and merits of your cause.

This was accordingly done. He desired to know where I lodged, and in less than an hour his chariot was at my door.

Except yourself, my cousin, the marquis had the most lovely and winning aspect and person that ever I beheld. I soon convinced him of the equity of my demand, and of the villainy of my trustee, and made him perfect master of the whole affair. But he still continued to visit and to stay with me a considerable part of every day, under colour of being better informed touching this and the other particular; the remaining time was spent in soliciting for me.

At length a hearing came on; and, after a short trial, honest Fairface was cast in principal and double costs. He was instantly taken into custody, and put under confinement, till he discharged the whole amount of the judgment in my favour. No sooner was one suit over, wherein I was plaintiff, but another was commenced, wherein I happened to prove but a very weak defendant. The marquis now became solicitor for himself, but with such a sweet timidity as seemed to doubt and greatly dread the success of his cause.

I could not refuse my time to him who had devoted the whole of his time and assiduity to me. We spent whole days together. But O, what floods of tears did that time often cost both him and me, while he pathetically and feelingly related your history, from the place where you broke off to the death of your Louisa, and your precious infants!

I believe, my cousin, that as grief is a greater softener, so it is a greater cementer, of hearts than any other passion. I gave the marquis, in my turn, my little story, and dwelt on every tender minuteness of my infant passion for you.—Ah, said he, what a pity that a heart so susceptible of all divine and human feelings, should sit as a lonely turtle, without a suitable mate!

I took him for that mate, my cousin; and in a husband I found the truest and tenderest of lovers. I became pregnant, for the first time in my life, and was delivered of a sweet and promising little fellow, whom we left at nurse in our country-seat, while I attended my lord on his embassy to Morocco.

But here I must stop, my brother; I am under the positive interdiction of an imperial thing called a husband, not to divulge a word further, till he sees you face to face. But I trust that he has blessed tidings for you, my brother; he says that he otherwise would not have dared to present himself before you, after his loss of your Eloisa.

Mr. Clinton smiled careless, as at the impossibility of any consoling event upon earth. Again, smiling archly—I protest, my sister, said he, you appear to me to grow younger for your years. I see no manner of alteration, save that you are something plumper, and not quite so slender as when we parted. But pray, when may we expect my brother? In about two months; at present he is engaged with the king, who is extremely fond of him, and lately created him a duke, on account of the services which he rendered the state in Africa. We received your kind letter, my dearest brother, at Paris, but wondered who the sweet fellow could be who was said to accompany you.

In the mean time, our hero and the young prince were in close combination. Abenamin stepped about and about Harry, and toyed with him, and twisted the curls of his careless locks around his fingers. Then turning and looking fondly up in his face—Ah, how fair, says he, does this black visage of mine show in those fine eyes of yours!—It is in truth, said Harry, so fair in my eyes, that I would not exchange it for fifteen of the fairest female faces in Britain. The prince then caught his hand, and pressed it to his bosom. —But what shall I call you? says he. You are a great lord in this country, and in my own country I am greater than a lord. But I hate the formality of titles between friends, and I will call you my Harry, provided you promise to call me your Abenamin.—A bargain, says Harry; let us seal it with a kiss!—No, no! says the prince, we never kiss lips in Africa; but I will kiss your head, and your hands, and your feet too, with pleasure. But tell me, Harry, what makes you so mighty clever a fellow; will you teach me to be a clever fellow also?—Ay, that I will, says Harry, and to beat myself too, provided you promise not to hit me over hard. Abenamin laughed, and aimed a little fist as though he meant to overturn him.

. As soon as Harry's grief for his late Maria would allow him to associate, he had been to seek his old friend and tutor, Mr. Clement; but he found only a single domestic at home, who told him that the old gentleman had been some time dead, and that the family were lately gone to take possession of a new seat that they had purchased in the country.

However, as Harry found himself quite happy in the

present society, he sought no further acquaintance or amusement in London. In less than three weeks the retinue of the prince and the duchess were well restored; and they all set out for Enfield, there to await the wished arrival of the duke.

On the third day, while they stopped at a village to repair the fractured harness of an over-mettled horse, Harry took a walk with the prince along the road. In their way they came to a long and waste cottage, where they heard the confused clattering of junior voices. Harry stepped to the door, and looking in, perceived about forty or fifty boys ranged on benches of turf, while a man of a pale aspect sat on a decayed chair, instructing them in their lessons.

Your servant, sir, says Harry. Pray, what language do you teach?—I can teach Latin and Greek, too, sir; but the people of this country choose to confine themselves to the language of old England.—If I am not too free, sir, pray, what is your name?—Longfield, so please your honour.—Longfield! Longfield! I have surely heard that name before. Pray, were you ever acquainted with a man called Hammel Clement?—Hammel Clement, sir? Yes, sir; and with a wife by whom he is greatly dignified.

Your friend Clement, says Harry, is come to great fortune, and, I dare answer for him, would be nearly distracted with joy at your sight, and would gladly divide his substance with you; but, if you please, you shall be no encumbrance upon his growing family. You shall instantly come with me; and, as Pharaoh said to Jacob—Regard not your stuff, for the good of all my lands lies before you, my Longfield; and I rejoice more in acquiring such a heart as yours, than if I had acquired the possession of a province.

Harry then called a few of the neighbours in, and giving them some guineas, to be changed and divided among the children, in order to enable them to see a new master, he and Abenamin took the threadbare Longfield on each side under the arm, and carried him away.

When they came to the turn that led to the mansion-house, Harry perceived with much pleasure that the two school-houses, which he had put in hand before the death of his father, were now completed. They stood opposite to each other, with the road between them. Their fronts were of hewn stone, and a small cupola rose over each, with bells to summon the children to meals and to lesson.

Here, Longfield, says our hero, is to be your province. You are to superintend these schools at a salary of three hundred a-year; and I will soon send you with proper means throughout the country, to muster me a hundred chosen children of each sex: for I yearn to be a father, Longfield, and to gather my family of little ones under my eye and my wing.

As soon as they alighted, Mr. Clinton and his Harry once more welcomed the duchess and her Abenamin to their home and their hearts, and the late house of mourning became a house of joy.

Above all, Abenamin inspired mirth and good-humour throughout the family, and melancholy fled before him wherever he turned. He was daily inventive of new matters of entertainment. He danced African dances for them with wonderful action and grace, and he sung African songs that imitated and exceeded the wild and inarticulate warblings of the nightingale; so that he became the darling and little idol of the whole household.

Harry had sent for the town-tailor, and got Longfield fitted with three or four suits from his father's wardrobe. He then sent him on his commission, in company with Mr. Trustly, the agent, whom he ordered to shew him the country, to introduce him to the several families of the peasantry, and to furnish him with whatever sums he should call for.

In the mean time, our hero and Abenamin became inseparable. He made the prince a present of his little dressed jennet, and at times rode out with him, and taught him the *manége*. At other times they would run and wrestle, and play a hundred gambols through the walks and the gardens.

Did you ever see the chase of the antelope, Harry?—Not I, truly.—You shall not be long so, says the prince. Go, gather me all the house—man, woman, and child—before the door here. You shall be the huntsman, and I will be the antelope; and, if any of your people can catch me in a mile's running, they shall have my cap for a kerchief.

Immediately the whole posse was summoned, to the amount of about sixty persons, male and female; and Mr. Clinton and the duchess, hearing what they were about, came laughing to the door to see the diversion.

Harry then gave his royal antelope about fifty yards law; then cried—Away! and instantly all heels and all voices were loosed after him.

The prince then turned, and bounded over a ha ha, that was sunk on the right side of the avenue; then clearing several other obstacles, whereby he threw out the greatest number of his pursuers, he at length reached the fields, and shot away like an arrow.

Our hero's huntsman headed about nine foreign and domestic footmen, who still held the chase, though at a distance, while Abenamin led them a round of about a mile. Then, turning short homeward, he came flying up the avenue, with only the huntsman and two followers puffing far behind. At length, reaching near the door, the prince threw himself precipitately into the arms of his friend, as it were for protection, crying—Save me, my Harry! save your little antelope!

Mr. Clinton and the duchess then successively embraced the victor, and wished him joy.—I protest, Harry, cried Mr.

Clinton, I will bet a thousand pieces with you on the head of my Abenamin against your famous Polly Truck.

That night, as our hero sat with the prince in his apartment—Have you ever been in love, my Harry? says he.—I confess, said Harry, that I have had my twitches and tendencies that way.

He then related to him the tragedy of his faithful Maria, which cost the prince the drenching of a hankerchief in tears.

Ah! exclaimed the prince, never—never will I forgive your Maria her death! Why was it not my lot, by some severer doom, to prove to you the superiority of my friendship and affection?—What! cried Harry, would you not leave me a single companion upon earth? When my Abenamin quits the world I shall also bid it adieu.

When their grief was over, the prince took his friend by the hand and said—I have a sister, my brother—a sister twinned with me in the womb, and as fair as I am black. All Africa is pleased to hail her as the beauty of the universe; but the truth is, that I think but poorly of her. The duke brought her with him to France; and, should he bring her to England, beware of your heart, my Harry! for, though I am prejudiced against her, she is the idol of all others, who bow down to her as before a little divinity. This has made her so excessively vain, that she holds herself of a different species from the rest of mankind, and thinks the homage of the world nothing less than her right. And now, my Harry, though I earnestly wish to be allied to you by a tie, nearer if possible than that of friendship, yet I would not wish my own happiness at the expense of your peace; and so I give you timely warning against this dangerous and haughty girl.

Our company had now been upward of six weeks at the mansion-house. Harry hitherto had never examined any part of the country, or any part of his own estate, above a mile from the house; wherefore—leaving his friend, Abenamin, in bed, in the presumption of his being tired with his last day's fatigue—he issued early forth, accompanied only by his huntsman and his agent's runner, who knew and was known every where.

With their staffs in their hands, they crossed and quartered the country at pleasure, without let or obstacle.

At length they came within prospect of a house sumptuously fronted, and of a happy situation. Harry stopped here with pleasure, comparing, as he approached, the acquirements of art with the advantages of nature: when a servant issued forth, and humbly besought him to walk in. Harry heard the voice of music.—What is your master's name? says he.—Fielding, so please your honour, and we are this dry celebrating the nuptials of his son, the young squire.

The master of the family met our hero at the outward door. Harry recoiled at recognizing the face of the Mr. Fielding whom he had seen at Hampstead; but, taking no notice, walked with him into the house.

Breakfast soon after was ushered in; and Mrs. Fielding, and Ned, with his blooming and blushing bride, came to the table.

Harry chuckled and rejoiced at heart, but still took no notice; when, after some cursory conversation, Ned looked at him with an eager disturbance, and cried—Bless me! my heart tells me that there is something in that face which is not quite unknown to me. If I could think, after my many and late inquiries, that my patron was alive, bating the difference of years, I should verily believe that you were——Your Harry Fenton! cried our hero, springing up; your Harry Fenton, my dear Ned!

Harry then opened his arms to receive his friend, while Ned leaped and catched at him, as the grappling-iron of a corsair would catch at a ship from which a great prize was expected.

All the family then, so highly as they had been obliged by our hero and his father, struggled who should be foremost in their acknowledgments and caresses.

After dinner, Harry rose to take his leave; but they all got in a group and opposed his passage, telling him he must be their prisoner for that night.—I consent only on this condition, said Harry, that you all promise to dine with me tomorrow.—Why, pray, sir, where do you live? says Mr. Fielding. At Enfield, with the young Earl of Moreland, says Harry; but he has a great friendship for me, and the house is as it were my own.

Much company arrived in the evening, and the ball was opened and held till late. But our hero declined dancing, that his friend Ned might stand forth peerless in the eyes of his bride.

Harry rose by the dawning, and footed it in an hour to Enfield. He flew up-stairs to salute the family, but found no one save Mr. Clinton, from whom he received at once a warm blessing and embrace.

Where is the duchess, sir, and my friend Abenamin—Gone, Harry, says his uncle, about breakfast-time yesterday.

A courier arrived with the joyful tidings that my brother was on the road, and so my sister and the prince hastened to meet him. By this time I suppose they are all on their return. And now take care of yourself, my Harry. The duke brings with him the sister of our Abenamin, the fair princess Abenaide. The duchess tells me that a lovelier creature never beheld the light; so that you must guard your heart with double bars against the power of this beauty. —She is vain and disdainful, sir—excessively vain, I am told; so that her pride will prove an antidote against the poison of her charms. However, I will haste to meet and welcome your most noble brother.

Harry was mounted on a haughty charger, that was bought when a colt in Mauritania: he was white as new-fallen snow, save a black main and tail, and three large blood-like spots on the off-shoulder. He was so perfectly instructed and subdued to the *manége*, that he seemed to have no will save the will of his rider; while Harry's least motion, like electricity, informed every joint and member.

The princess came foremost in an open chariot drawn by four spotted Arabians, and the eye could scarcely support the brightness of the wonderful beauty who sat within it.

Harry bowed twice as he approached, but she scarce deigned a perceptible nod of acknowledgment to his salute. Our hero felt himself piqued.—Proud beauty! thought he, I thank you for your timely prevention of a passion that, perhaps, might have proved unhappy to me. He then passed forward with affected carelessness to salute the duke.

When he came up, the coach stopped, and Harry, flying from his saddle, approached the window, while his steed stood trembling but motionless behind him.

My lord, said Harry, seizing the duke's hand and respectfully kissing it, if you were sensible of the joy that my heart receives from your presence, I think it would make you nearly as happy as myself.—My sweet fellow, said the duke, I have often heard of you at Paris, as also by the letters of my love here; my longing at last is gratified, though my wonder is increased.

But madam, says Harry, what have you done with my little playfellow? what's become of my Abenamin? O, cried the duchess, laughing, he is forthcoming I warrant you; but what has so bewitched you to him? I think you could not be fonder if he were a mistress.—True, madam, answered Harry, sighing; I never look to have a mistress that I shall love half as well; but pray put me out of pain, and let me know where he is.—Be pacified, said the smiling duke, he is not far off; and here is my hand and promise that you shall see him before night.

Our hero then turned and vaulted on his horse: the coach now began to move, and Harry put his wand to the flank of his horse, who, turning his head to the carriage as of his own accord, moved sidelong towards Enfield with a proud but gentle prancing; while the duke cried out—Look, look! O the boy, the graceful, lovely boy!

While our hero attended the carriage of the duke, the princess and her train had got to the house and alighted, while Harry opened the coach-door, and handed out the noble pair, who alternately kissed and took him to their arms. Mr. Clinton then came forth and received them all with transport. But Harry, under some pretence, walked away ruminating, in order to avoid the disdainful regards of the young lady.

In the mean time, our company, rejoicing and caressing each other all the way, had got slowly, though very lovingly, to the great mansion-parlour. The duke then respectfully taking the young lady by the hand—Permit me, brother, says he, to recommend to you my lovely ward, the fair Princess of Morocco. The lady then gently bent one knee towards the ground, while she received the cordial blessing and salute of the old gentleman.

They then took their seats. When Mr. Clinton, while he looked more earnestly on the princess, grew suddenly affected, and called out for a glass of fair water and hartshorn. When he drank it, he found himself in a measure restored; and lifting his hands, he cried—I protest one would think that nature had copied this young and lovely creature from an image that has lain impressed upon my heart near these forty years.

You are in the right my brother! exclaimed the duke; it is even as you surmise. Allow me then, once more, to introduce to you the counterpart of our once adored Louisa; to introduce to you my niece, and your own offspring, my brother—even the daughter of your still living and ever precious Eloisa! The princess then sprung forward, and, dropping precipitately at the feet of her grandfather, she put her face between his knees, and seizing both hands, she bathed them with her tears, crying—My father! O my father! my dear, my dearest father! how inexpressibly blessed I think myself to be the offspring of such a father! Mr. Clinton then raising her, and seating her fondly on his knee, and grasping her to his bosom—I will not ask, he cried, how these miracles came about; it is enough that I feel the attraction which pulls you into my heart. And so saying, their tears flowed and mingled in a happy emotion.

Go, my angel, said Mr. Clinton, and take yonder seat, that I may view and delight my soul with your sight at leisure. My eyes begin at these years to see best at a distance.

At length the soft voice of our Harry was heard in the hall; and the duke, whispering his brother, requested him for a little time, to take no notice of what had passed.

Our hero then entered, bowing respectfully and gracefully, but carelessly, towards the side where the princess sat. He then took his seat beside the duke, and bending fondly to him, and seizing a hand with both his hands, he pressed it to his lips and cried—Welcome, welcome, my dearest lord, to the house and the hearts of your truest lovers!

Then, giving a glance to the side where the princess sat, he caught a glimpse of her attractions, and sighing, said to himself—O the pity, the pity! But no matter; her pride shall never suffer a single charm to take place; and so thinking, he turned his eyes aside.

Mean time, Abenaide arose with as little noise as a hare from her seat; and stealing round, like a cat circumventing a mouse, she came behind Harry's chair, and reaching, and covering an eye with each of her hands, she turned his head to her, and made a sound with her lips as though she had kissed him. Harry opened his eyes in utter astonishment; while in a twinkling, standing before him, she chuckled a laugh, and cried—My Harry! what, have you forgot me? Don't you remember your old playfellow, your little friend Abenamin?

Harry's eyes were now opened, in the midst of the hurry and agitation of his soul. At a glimpse he took in the whole oppression of her beauties; and casting himself, quick as a glance of lightning, at her feet, he seized the hem of her robing and glued it to his mouth.

At length, lifting up his eyes, he cried—Ah! what are all these wonders to me, or my happiness, unless my Abenamin will also become my Abenaide?—That, replied the princess, is not at my option: there sits my lord and father, at whose disposal I am.

Harry then rose, and throwing himself at the feet of his revered patron, embraced his knees in silence, while Mr. Clinton cried out—Yes, my Harry, I understand you; nothing shall ever be wanting to the happiness of my darling, that the power of his tender parent and loving uncle can effect! I can have nothing in heaven or earth that is not the property of my Harry. Harry kissed his hands and sprung up.

Mr. Clinton then continued—I aver I am still in a labyrinth. Did you not say, my Abenaide, that you were also our Abenamin?—I did, my father, says she, but I did not dare to avow myself. Ah! what a painful struggle did that restriction cost me, while I panted to catch and to cling to your honoured feet; while I used to look and gaze upon you unperceived; while my heart swelled with affection, and my eyes with restrained tears; and while I kissed in secret the book that you read, and the ground that you trod on.

Abenaide then sat down, and Harry, lightly throwing himself on the ground beside her, looked beseechingly around, and cried—My lord—my dearest lady—our still precious Fanny Goodall—can you vouch—can ye warrant that I am safe in this matter? Then looking up to the princess, and drinking her in—No! he cried, you cannot engage it; I feel that I shall perish in the very ecstasy of the expectation of being united to her.

Just then Mr. Meekly came in. He had been long and far away, upon many a blessed tour of doing good through the earth. But as soon as he learned of the arrival of his beloved patron and young lord, he rode post to embrace them.

Harry sprung from love to friendship, and, catching him in his arms, cried—O my Meekly, my dearest Meekly! how seasonably you come, to temper by your advice the insufferable transports of my soul! Behold the regent of my heart —behold the queen of all my wishes!

Meekly then fixed his eyes upon the princess, and soon after exclaimed—Gracious father! what do I see? Can the Louisa be resuscitated, and new raised from the dead? O, then, it must be so—she must be her descendant. No one save my peerless patroness could produce the likeness of my patroness. But how this blessed miracle was brought about is the question.

That is my question too, my dear Meekly, said Mr. Clinton, if my most noble brother would be so good as to solve it.—I will gratify you, gentlemen, said the duke, in as few words as possible. Meanwhile the princess withdrew.

On my embassy to the court of Morocco, I had several private interviews with the emperor before my credentials were opened in public. I had the good fortune to be liked by him, so that he suffered no day to pass without seeing me. His name was Abenamin; he was accounted a great captain; he exceeded all in his dominions for grace of person and beauty of aspect; and that which rendered him still more singular was, that he had given liberty to all the ladies of his seraglio, and for many years had kept constant to the reigning sultana, said to be the most exquisite beauty on earth.

As we grew more intimate, in the exuberance of his affection for his empress he could not refrain from speaking of her to me; and he promised that, before I departed, I should see and converse with her—a grace, he said, never granted to any other man.

At length the day being appointed for my public entry, I rode through the city attended by a sumptuous train, and, alighting before the palace, advanced to the hall of audience.

The emperor was seated, with his sultana at his right hand, upon a throne of ivory. As soon as I had approached the presence, and began to open my commission, the empress gave a great shriek, and fell over in a swoon upon the bosom of her husband.

The royal Abenamin instantly turned pale as death—tore off her veil with trembling hands to give her air—and called me to his assistance, as it is accounted profanation for any Moor to touch the person of the empress. But O heaven! O my friends! think what was my astonishment when, in the pale face of the queen, I beheld the loved features of our darling Eloisa!

The court broke up in confusion, and her women came hurrying with drops and essences. As soon as she recovered, she opened her eyes upon me, and reaching out her arms, and catching me to her, she cried—O my uncle, my dearest uncle! am I so blessed, then, as to behold you before I expire?

The monarch, in the mean time, looked upon me with a jealous eye, and twice put his hand to the haft of his dagger, but checked his rising indignation till he should have the mystery of his queen's behaviour explained. The women then raised her up and bore her to her apartment; while the emperor, turning to me with no very friendly aspect, ordered me to follow him.

When I had attended a considerable time in the antechamber, he came forth with a serene and joyous countenance, and embracing me, cried—O my friend! my dear kinsman! how transported I am to find and acknowledge you for such; the parent of my angel becomes a part of myself!

He then led me by the hand into the bedchamber of my Eloisa, where we renewed our caresses without restraint. But the monarch, fearing that these emotions would be too much for her, told me that he had something for my private ear till dinner, and took me into an adjoining closet.

There seating, and taking me affectionately by the hand, I will now tell you, my uncle, says he, how I came by this inestimable treasure of your niece.

I had fitted out a royal ship of my own, not as a corsair, but rather for trade in the Mediterranean. On their return from the coast of Egypt, as they passed, after a violent hurricane, within sight of old Carthage, my people perceived at a distance a sloop stranded on a shoal of sand about a league from the shore. Immediately they sent out a boat, and took the distressed company in, consisting of my charmer, two female companions, and three servants in livery, besides the boatmen.

The intendants of my ship behaved themselves with all possible respect towards the young lady and her attendants; and endeavoured to quiet her terrors by assuring her that she was free, and that their prince was a person of too much honour and humanity to derive any advantage from the disasters of the unfortunate.

The moment that they brought her before me, pale, trembling, and in tears; while she dropped on her knees, and lifted to me her fine eyes in a petitioning manner; the gates of my soul opened to the sweetly affecting image, and ever after closed, of their own accord, upon it.

Ah! I cried; heavenly creature, calm, calm your causeless fears! I swear by our prophet, and the God of our prophet, that I would rather suffer the gaunch than put the smallest constraint on your person or inclinations. You are free, madam; you shall ever be free, save so far as I may bind you by my tender offices and affections.

I raised her, and she grew something better assured; when, bending a knee in my turn, I kissed her robe and cried—Look not upon me as your tyrant, look not on me as your lover; but look upon me as your friend—the tenderest and truest of friends—who shall ever be ready to sacrifice his own happiness to yours.

From that time I studied every amusement, every diversion, that might serve to dissipate the timid shrinkings of her remaining apprehensions; while I conducted myself towards her with a distant though fond respect, not even presuming to touch her ivory hand.

In the mean time my soul sickened, and grew cold to all other women. If you were ever in love, my dear D'Aubigny, you know that it is a chaste as well as a tender passion. I languished indeed for her—I longed and languished to death; but then it was rather for her heart than her person that I languished.

One day, as she heaved a heavy but half-suppressed sigh— Ah, my angel! I cried; I can have no joy but yours, and yet you have griefs to which you keep your friend—your Abenamin—a stranger.—True, my lord, says she, tears breaking from her; all your bounties have not been able to silence the calls of kindred or claims of nature within me. Ah, my parents! my dear parents! I feel more for you than I feel even for myself, in being torn from you.

The weight of her affliction fell like a mountain on my soul, and crushed me to her feet. You would leave me then, Eloisa—you wish to leave me; but your generosity delays to tell me so, for fear of breaking my heart. Well, be it so —go from me—you know I cannot survive you; but my death is of no consequence, my Eloisa shall be happy. I will go this instant, I will despatch my swiftest galley to Languedoc, I will write word to your parents that you are safe, that you are beloved, and yet pure and untouched, since respected as a deity. I will invite them to come and take possession of my treasures, my dominions, my heart; but, should they reject my suit, I again swear by Allah to send you to them laden with wealth, though I myself should drop dead at the instant of your departure!

The noble soul of my Eloisa became instantly affected. She caught a hand between both of hers, and, bathing it with tears, cried—O, now indeed you have bound me by chains infinitely stronger than all the shackles that fasten the slaves to the galleys of Africa.

I kept firm to my engagement, and in a few weeks my winged messengers returned. But, O the tidings, the very doleful tidings, for my beloved! They brought word that they found no creature save two ancient domestics in the great hotel, as two ravens in the midst of a lonely forest.

From these they learned that my Eloisa's mother and little brother were dead; that her grandmother was dead; her aunt the marchioness also dead; and that the marquis had retired they knew not whither.

She wept incessantly, and I wept with her. At length she softly said—You have conquered, my lord, you have conquered; I am subdued by your weight of affliction. O that you could but conform to one article more, that we might be united as one heart, and one soul, and one sentiment, for ever!

It was now, for the first time, that I dared to seize her hand; I crushed it to my lips, and thrust it to my soul. What would you enjoin, I cried?—I would do any thing, dare any thing, to be united to my Eloisa? in life and in death, body to body, and dust to dust, never—never to be sundered till her spirit should make the heaven of my spirit hereafter!

Ah! she suddenly exclaimed, that is the very thing I so eagerly desire. Let the God of my heart be the God of your heart; let the God of my spirit be the God of your spirit; so shall we be united in him, and jointly partake of his blessedness through eternity.

Ah! I cried; can I forego the divine precepts of our prophet?—Your prophet, says she, preaches only to the eye and the ear, and that is all that he does or can pretend to; but CHRIST, my prophet, preaches in the heart to the affections. From him is every good motion, divine or human. He is the unknown God of your spirit, my master, my Abenamin; and you feel his precious power while you disavow his name.

I was puzzled—I was silenced. I bent a knee in reverence, kissed her hand, and withdrew.

I sent for the chief of the Christian missionaries throughout the city and country. I consulted each of them in private, but received no satisfaction from them. They all appeared equally zealous for my reformation, but attempted it by different, and even by opposite, arguments.

Some would have persuaded me to be a Christian by shewing the absurdity of every religion that was not Christian. Others affirmed that my eternal salvation depended on my conformity to certain external rules and penances. While the greatest number inveighed against the Christians of every other denomination; and would have thrust me wholly from Christ, if I did not consent to receive him within their stinted pale.

I knew not what to do; I was put to a stand, and quite confounded by this multiplicity of conflicting opinions. At length a countryman of my own came to me from the desert. He had been a great sinner, but was converted by the sense of his sins; and he was revered and resorted to by all the friendless and afflicted.

I opened my soul to him, with all its doubts and difficulties. My friend in Christ, said he, with a gentle and still voice, they have been leading you all astray, quite away from the haven that stretches forth its arms for the reception of long-toiled mariners, whom storms have at length compelled to seek a final port.

The God of your creation can alone be your redemption; the God of your nature can alone be the salvation of the nature that he imparted. But who shall convince you of this? Not all the angels in heaven, nor all the doctors upon earth, till the Christ of your heart shall be pleased to convince you that you are, as indeed you are (however mighty a monarch), a poor, frail, erring, vile, and despicable creature; subjected to innumerable lapses and infirmities, sickness, passions, and crosses, griefs, agonies, and death. When this is effectually done, the whole of the business is done. You will call for and catch at a Saviour, in the sensibility of your want of him. When you come thus laden with your sins to him, he will in nowise cast you out. But he will take you, as Noah took the wearied dove into the ark—he will take you within the veil of his own temple of rest; and all sects, forms, and ceremonies, will be as the outward courts, with which you shall have no manner of commerce or concern.

My heart felt the weight and the fulness of conviction. I took him to my arms and requested instant baptism. My Eloisa was called; we locked ourselves in; and I was washed by water and faith into Christ, while my kneeling angel wept a stream of delight beside me.

It is said that possession cloys. But I experienced, my dear D'Aubigny, that love never cloys. Every day with my Eloisa seemed to triumph, in heartfelt happiness, over my first bridal day. But O! what was the joy, the exultation of my fond heart, when she gave me to be the father of a little daughter of paradise!

One day, while we were toying and fooling with the smiling infant, and throwing her, as she crowed, from the one to the other—Ah, my husband! cried Eloisa, how poor I was lately; no parents, no kindred, nothing but my Abenamin upon the whole earth! and now God has been pleased to make my afflictions to laugh, and to give this babe for a further band, a precious link of love between us.

He was just in this part of his narration when the music sounded to the banquet. We instantly rose and joined our Eloisa.

When the collation was removed—Madam, said I to the empress, have you ever heard of a relation of yours, christened by the name of Fanny Goodall, and lately Countess of Maitland?—I have, said she, often heard my fond father speak of her with filling eyes.—She is in this city, madam. She is no longer Countess of Maitland. She is now doubly your relation, you aunt as well as your cousin; and goes by the title of the Marchioness D'Aubigny. With the good leave of my lord here, I will bring her to you directly.

I went to the palace appointed for my residence: I there gave my Fanny a few heads of the story of our Eloisa, and took her hastily to the presence.

The ladies looked at each other in long and silent admiration. Then opening their arms, and rushing together, they continued some minutes locked in mutual embrace.

Madam, said the emperor, smiling, I think I ought to be allowed the same liberties with my aunt that your husband took with his niece. Whereon he welcomed and caressed her with an affectionate fervour.

O! exclaimed the royal fair, how very poor, and how very rich our God can suddenly make us! But then, lord of my life, to think of parting—of parting with these dear friends again, perhaps never to see them more—that's what sinks and wrings my heart in the very midst of exultation.

That, my love, said the emperor, is the very important article on which I wish to consult with you and our friends here, our dear kindred in Christ. But I must first shew them their young relation, my little enchantress, my precious pearl, my eye-delighting Abenaide.

He then stepped forth, and, after a while, led in a gracefully moving creature, but veiled from the head to the waist. Throw up your veil, my love, says he; here are none but your friends, your very dear relations—your lovely aunt, and your uncle, the Marquis and Marchioness D'Aubigny.

She did as she was ordered; and instantly broke upon my sight, like a new glory arisen upon mid-day.

My Fanny seized upon her, as desirous of devouring her. And I, in turn, took her to me with tearful eyes, as almost persuaded that I embraced the newly-revived person of my dearest sister Louisa; so perfect was the resemblance in every grace and feature.

Her royal father then gave a beck, and she instantly vanished; while her absence seemed to cast a shade throughout the room.

The monarch then, deeply musing and heavily sighing, began—I am now, my dearest friends, friends beloved above the world, and all that it contains—I am now to open to you my inmost heart, and to reveal a purpose whereon I have been ruminating these many months, but could not hit on an expedient for bringing it to pass. How opportune has our JESUS sent you to us on this occasion!

I have but two children living; my Abenaide, and a son by a former woman of my seraglio. His name is Abencerrage; he is a youth renowned in the field, but of a proud and impetuous demeanour. He had long conceived an illicit passion for his young and lovely sister. At length the fire broke forth, and he lately attempted to carry her away.

I would have instantly put him to death, had I any other heir to succeed to my dominions. I therefore contented myself with banishing him my court and my presence; though I am sensible that this has not availed for the extinguishing his horrid flame.

Now, my friends, should I die, or should this violent boy break into rebellion—for he is the favourite of the licentious soldiery—I tremble to think what would become of my bright-eyed dove within the talons of such a vulture.

This, together with my eager desire of quitting the kingdom of infidels, and of joining with the blessed society of Christian people, has, after many struggles, determined me to abdicate my throne, as soon as I can amass and transmit a fund sufficient for supporting my Eloisa and myself, with becoming dignity, in her native country.

Ah, my lord! I cried, clasping him passionately in my arms, regard not your treasures, delay not a moment for that! Your Eloisa's relations, both by father and mother, are possessed of princely fortunes, and they will be all freely at the disposal of your majesty.

Ah, my D'Aubigny! said he, I am not yet so duly mortified a Christian as needlessly to elect a state of dependence, or willingly to descend at once from the king to the beggar. I have, however, been preparing: I have already converted a large part of my effects into bills and jewels, of high value but light portage, to the amount, as I think, of about forty millions of French money. This I will transmit by you; and, as soon as I shall have compassed an equal sum, I will stay no longer in Africa; I will fly to your bosoms, my precious friends.

In the mean time, this violent and unprincipled boy gives no rest to my apprehensions. It is therefore necessary that I commit my Abenaide to your trust. It is necessary, I say, that I tear away my choicest limb, the dearest part of my vitals! Support me, CHRIST, in the trial; but it must be gone through.

This, however, must be done with all possible privacy. I am persuaded that my young villain has his spies in and about my palace. I shall therefore request my dear aunt to disguise my little girl in boy's apparel, and to blacken every part of her visible complexion, that she may pass unnoticed, as your page, through the midsts of my attendants.

At length the time approached, and pressed for my departure; but how to part was the question. All attendants were ordered to avoid the presence far away. Our metamorphosed Abenaide stood weeping beside us, while her father and mother crushed us successively to their bosoms. All was passion, a gush of tears, but not a word was uttered on any part.

Oh, my D'Aubigny! cried the emperor at length, friend, brother of my heart, can you conceive what I feel at this instant? I regard not the world, nor the things of the world. Omit such necessary accommodations as are common to us with brutes; and all belonging to the immortal and divine humanity of man, is magnetism, is fellowship, the feeling as of steel to adamant, and of adamant to steel. There is the friendship, the endearment, the love passing love, and surpassing all other enjoyment. If we meet again, my D'Aubigny, I shall anticipate my heaven.

Again he embraced his little angel; and again he embraced his queen, and besought her to be comforted. We then took leave, as for the last; and again they called us back, and embraced and took leave again; till, seeing no end, I suddenly broke away, hurrying with us our Abenaide for fear of observation.

I have little further to say, my brother. We arrived safe at Paris, where we received your letter; and, impatient to make you happy, I despatched my Fanny with her train and the princess before me; enjoining them, however, not to reveal our secret till my arrival. For, as I had charged myself with the loss of your Eloisa, I deemed myself best entitled to make you reparation in person. But I ought not to omit that, before I left Paris, I received a further remittance of a large sum from your son-in-law, so that we may speedily look to have the royal pair in England.

Soon after, a post-chaise whirled into the court, and Harry flying out, caught Clement and Arabella into his strict embrace. He then hurried them in, where Mr. Clinton received, and caressed, and introduced them to the duke and duchess as persons of great merit, and his highly valued friends. He then presented to them his Abenaide, who saluted Clement, and embraced Arabella with an affectionate familiarity.

Oh, sir! cried our hero, kissing his uncle's hand, am I to be the last person in the world whom you will honour with a salute from your bewitching daughter?—I ask your pardon, my lord, said Mr. Clinton solemnly; allow me then, at length, to repair my omission, by presenting to your earlship her little highness Abenaide.

The duke and duchess and Meekly laughed; but Harry was not a whit the slower in laying hold of his advantage.

He kissed her forehead, her eyes, her cheeks; and lastly dwelt upon her lips, as though he would have infused his soul between them.—Harry, Harry! cried Mr. Clinton, I will never introduce you to my girl again, unless you promise not to kiss so hard, and bring so much blood into her face.

Just then a footman entered—My lord, says he to Harry, there are three carriages and several horsemen waiting without the gate. They inquire for one Master Fenton, who, they say, lives with the Earl of Moreland; but I assured them there was no such person in the house. Oh, sir! said Harry, these are our old friends the Fieldings, and out he flew.

As he approached the carriages, the company gave a shout of joy.—Why, sir, said Mr. Fielding, a servant denied you to us, and said that no one of the name of Fenton lived here.—Oh! says Harry, don't heed the blockhead, he is but a new-comer.

He then opened the doors of the carriages, and handed and caressed them in turns, as they came out, Mr. and Mrs. Fielding, and Ned and his blooming bride.

Mr. Clinton received them at the door, with the joy of his heart apparent in his countenance. He then introduced them to his most noble brother and sister, to his friend Meekly, and lastly he presented his Abenaide to them, on whom they all gazed in mute and reverential astonishment.

Harry then observing that his uncle had not equally presented his daughter to Ned—Sir, said he, I apprehend that this is not quite fair; I have already kissed the fair bride of my friend with all my heart, and it is but honest that he should be favoured with a salute from mine in turn.

Harry then took Ned by the hand and presented him to his beloved. While Ned bent the knee, and, touching her hand tremblingly, looked awfully to her face, and said—Yes, bride of Eden, lovely extract of every beauty! you alone can reward, you alone can deserve him; you alone are fitted to be the mate of my incomparable lord and master, my patron and preserver! So saying, he lightly touched his lips to the polished hand. But the praises of her Harry had gone with a pleasant trickling to the heart of Abenaide, and, gently raising Ned, she affectionately saluted him with a glistening eye.

Pray, sir, said Mr. Fielding whisperingly to Mr. Clinton, is the Earl of Moreland in company?—That is he, sir, pointing to Harry.—Oh, then, cried Fielding, he is titled below his merits; it was for an emperor that nature intended him!

Dinner was then served. During the repast the Duke said —Let us not, my brother, keep our Harry in pain; why should we delay the happiness of children so very dear to us? With regard to your child's marriage to some mighty prince, as your son-in-law hinted, I think her more ennobled and more illustrious by her marriage with our hero here, who purchased her at his peril, than if she were mated to the greatest potentate on earth.

You must excuse me, my noble brother, said Mr. Clinton; I will have no clandestine doings in this business. My girl shall be married in the face and witnessing of thousands; lest hereafter this young rogue should have the effrontery to deny her. What day of the week is this? Thursday, I think; let Monday se'nnight be the day.

Harry rose, and pressed and kissed the hand of the duke with rapture, and then kissed the hand of his patron in silent submission.

In the mean time, all preparations were pushed into forwardness by Mr. Clinton. The many shops of the many towns within many miles around, were emptied of their boards and sheeting, their knives and forks, etc. Hundreds of tables and forms were framed, hundreds of tents were erected. Proclamation was made in every village, and all people within ten miles were invited to the wedding.

When the day approached, one hundred oxen were slain, one hundred sheep, with fifty fat deer, etc. etc. The spits fried and the caldrons smoked over the fires of many a field.

At length the auspicious morning rose; and Harry and his bride were already up and dressed in their respective apartments.

The princess was habited, after the Persian fashion, in a vest of silver brocading, scalloped over a petticoat of the same fabric, that flowed in a train behind. A scarf of cerulean tint flew between her right shoulder and her left hip, being buttoned at each end by a rose of rubies; her shining tresses of jetty black, bound together at her neck beneath a huge amethyst, fell down in luxuriant ringlets, and shaded and revealed by turns the fine bend of her tapering waist; a coronet of diamonds, through which there waved a white branch of the feathers of the ostrich, was inserted on the left decline of her lovely head; and a stomacher of inestimable brilliance rose beneath her dazzling bosom, and, by a fluctuating blaze of unremitted light, checked and turned the eye away from too presumptuous a gaze.

Our hero coming forth, beheld her, as a pillar of light, just issuing from her antechamber. He stepped back as she advanced, and fixed his eyes upon her in mute astonishment; then springing forward, he fell prostrate and kissed the hem of her robing.

Arabella attended her royal friend, and Clement his noble pupil, just as Longfield entered to give an account of his expedition. But he had scarce begun his detail, when catching the images of his long-parted friends, he cried—Bless me, my lord, Mrs. Clement, I think!—Yes, my Longfield, said Harry, and here too is your old and fast friend, Hammel Clement. Clement would not have known Longfield in his present genteel plight; but hearing his name, and recollecting him at a glance, he flew and seized upon him with a strenuous embrace. Arabella then advanced to welcome her old preserver; but Longfield respectfully bowed and shrunk back.

You shall not escape me so, my dear Mr. Longfield, says she. I cannot forget what I owe you, even my life and reputation; and I bless the Father of mercies, who has put it in our power to pay part of our debt, and so saying she embraced him with freedom and cordiality.—Yes, my dear Longfield, cried Hammel, yours is the half of our fortunes, and more than the half of our hearts.—Your heart, sir, said Longfield, will ever be most valuable; but as to any thing additional, the bounty of my young master has rendered all further fortune quite superfluous to me.

Longfield then beckoned his lord forth, that he might relate to his eye, rather than to his ear, the success of his commission. They hastened to a long barn, where he shewed Harry two ranges of beautiful children, one of a hundred chosen girls, another of a hundred chosen boys, all dressed in a clean and elegant uniform. Harry walked between the ranks, his heart exulting in the sense of its own genial humanity. Then embracing his agent—Yes, dear Longfield, he cried, these shall be indeed my children; and I will prove a true and affectionate father to them. But let us hasten to bestow upon them a tender mother too, I trust.

He flew back as a glimpse of lightning, and seizing and half-devouring the hand of his bride—Will you pardon me, my beloved, says he, some matters that happened before our union? I have collected all the children I ever had before marriage. They wait for your inspection; and I hope that you will not prove a hard stepmother to them.—You are a rogue, says she, archly smiling, and giving him a pat on the cheek; but come along, and, so saying, away they tripped.

The princess walked, with a silent and musing attention, up and down the ranges. Her heart grew strongly affected, and, taking out her handkerchief, she wiped away the dropping tear.—And has my lord, says she to Longfield, has he indeed taken upon him to be a father to all this pretty host of little ones?—He has, so please your highness, says Longfield, and has accordingly clothed and provided for them.— O, she cried, under the FATHER which is in heaven, he is the dearest father that ever was upon earth! So exclaiming, she turned to Harry, and, hiding her face on his shoulder, she pressed him to her heart.

On their return, they perceived Mr. Clinton, the duke and duchess, all standing in the great folding-door; and, flying up the marble steps, they both bent the knee, and received the joint blessings and successive caresses of their three exulting parents.

Just then Harry spied Goodman Dobson and his dame coming diffidently but puffingly up the avenue. Instantly he caught his angel by the hand, and hastened to meet them. He took them successively in his arms, and saluted them with warm affection, while with yearning hearts and bowels they wished him joy upon joy. They then kneeled down on each side of the princess, kissing her hands and garments, and blessing her for bestowing such a heaven of beauty upon their Harry. But as soon as Harry told her that they were his fosterers, she raised and kissed them in turns, with her arms about their necks. Harry then gave them into the hands of his huntsman, with orders to take them to the larder.

The multitude, before this, began to thicken apace. And the youth had got together in the great lawn, casting the quoit and the sledge, and leaping over a cord that was raised between two posts.

My dearest Harry, cried the duke, I have heard things almost incredible of your prowess and action, but never saw any sample save the mounting of your Bucephalus. Will you be so good to give me some instance of your excellence among yonder young competitors, whom I suppose to be the most eminent that the shire can exhibit?—Do, my Harry, said Mr. Clinton, indulge my dearest brother on this our day of jubilee.

Harry bowed, and ordered his page to bring him his quarterstaff, and despatched another for a cord and two long poles. He then walked down the avenue, attended by the males and females of the whole family.

As they approached the lawn, a youth of uncommon vigour had cleared the former cord, though raised to something upward of five feet in height; but all who attempted to follow either recoiled or pitched over.

Harry then caused his two poles to be erected to an elevation of ten feet, with a cord reaching from top to top. The multitude came down in thousands to see what they were about. When Harry, having cleared the contested cord, went backward from his lofty poles about the distance of thirty paces; then rushing forward, he advanced one end of his staff to the ground, and springing, and raising, and rising upon the opposite end, he pitched himself over the elevated string; while the multitude beheld him, as a new-risen phœnix, suspended and glittering in the air, and then alighting as winged on the other side.

The elements were rent by an universal shout, which followed and undulated after our company till they sheltered themselves within the house.

The Fieldings then arrived with the Reverend Mr. Catharines, who was appointed to join the noble pair.

After breakfast the carriages were, ordered out, first, Mr. Clinton and Mr. Meekly moved away in the former's coach and four to the church. The family of the Fieldings then followed in a coach and four. Next went Clement and his Arabella in their post-chaise and pair. The duke and duchess then succeeded, in a sumptuous coach proudly drawn by six German greys, attended by a long retinue of French liveries. and the duchess's women in a coach and four. And last of all came our hero and his Abenaide, enthroned in her open chariot; her four spotted Arabians, restraining their impatience, beat measures with their feet, scarce seeming to advance the pace of a tortoise.

Harry's page closed the rear, mounted on his lord's charger, who stepped foaming behind the chariot; and the long cavalcade nearly reached from the great hotel to the entrance of the town.

The crowd, however, extended wide and far beyond the cavalcade. They bowed respectfully, and paid obeisance to Mr. Clinton, the duke, etc., as they passed; but, as soon as they got a glimpse of the chariot of their young Phaeton, their acclamations became unremitted, and almost insufferable to the ear, like the shouts of a Persian army at the rising of the sun.

Slowly as our Harry moved, the multitude strove to retard him, by throwing themselves in his way, that they might satiate their eyes and souls with the fulness of the sight. Bended knees and lifted hands, prayers, blessings, and exclamations, were heard and seen on all sides; and all the way as they went, hundreds upon hundreds shouted forth the hymeneal of the young and happy pair.

THE END.

www.ingramcontent.com/pod-product-compliance
Lightning Source LLC
Chambersburg PA
CBHW030406230426
43664CB00007BB/769